The Psychology of Environmental Problems

Second Edition

THE PSYCHOLOGY OF ENVIRONMENTAL PROBLEMS

Second Edition

Deborah Du Nann Winter
Whitman College

Susan M. Koger
Willamette University

Printed on 30% post-consumer recycled paper

Proceeds from this book will be donated to
Psychologists for Social Responsibility,
Environmental Protection and Justice Action Committee.

 LAWRENCE ERLBAUM ASSOCIATES, PUBLISHERS
2004   Mahwah, New Jersey   London

Lawrence Erlbaum Associates, Inc., Publishers
10 Industrial Avenue
Mahwah, New Jersey 07430

Cover design by Kathryn Houghtaling Lacey

Library of Congress Cataloging-in-Publication Data

The Psychology of Environmental Problems, Second Edition,
by Deborah Du Nann Winter and Susan M. Koger.

ISBN: 0-8058-4630-1 (cloth: alk. paper) — 0-8058-4631-X (pbk: alk. paper).

Includes bibliographical references and index.

Copyright information for this volume can be obtained by contacting
the Library of Congress.

Books published by Lawrence Erlbaum Associates are printed on acid-free paper,
and their bindings are chosen for strength and durability.

Printed in the United States of America
10 9 8 7 6 5 4 3

*To John, who keeps me noticing
the physical world—DDW*

*To Jen, "we are of this world to change
it and change with it"—SMK*

Contents

Foreword

I love this book! In discussing the momentous environmental problems that threaten our Earth, it explains many of the crucial ways that human behavior—by individuals, organizations, businesses, and governments—has caused these problems, and it also explores ways that human behavior can help to resolve them. It says the things that need to be said, both unflinchingly and insightfully. It also says them gracefully, with a clear, readable, and engaging style that captures readers' attention and interest. Moreover, the authors, Deborah Winter and Sue Koger, share human, personal glimpses of themselves, which will evoke readers' empathy and provide excellent models of self-understanding and personal development.

In reviewing the first edition of this book, I said it "has given voice to key environmental issues that have ultimate importance for all human beings, yet are usually ignored by most of us." The second edition continues that excellent tradition, and I believe it does so even more successfully than the first edition because it focuses its full attention on psychological aspects of environmental problems. That is a major service to both fields—psychology and environmental studies—and I greatly appreciate the authors' dedication and creative flair in tying the fields together so lucidly.

Importantly, the authors do not stop with merely explaining how badly people have been treating Earth's life-sustaining environment. They state their goal as helping "readers in their roles as decision makers and active citizens in the design of a more sustainable world." To that end, they concentrate on showing how a wide variety of psychological theories and approaches—psychoanalysis and behaviorism, social psychological and cognitive viewpoints, physiological/health and holistic approaches—can illuminate understanding of environmental problems and can point the way toward ameliorating or overcoming them. They even offer an appendix with concrete suggestions about "how to do it" and where to get all kinds of useful information from on-line sources.

Here is a brief sample of some of the intriguing highlights that you will encounter in this volume. Many cartoons, drawings, analogies, and humorous references add a light touch to its serious message—for example, look for Sir Francis Bacterium in Chapter 1. It offers many surprising insights, such as that the U.S. is really a highly overpopulated nation, and that forests are like the lungs of the Earth. The book ties principles from each of the areas of psychology tightly to practical behavioral applications, such as support for the Endangered Species Act, or the power of situational norms to produce overconsumption. It notes that evolutionary patterns in human perception, thought, and behavior can cause serious misunderstanding of environmental problems; for instance, see "confirmation bias" in Chapter 6.

Other eye-opening examples include: If we paid the total real costs of our consumption of natural resources, a hamburger made from cattle raised on cleared tropical rainforest land might cost $200. Persistent organic pollutants (chemicals such as DDT and PCBs) can build up in plants, animals, and human bodies, and can cause lowered IQ scores, cerebral palsy, and poisoning in children; the book offers guidance in ways to avoid exposure to them. The process of assessing the risks of environmental damage requires setting a value on a human life—what amount should it be?

The Gaia Hypothesis proposes that the earth is a living system, and its processes will persist regardless of whether human beings continue to survive or not. Accordingly, the authors emphasize that environmental policy decisions must consider "the interconnectedness of all people and species, and a sense of awe for the exquisite beauty of creation." In their final chapter they present six principles to guide our actions aimed at building a sustainable world. I particularly liked the principles of visualizing how an ecologically healthy world might look, and working toward that vision by taking small steps to work on these big problems.

The authors have read widely and brought together many recent references from diverse sources. They are sensitive and thoughtful in their presentation of both "doomster" and "boomster" views of our ecological situation. And they call for both psychological and lifestyle changes as well as technological and societal structural ones in working toward the goal of a sustainable world that we can pass down to our descendants. They conclude that psychology has a lot to offer in this process—and so does their book!

I hope you enjoy and profit from reading it as much as I did.

Stuart Oskamp
Claremont Graduate University
Claremont, CA

Preface

This book is about the psychology of environmental problems, and is the second edition of Deborah's (1996) text, *Ecological Psychology: Healing the Split Between Planet and Self*. Deborah was moved to do the first edition after being profoundly affected by an experience while she was living in Europe. Although it would be simplistic to claim just one event could change one's life, there was one that substantially affected her life path. Deborah was on a sabbatical from her teaching position at Whitman College, living in Copenhagen in the winter of 1988, when she visited a friend in Hamburg. One dreary November afternoon, they walked along the shore of the Elbe River past some beautiful Victorian homes. Deborah tried to visualize how pleasant these houses would be in the summer sun, facing the water. She pictured well-dressed little children in white lace, frolicking along the water's edge, with their nannies looking on. As they continued on, her friend asked what she would like to eat for dinner that evening. Deborah suggested fish, because they were at the waterfront. Her friend answered that fish is very difficult to get and not very good. But why, she asked, when we are so near the water? Her friend responded, "The water is dead here. It's been dead for years. Nothing grows in it." "Oh, that's ok," Deborah said, and suggested pasta instead.

As they continued on, Deborah's thoughts returned to the problem of dead water. Suddenly, she stepped into a new world: a world where the industrial pollutants of a city could actually kill water. Not just water in an isolated lake, but water in a big river. She looked at that water, then, and saw it was black and ominous. It looked like liquid death. Deborah had never thought of water as alive or dead before. It was just the backdrop for the more interesting and tasty beings who inhabited it. But, at that moment, she saw the graveyard of an entire ecosystem in which no living organisms existed. No seaweed, no fish, no amoebae, nothing but blackness, lapping up against the landscaped grounds of the beautiful estates.

What she experienced in those next steps was an important shift in her worldview. As a psychologist, Deborah had always thought of the physical world as the mere background against which more fascinating animals called human beings loved, fought, conquered, created, suffered, and enjoyed pleasures, such as those in those lovely estates. Walking along the shorepath in Hamburg, she saw that the physical world made human civilization possible: The Victorian estates rested on industrial wealth from shipping, manufacturing, and merchandising. But human civilization was destroying the physical world in return. These beautiful estates, financed by the wealth of Hamburg's industries, now face the deathly result of that civilization, the black liquid that laps up against their shores.

As a U.S. citizen living in Europe, Deborah immensely enjoyed many pinnacles of human civilization so salient there: the music, the art, the ballet, the cathedrals, the cuisine, and the ambiance of urban sophistication. But as glorious and magnificent as human civilization is (and in Europe, that glory and magnificence is absolutely stunning), *Western civilization is not sustainable*. In Germany and northern Europe, it is easier to see the ugly ramifications of too many people and too much pollution, where trees in the Black Forest are dying from automobile pollution from the autobahn, no wilderness exists anymore, and an entire river can die. In the United States, unsustainable patterns are less obvious because there is more space per person. But we are not far behind our European friends. The realization that we are living in an unsustainable culture has stayed with Deborah ever since.

Sue can also trace her concern about environmental issues to one event. While at a party for graduate students at the University of New Hampshire in 1989, she offered to get a friend a piece of cake. He declined because it was being served on styrofoam. Sue put two pieces on a napkin, sat down, and realized that every action has an impact and that we can make choices that reduce our adverse impact. Over the next several years, Sue became more conscious of her everyday behaviors, and to this day she strives to live as lightly on the planet as possible.

As psychologists, Sue and Deborah continually ask themselves "What does psychology have to say about the fact that we can't continue to sustain human life on the planet unless we change a lot of what we're doing? Given that our culture is unsustainable, why are we[1] even teaching psychology?" Students at Willamette University and Whitman College keep these questions alive for us with their fundamental concerns about their futures, choice of livelihoods, and the reasons, if any, as to why bother studying psychology. We have found that many of our students feel uncertain and unhopeful about the future. Although they plan and hope to "get a good job," few think their lives will be as comfortable as those of their parents. In fact, there is a foreboding among most of our students, a feeling that collectively we are quickly approaching the limits of industrial growth, and that their generation will have to pay the costs of the unsustainable practices instituted by the generations before them. Most of the time, this gloomy vision is buried beneath the demands of academic loads, social lives, and personal development, which are so crucial in the undergraduate years. But behind the layers of busy activity, pessimism prevails.

Yet our students are also idealistic, and it is their idealism for which we are most grateful, and to which we wish to speak. In our many years of college teaching, we have seen that most of our students truly want to help the world; they seek careers not only for good money but for good meaning; their hearts are still as open as their minds; and they ask really good questions about values, choices, and purpose. Whereas most of their parents' generation is locked into mortgages, family responsibilities, and firmly set identities, our students have less certainty, as well as less confidence, about their own lives. Consequently, they have more motivation and more authenticity in their struggle to make good value choices.

In *Varieties of Religious Experience* (1929), William James argued that conversion experiences are real, but only if supported by many other congruent events. Deborah's walk in Hamburg and Sue's lesson in styrofoam were pivotal only because many other experiences came both before and after them. In addition to continual work with students, Deborah married a geologist who has taken her to extraordinarily beautiful wilderness areas and taught her that rocks and dirt are crucial features of ecosystems. Before she married John, she was a typical social scientist who thought of rocks and dirt as a stable (and boring) background, on which the interesting stuff like plants and animals (especially people) grew. But John helped her recognize that the

---

[1]Although we want to keep our personal experiences salient in this book, we've struggled with how to refer to ourselves in the clearest way. The first person "I," "we," or "our" is most direct, but not always accurate when we are referring to one of us. So when we speak of both Deborah and Sue together, we will use the first person "we"; but when we refer to one of us, we will use her specific name. We hope this switching between first and third person will be clear for you, our reader.

biological world is possible because of the nonbiological (inorganic) world; in fact, there is no easy figure–ground separation like she had assumed. The inorganic world is just as dynamic and fluid and dramatic, although it takes a different sense of time to perceive its impressive changes through melts, flows, and tectonic dances.

After Sue's "epiphany," she joined environmental groups and became an activist. During a sabbatical from teaching at Willamette University, she decided to integrate two of her passions: her environmental concerns and academic psychology. When Sue discovered Deborah's book, she wrote to inquire about collaborating on a second edition. They both felt like they had found soul sisters, especially when they discovered that they both had graduated from the same doctoral program (although 15 years apart). Happily, this book is the outcome.

Deborah and Sue have many things in common: We share a common worldview because of forces that at first seem tangential. Both of us were born during the baby boom, and are white, middle-aged, professional females who enjoy the fruits of industrialized civilization while struggling to reconcile what we know about the ecological world with how we live. As privileged people, we are economically secure enough to have the luxury of considering larger questions of survival than just our own. And as neither of us have children, we may be more concerned about the future of the planet than our friends, whose parenting responsibilities understandably require more immediate focus on much smaller numbers of people.

These are a few of the biases pervading this book. Many statements about overconsumption will seem irrelevant or self-indulgent to those who are struggling to support a family, stay employed in an extractive industry, or just survive in an economically and socially insecure world. Environmental devastation is greatly enhanced through overconsumption by the world's rich, and desperation of the world's poor, but we will focus more on the former because we fall into that category, and we expect that most of you, our readers, do as well. We also focus on North Americans and people in other industrialized settings because we believe that relatively wealthy people such as ourselves have the most opportunity, and thus most responsibility, to design crucial changes. We hope this book will help our readers in their roles as decision makers and active citizens in the design of a more sustainable world.

We tell you these things about ourselves and why we wrote this book because authors are always alive and potent in any intellectual work, no matter how stringent their attempts to be objective. Knowledge is always shaped by values, assumptions, cognitive styles, and the peculiar and arbitrary conjunction of sociological factors over which we have no control, but from which our sense of meaning is derived.

Having disclosed our idiosyncrasies to you, we also call on Erik Erikson to help illuminate the path toward wisdom. Erikson proposed that wisdom comes from what he called *ego integrity*, by which he meant living with the paradox of being able to see the arbitrary, accidental basis for one's deepest beliefs, and at the same time, employing the courage to stand by them with utter conviction. Recognizing the personal and sociological reasons for our views, we offer them to you with the hope that they are clear and vivid enough to illuminate the ones you share, as well as the ones you must rework to support your own ego integrity.

THE ORGANIZATION OF THIS BOOK

This text applies psychological theory and research to environmental problems. We think this endeavor is important because, as a colleague noted, there really are no "environmental problems." Rather, we are seeing symptoms of the mismatch between how humans meet their needs and wants, and the natural order of things. Chapter 1 begins this project by outlining current environmental difficulties. Here we argue that because environmental problems have been caused by human behaviors, beliefs, decisions, and values, psychology is crucial for finding solutions to them. Chapters 2 through 7 examine a particular subfield or perspective in psychology, as applied to environmental issues. The last chapter compares the different theories, and offers six operating principles for how to approach solutions. We wrote with novice and upper level psychology and environmental studies students in mind, as well as the layperson who may wonder if psychology has anything useful to say about mounting ecological difficulties. We retained much of the organization and content from the first edition, but many sections were significantly revised: We updated the literature wherever possible, added a new chapter on the effects of environmental toxins and stress, and eliminated the second chapter, "The 'Nature' of Western Thought," while incorporating some of its points in other chapters. We also added a "key concepts" section at the end of each chapter.

This book not only talks about ecological thinking, it also illustrates it. As Warwick Fox (1990), an ecophilosopher, once wrote,

> I do not see how anyone can write about ideas and not develop at least some degree of ecological consciousness. Such writing inevitably leads one to realize just how much one's "own" ideas are a complex interactive function of the ideas that one has absorbed from others—others whose "own"

> ideas are in turn, a complex interaction of the ideas they have absorbed, and so on. (p. xiii)

We are grateful to the countless people who inspired and supported us through our efforts in developing, writing, and revising this text. We particularly appreciate Debra Riegert at LEA for signing the second edition, the good work of Jason Planer and Eileen Engel at LEA who helped make this edition a physical reality, and the valuable help from our student assistants, Shannon May-Comyns Westfahl, Matt Snodgrass, and Kristi Thane. We also thank Whitman College and Willamette University for financially supporting administrative costs for this edition.

Deborah's husband, John, recently noted that nobody in their right mind would agree to write (or revise) a book if they realized how much work it would turn out to be. At the end of this year-long project, we smile in acknowledgment of his observation, but are also grateful for the chance to work together, learn from each other, and create our little intellectual ecosystem contained herein.

1

What on Earth Are We Doing?

> The environmental crisis is an outward manifestation of a crisis of mind and spirit. There could be no greater misconception of its meaning than to believe it is concerned only with endangered wildlife, human-made ugliness, and pollution. These are part of it, but more importantly, the crisis is concerned with the kind of creatures we are and what we must become in order to survive. (Lynton K. Caldwell, quoted by G. T. Miller, 2002, p. 1)

What will your future be like? If you are like most people, you have hopes of a happy life with your family and friends. You desire secure, meaningful work, good physical health, rewarding interests, and enough leisure time to enjoy them. Yet most of us also have a notion, ranging from an inkling to a grave fear, that our future will not be pleasant, or at least not as comfortable, as our present. National and world events compound the vague realization for many of us that we are operating in a way that cannot be sustained for more than a few decades. Human beings are running out of available resources, polluting our natural habitat, and reproducing too quickly.

Yet we proceed to live as if our normal lives will continue. We bear a vague sense of pessimism about our future while we carry on with business as usual, and we worry more than we act. A strong majority of U.S. citizens, 83%, express concern about the environment and believe that at least some (if not immediate and drastic) action must be taken to address environmental problems, yet only 18% regard themselves as active participants in such efforts (Dunlap & Saad, 2001). Instead, we go to school or work, do the shopping and laundry, visit friends and take vacations when we can, and try not to think about the claim that the planet cannot possibly sustain our current lifestyles for very much longer. Perhaps we hope that the doomsday scientists will decide they got it wrong, or come up with some good technological fixes. If we wait it out, we may find that all will be well, after all.

That seems doubtful, however. Although trusting technical specialists might make us feel more comfortable, we are unlikely to be saved by them. The physical problems that threaten the survival of human life on the planet are too huge, too complicated, and too serious to be solved by a small group of scientists, although we will certainly need their knowledge to reverse our plight, just as we required their knowledge to produce it. Human beings have always altered their physical environment in order to survive, but the pace and scale of current environmental changes knows no precedent. And the longer we wait, the worse the problems become, making solutions seem more and more difficult. In short, betting on the smaller and smaller odds of technological solutions is likely to become more and more irrational.

Besides, deciding whether or not to entrust our fate to scientists misses an important cause of the current predicament. We cannot leave our problems solely to physical scientists to create physical solutions, because environmental problems are also psychological in origin: They have accrued because of the thoughts, beliefs, values, and worldviews that human beings have historically acted on and continue to act on. Human behavior is ultimately responsible for quickly deteriorating ecosystems. Deforestation doesn't just happen: Human beings cut down trees. Ozone holes aren't natural phenomena: They are caused by humans who manufacture and release dangerous amounts of chemicals into the stratosphere. Greenhouse gases may be threatening our very survival because billions of people do what they do every day. Behavior is accompanied by beliefs and attitudes that make business as usual seem sensible, even though business as usual is jeopardizing future survival. Thus, solutions to environmental problems will require more than just technological answers. We will also have to make psychological changes: changes in the way we behave, see ourselves, see our relationship to nature, and even, perhaps, the way we see the meaning of our lives. As Einstein's dictum put it, problems cannot be solved from the same mind-set that created them (Hawken, A. Lovins, & L. H. Lovins, 1999, p. 6).

For most people, environmentally irresponsible behavior is rooted in many structural dimensions. For example, both of us (Deborah and Sue) are planning to take airplane flights soon after this book is completed. Purchasing airplane tickets is financially affordable because of massive government subsidies to airlines, an international trade system that makes petroleum and planes inexpensive, frequent flyer miles that make the flights seem "free," and federal regulations on airways that make commercial flights numerous and cheap. We will board these flights knowing that they are environmentally irresponsible actions, while we are also looking forward to the sun-filled vacations they will deliver. Although it is important to consider the political and economic institutions that sponsor our environmental irresponsibility, only people can change those structures (Bazerman & Hoffman, 1999). We therefore write this book in the hope that it will demonstrate the breadth and utility of psychology for understanding and mitigating the disconnection we all feel between recognizing the potential danger of irreversible ecological collapse, and maintaining lifestyles that contribute to it.

Psychology is defined as the study of behavior and mental life, and recently celebrated its first century of existence as an independent discipline. Although psychology has had much impact on modern industrialized culture, it has rarely been seen as an environmental science, having something relevant to say about how we got into such a mess and how we might get out of it. Instead, psychology seems to have two very different manifestations. In the college classroom, it is taught as a science: Empirical studies, including statistical analyses, are used to illuminate basic behavioral and mental processes like learning, perception, motivation, and thinking. In the shopping mall, however, psychology looks very different. Much to the academics' consternation, the trade bookstore places psychology books alongside self-help books and books on the occult; there psychology looks like a do-it-yourself method you can use to manage a divorce or experience your past lives.

Neither the academic nor the trade book version of psychology is completely correct or completely wrong. Psychology has been both a science as well as a practical tool for public use ever since its beginnings, and although these two wings often offend each other, they have also learned to live side by side. Neither the purely academic wing, nor the "pop" wing, represents the biggest constituency anyway. The ma-

jority of psychologists (over 60%) are applied psychologists, trained
professionals who bring psychological principles to the problems of
mental health, personnel management, industrial design, and consumer marketing, to name just a few. Using psychology to examine environmental problems offers yet another opportunity to integrate the
scientific and the applied sides of the discipline.

Most of us are somewhat familiar with the sobering environmental
problems we face, and certainly you have already heard at least some
of what is to follow. Thus, before we discuss some current ecological
problems, we invite you to think about the issues as a psychologist
would. You will learn more if you consider your own behavior and
mental life as you read the rest of this chapter and this book. Keep
track of your own reactions: your thoughts, feelings, and behaviors,
which are the raw data of psychology. They will enable you to judge
the adequacy and relevance of the theories discussed in the chapters to
come. We encourage you to jot down reactions as you experience them.
Psychological responses are what this book is about, so treat your own
with respect: They will enhance your understanding of the material, as
well as of yourself.

THE NATURE OF THE PROBLEM

Ever since Rachel Carson's widely read book *Silent Spring* (1962), we
have been exposed to information about environmental damage. In
the 1990s, we read about a slew of environmental problems threatening the survival of our entire planetary ecosystem: ozone depletion,
global warming, overpopulation, deforestation, air and water pollution,
topsoil loss, and coral reef destruction, to name a few. In 1992, 1,670
prestigious scientists, including over 100 Nobel Laureates, signed a
"World Scientists' Warning to Humanity," urging public attention to
the "human activities which inflict harsh and often irreversible damage on the environment and on critical resources" (Union of Concerned Scientists, 1992). The news is bad, and it continues to get
worse. No wonder we cannot stay tuned for very long: To do so would
be too depressing, perhaps too terrifying. So we turn our attention to
our present concerns: family obligations, work or school, enjoying
friends, paying bills.

Such a response is understandable and is consistent with an evolutionary perspective. Our perceptual systems evolved in an environment where any threats to safety were sudden and dramatic, and our
ancestors had no need to track gradually worsening problems or as-

saults that took many years to manifest (Ornstein & P. Ehrlich, 2000). In fact, attending to such events may have actually been maladaptive. As a result, our species is short-sighted and has difficulty responding to potentially catastrophic but slowly developing and harmful conditions. Rather than working to prevent such conditions, we have a strong tendency to delay action until the problems are large scale and readily apparent, at which time we attempt to respond. Unfortunately, by then it may be too late.

Despite such "hard-wiring," our species is also capable of dramatic and rapid cultural evolution, as the pace of the industrial and technological revolutions reveals (Ornstein & P. Ehrlich, 2000). For example, as undergraduates, both Deborah and Sue used typewriters for writing papers after engaging in grueling research with massive publication indexes. Now, the idea of using anything other than high-speed word processing programs, and sending and editing drafts via e-mail, feels impractical and inefficient. The World Wide Web has made research fast and convenient, and computerized networking between libraries enables access to collections far more extensive than any single library's holdings. While it is easy to "blame" technology for our current predicament, the human capacity for rapid behavioral change could also reverse current ecological trends.

In any event, it is becoming clear to most people that we cannot continue on our present course. By 2001, 42% of U.S. citizens reported that they worry "a great deal" about the quality of the environment, and 77% reported they were in favor of "more strongly enforcing federal environmental regulations" (Saad, 2001, p. 34). Ninety-one percent favored investments in renewable energy sources, including solar, wind, and fuel cell technology (D. W. Moore, 2001).

Unfortunately, "the U.S. government has frequently played an obstructive role" in progress toward sustainable practices (ones that do not harm the environment or endanger future generations' ability to support their lifestyles) (Oskamp, 2000, p. 502). For example, the George W. Bush administration reduced funding for research into cleaner, more efficient vehicles, and proposed a 27% reduction in renewable energy research and development, creating the second lowest budget in over 20 years (Renner, 2001). The administration also reversed regulations on various forms of pollution, planned to open ecologically sensitive regions to oil and gas development, and abandoned the international Kyoto protocol, which commits industrial nations of the world to collectively reduce emissions to 5% below 1990 levels by 2010. At meetings in Marrakech in fall 2001, all other countries reaffirmed their commitment to move ahead on the Kyoto targets, even without U.S. participation. Yet the United States is the world's biggest contributor of greenhouse gases: With only 4% of the world's population, we account for 25% of global emissions.

The list of environmental setbacks is long, but we cannot blame it all on George W. Bush. Environmental problems have taken centuries to develop, and rest largely on a Western worldview, which provides a set of beliefs that encourages us to use and abuse nature. The major thinkers who formed our modern worldview all promoted environmentally problematic and unsustainable practices. For example, Francis Bacon (1561–1626) argued for human control of nature, John Locke (1632–1704) emphasized material wealth and land ownership, and Adam Smith (1723–1790) posited that the state should not interfere with individuals' accumulation of wealth, because he believed that what is good for the individual is good for the state.

The American Declaration of Independence argued the same point: "All men [sic] are endowed by their Creator with certain unalienable Rights, that among these are Life, Liberty, and the pursuit of Happiness." This primacy of the individual over the state became a hallmark feature of the U.S. government, and thus our modern worldview was written into a federal constitution and into a national psyche: No longer did we have primary moral or psychological responsibilities to the society. Similarly, U.S. expansionism "by the right of our manifest destiny" expressed a moral imperative to use whatever needed to be used in order for the great experiment of liberty to grow and "possess the whole of the continent" (White, 1991, p. 73).

Admittedly, we enjoy many positive effects of the modern emphasis on individualism: a sense of freedom, mobility, opportunity, and accountability that we wish more people on the planet could also experience. But excessive individualism at the expense of group responsibility has its costs. It can sponsor self-indulgence and lack of concern for others. In order to build a sustainable society, we must look at some of the problems that this heritage has delivered.

BIOLOGY'S BOTTOM LINE: CARRYING CAPACITY

An array of interconnected problems created our current crises, but the bottom line that causes so many of us to worry is that the Earth has a limited carrying capacity. Globally, we cannot go on much longer in our present mode because the physical resources of the planet have limits and we are quickly approaching them. **Carrying capacity** is a concept developed by biologists to describe the maximum number of any specific population that a habitat can support. If the habitat is iso-

Source: Reprinted with special permission of King Features Syndicate.

lated and the population cannot migrate to a new one, the population must find a balance with the resource base. If it doesn't and the population grows too quickly so that it depletes its resources suddenly, the population will crash.

Such crashes have actually happened in both nonhuman and human populations. Islands, which segregate ecosystems and prevent migration, provide the clearest examples. For instance, in 1944, the U.S. Coast Guard imported 29 yearling reindeer to the isolated St. Matthew Island in the Bering Sea (between Alaska and Russia). The island was ideal for the propagation of reindeer, so that by 1963 the population had grown from 29 to over 6,000. However, the terrain became badly overgrazed and food supplies dwindled, and the population crashed in winter 1964. The island could have sustainably supported about 2,300 reindeer, but after the crash, only 3% of that figure survived (Catton, 1993).

Population crashes also happen to humans. Archaeological evidence from Easter Island, off the coast of Chile, shows that a very complex but unsustainable human population grew there for 16 centuries. To support themselves, the islanders cut more and more of the surrounding forests, so that eventually soil, water, and cultivated food supplies were depleted. The population crashed in the 17th century, falling from 12,000 in 1680 to less than 4,000 by 1722. In 1877, only 111 people still survived (Catton, 1993).

When carrying capacity is exceeded in mainland civilizations, the picture is more complicated because declining wealth makes the civilization more vulnerable to armed conflict. However, the Sumerians of Mesopotamia and the Maya of the Yucatan region provide two clear examples of exceeded carrying capacity. The Sumerians were the first literate society in the world, leaving detailed administrative records of their civilization and its decline between 3000 B.C. and 2000 B.C. The complicated agricultural system that supported their population also depleted their soil through salinization and siltation. Crop yields fell 42% between 2400 B.C. and 2100 B.C. and by 65% by 1700 B.C. In the words of Ponting (1991):

> The artificial agricultural system that was the foundation of Sumerian civilization was very fragile and in the end brought about its downfall. The later history of the region reinforces the point that all human interventions tend to degrade ecosystems and shows how easy it is to tip the balance towards destruction when the agricultural system is highly artificial, natural conditions are very difficult and the pressures for increased output are relentless. It also suggests that it is very difficult to redress the balance or reverse the process once it has started. (p. 72)

Similarly, the Maya, who developed what are now parts of Mexico, Guatemala, Belize, and Honduras, built a complex civilization on the fragile soil of tropical forests. Clearing and planting supported a population from 2000 B.C. to 800 A.D. As the population grew, land that needed to recover between plantings was overused. In about 800 A.D., the population crashed; within a few decades, cities were abandoned, and only a small number of peasants continued to live in the area. The remains of their civilization, buried under the tropical jungle, were not discovered until the 19th century. Skeletal samples show that widespread malnutrition killed massive numbers of people.

In the past, population crashes have occurred in one part of the world without seriously affecting those in another. Today, however, "the great life-supporting systems of the planet's biosphere [are deteriorating]—the climate and chemical cycles, the accumulation of wastes, the exhaustion of soils, the loss of forests, and the decline of ecological communities" (Speth, 1993, p. 27). Thus, global structures are being weakened, threatening an ecological catastrophe on a *planetary level*. The Earth is, in this sense, a large island, with no known way to borrow resources or dump pollution anywhere else. Because of the array of interconnected global problems described below, many of us believe that we are heading for a similar kind of population crash at a global level. We are using resources unsustainably, and at the same time, polluting the ecosystems, thereby weakening their ability to restore and supply the basic physical requirements for human biological needs. Furthermore, both human population growth and resource depletion are accelerating at exponential rates, which is what makes the problem so pressing, yet so difficult to directly perceive.

Exponential growth is deceptive because it starts off slowly but quickly accelerates. It occurs when a quantity increases by a fixed percentage of the whole, meaning that it will double after a certain interval, rather than grow incrementally (which is linear growth; see Fig. 1.1). The concept of exponential growth is so important to understanding the current predicament that it is worth spending a moment with a conceptual example. Imagine that you have a bottle with one bacterium in it, which will double every minute. Assume that it is now 11:00 p.m. and the bottle will be completely full by midnight. When will the bottle be half full? If you suggest 11:30, you are thinking in terms of linear, rather than exponential, growth. Actually, the bottle would be half full at 11:59 because the bacteria will double every minute. Next question (and this involves a little more imagination): When do you think the bacteria might start to notice that things are getting a little crowded? Probably not even at 11:55, because at this point the bottle is still only 3% full. Remember, exponential growth begins slowly but ac-

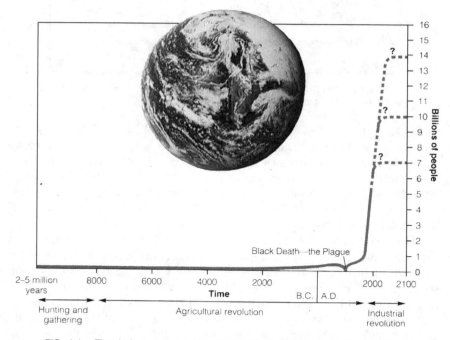

FIG. 1.1. The J-shaped curve of past exponential world population growth, with projections beyond 2100. Notice that exponential growth starts off slowly, but as time passes the curve becomes increasingly steep. The current world population of 6.1 billion people is projected to grow exponentially to 7–14 billion people sometime during this century. (This figure is not to scale.) (Data from World Bank and United Nations.) From Miller (2002), *Living in the Environment*, 12th edition, p. 2. © Wadsworth/Thomson Learning, Belmont, CA. Reprinted with permission of Brooks/Cole, a division of Thomson Learning: www. thomsonrights.com. Photo courtesy of NASA, http://images.jsc.nasa.gov/.

Source: Toles © 1994. The Washington Post. Reprinted with permission of Universal Press Syndicate. All rights reserved.

celerates quickly. Final question: Suppose the Royal Bacteria Society sponsored Sir Francis Bacterium to leave the bottle and go exploring for new space, and suppose Sir Francis got really lucky and found three new bottles, quadrupling the space for the society. How much time did he buy? Although it may seem at first that their problems are solved, it would actually only give them two more minutes until all four bottles were completely full.[1]

Unfortunately, the human population picture is even worse than this example, because exponential growth rates have themselves increased, meaning that the doubling time has grown shorter and shorter. In 1650, it would have taken 250 years to double the human population, but at present the population is expected to triple in the 48 least developed countries, and to double in many more nations, by 2050 (Engelman, Halweil, & Nierenberg, 2002). In 1999, population was increasing at the rate of 1.3% per year, creating a net increase of 78 million people (United Nations Secretariat, 1999), the equivalent of 10 New York Cities, each year. Engelman estimated that the world population will increase from 6.2 billion people in 2002 to between 7.9

---

[1]Special thanks to John Du Nann Winter for this teaching example.

and 10.9 billion by 2050 (Engelman et al., 2002). Like the bacterium example, finding new supplies of food or energy, or even a new planet or two, would only temporarily solve our problems.

Although industrialized countries have managed to bring their birth rates down, population continues to explode in the world's less developed countries, which are home to four fifths of the planet's human beings. There, improved medical care has lowered the death rates, without a corresponding decrease in birth rates. Campaigns to curb birth rates have failed largely because families who live at subsistence levels must have as many children as possible to help provide the family food supply, and insure parents some measure of protection during old age. Because infant mortality rates are high, more children must be born than can be expected to survive. Gender bias contributes as well, as families keep on producing children until enough boys are born to provide the family with economic security or social status in the community. Thus, poverty and sexism together drive population growth. U.S. foreign policy also contributes to these trends by reviving the "global gag rule," originally instituted by former President Reagan. This ruling "prohibits foreign family planning organizations from receiving U.S. government aid if they provide abortions . . . counsel women about abortion . . . or advocate less restrictive abortion laws" (Hwang, 2002, p. 24).

Some experts argue that until the world's distribution of wealth is altered, population will not be controlled. For example, Piel (1994) proposed that population control closely follows economic development, which enables people to escape from the poverty cycle. In other words, as poverty lessens, birth rates also decrease because women have better educational and professional opportunities as well as access to birth control (Engelman et al., 2002; G. T. Miller, 2002). Lowered infant mortality accompanies economic development, and improved nutrition and medical care also helps to reduce birth rates. But unfortunately, poverty has been growing. One fifth of the world's population, or 1.3 billion people, live in desperate poverty without the basic resources of clean water, adequate food, shelter, or sanitation (World Resources Institute, 1998–1999). Even in developed countries such as the United States, more than one person in nine (11.3%) fell below the official poverty line in 2000 (U.S. Census, 2000). If current practices continue, one half of the world's population will live in absolute poverty by 2050, meaning too poor to grow or buy enough food, or maintain a job (G. T. Miller, 1993, p. 7).

At the same time that human population has been increasing super-exponentially, so has consumption of the resource base, but at an even greater rate. Energy is the most basic natural resource, and we can measure consumption of it in terms of the daily number of calories people use for food, shelter, clothing, and other human creations, including cities, movies, and razor blades. One million years ago, about a million people on the planet engaged in hunting-gathering subsistence and each consumed a daily average of 3,000 calories for all their activities. By the early agricultural stage 10,000 years ago, energy consumption had jumped to 15,000 calories per person as cities were built and wealth was accumulated. Today, each of the globe's people consumes an average of 89,000 calories per day (Clark, 1989), with people in the United States consuming a whopping average of 260,000 (G. T. Miller, 2002). Overall, industrialized nations currently consume 390,000 calories per person each day.

Some of this utilized energy is renewable (e.g., sun, food, wind, and hydropower) and some is nonrenewable (e.g., oil, coal, gas, and uranium). At present, humans on the planet get only about 9% of their energy from renewable sources, withdrawing 91% from nonrenewable sources (G. T. Miller, 2002). Some energy deposits of nonrenewable energy are identifiable and extractable right now, some are identifiable but too expensive or difficult to extract, and some are unidentified. At present rates, we cannot expect the known major sources of nonrenewable energy to last for very long (see Fig. 1.2). Even if we did not increase our rates of population or consumption from this point on, we would use up identified reserves of gas and oil in less than one lifetime. Because of exponential growth, even doubling our supply of oil (from, say, getting lucky in Alaska) would extend our consumption only by 20 or 30 years. During the energy crisis of the 1970s, sudden price escalations and shortages of gasoline helped us understand the nation's dependency on petroleum products, and we learned to conserve where we could. However, the "crisis" ended, and old habits returned. But, "if the United States had continued to conserve oil at the same rate that it did in 1976–85 or [its citizens] had simply bought new cars that got 5 mpg more than they did, [the United States] would no longer have needed Persian Gulf oil after 1985" (A. B. Lovins & L. H. Lovins, 2001, p. 77). Such conservation measures might have prevented the Persian Gulf War in the early 1990s, and provided insulation from price shocks in the international oil market. At present, an average improvement of fuel efficiency of just 2.7 miles per gallon would eliminate our need for all Persian Gulf oil (R. F. Kennedy, 2001). Unfortunately, in 2002, the U.S. Congress voted against increasing fuel efficiency standards (Masterson, 2002), and in 2003, the U.S. invaded Iraq for what many observers believe was control of oil supplies (Winter & Cava, 2004).

Although experts are hopeful that we can convert to alternative energy supplies, other forms of resource depletion threaten the carry-

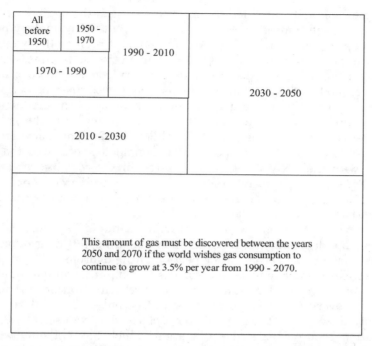

FIG. 1.2. If the rate of growth of natural gas consumption continues at 3.5% per year, every 20 years an amount of new gas must be discovered that is equal to all the previous discoveries of history. From Meadows, Meadows, and Randers (1992), *Beyond the Limits*. © Chelsea Green Publishing Co., White River Junction, Vermont. Reprinted with permission.

ing capacity of the planet to support human populations, and these forms have no clear alternative technologies. These depletions interact, accelerating their damage to the ecosystem. For example, whereas population has doubled over the last 40 years, the land area available for food production shrunk because we converted farmland to residential use. Because of urbanization, desertification, and population growth, harvest area per person has decreased to almost half of what it was in 1960 (Engelman et al., 2002). The Green Revolution, including widespread use of chemical fertilizers, substituted for shrinking land availability and more than doubled crop production since 1940 (G. T. Miller, 2002). However, per capita grain production is now *falling* because of shrinking land base, continued population growth, and because inorganic chemical fertilizers quickly damage land by acidifying and compacting soil (Halweil, 2002; G. T. Miller, 2002). Topsoil is also being lost at an astonishing rate: About 7% is eroded or blown into streams, lakes, and oceans each decade.

Some scientists and legislators propose genetic engineering of crops as the solution to world hunger, although this technology poses troubling risks of its own (E. O. Wilson, 2002). Specific effects on human health are unknown but seem likely given that some illnesses and allergies have already been traced to genetically modified corn originally intended as feed for farm animals. Biodiversity can be seriously compromised by the use of genetic engineering, as engineered species mutate and migrate, take over native habitat, and alter the genetic characteristics of wild species (G. T. Miller, 2002). There are ethical concerns as well, such as proposals that animals be reconstructed and crossed with the DNA of vegetative matter for the convenience of humans. For example, researchers have already transplanted a gene from spinach into a pig in order to improve the nutritional value of the meat ("Researchers Implant," 2002).

Meanwhile, the clean water supply is shrinking. Agricultural, industrial, and domestic uses of toxic chemicals are polluting ground water, lakes, rivers, and oceans. The portion of the hydrological cycle that provides fresh water to wells and springs is being interrupted. Rainwater can no longer replenish aquifers because deforestation, urbanization, and overgrazing make it more likely that water will run off, rather than seep into the ground and replace what we use. The Green Revolution required extensive irrigation, which has not only waterlogged and salinized soils, but also has quickly depleted aquifers. At current rates of population and economic growth, by 2025, two thirds of the world's population will be facing water stress, conditions where it is difficult if not impossible to meet their water needs (Gardner, 2002). Already more than one billion people on the planet lack safe drinking water, and nearly half of all people live without access to basic sanitation. Even in the United States, at least one quarter of the groundwater that is withdrawn is not replenished, and many regions are experiencing severe water shortages as a result of droughts.

While usable water and land supplies are shrinking, so are the forests. Because forests act like the lungs of the Earth, converting carbon dioxide to oxygen, the planet's available oxygen supply will dwindle, and forest loss increases erosion, desertification, and siltation of waterways. Deforestation has devastated communities and cost many lives. For example, in 1998, a landslide in India killed 238 people and flooding in China caused 3,000 deaths (Gardner, 2002). Only about one half of the world's original forest cover still remains, but the rate of cutting continues to accelerate. Some of what was cut has been replanted, but replacement crops are much more homogeneous genetically, and thus vulnerable to disease. Tropical forests, home for most of the planet's astoundingly varied life forms, are disappearing at record rates, caus-

Source: Reprinted with permission of Kirk Anderson.

ing the extinction of life forms faster than when dinosaurs became extinct about 65 million years ago.

If loss of natural resources were not threatening enough, along with them comes another array of problems from their use and misuse: pollution. Burning tropical forests is producing huge releases of carbon dioxide, which join emissions from automobiles and other fossil fuel-driven technologies to dramatically increase atmospheric levels of greenhouse gases: Carbon emissions into the Earth's atmosphere have increased by 31% since 1750, "with more than half this increase occurring in the last 50 years. Current concentrations are the highest in the last 420,000 years, and probably in the last 20 million years" (Dunn & Flavin, 2002, pp. 27–28). Greenhouse gases trap heat in the atmosphere, creating the greenhouse effect, which is necessary to stabilize atmospheric temperatures and maintain a climate suitable for life on this planet. However, the excessive levels generated by human activities are responsible for the phenomenon of global warming.

The scientific debate regarding global warming effectively ended in 1995, when the Intergovernmental Panel on Climate Change (the IPCC, an international coalition of 2,000 eminent climatologists and other scientists) reviewed decades of research and found that the balance of evidence pointed to human-induced warming. Over the last 7 years, more evidence has poured in, strengthening the scientific consensus, and raising forecasted temperatures. In its 2001 report, the

IPCC found that the Earth was warming faster than anticipated, and predicted that the globe would heat up by a further 2.5°F to 10.5°F over the next 100 years (IPCC, 2001; National Research Council, 2001). To put that number in perspective, during the last ice age, the world was only 9°F cooler than it is today. Thus, we are looking at the very real possibility of changes in planetary temperature of ice age magnitudes over the next century.

Although it may seem inconsequential, even attractive, that the climate would warm a little in a few years, only a few degrees increase will produce multiple and extremely adverse environmental and human health effects (e.g., Epstein, 2000; Trenberth, 2001). Because of the effects on farmlands, agriculture will have to move toward the poles, causing disruptions in food supplies, requiring new dams and irrigation, and migration of human populations. Tropical climates will replace temperate ones, speeding the decay of organic matter in the soil, releasing more greenhouse gases, and spreading tropical diseases. Sea levels will rise, causing flooding and severe threats to the half of the human population now living in the planet's coastal regions. Property damage, insurance claims, loss of crops, and other economic costs will result in a bankrupt global economy during the middle to late part of this century (Gelbspan, 2001).

Scientists continue to argue about some of the specific numbers and rates of resource depletion and pollution. Nonetheless, it is commonly understood that the planet is losing its ability to protect life, regenerate resources, disperse pollution, and provide food for the quickly escalating number of human inhabitants. On our current course, we are quickly approaching the limits of Earth's carrying capacity, if we have not already "overshot" them.

PSYCHOLOGICAL REACTIONS: BOOMSTERS VERSUS DOOMSTERS

Most people are familiar with the outlines to these problems, but reactions to confronting them are a psychological issue that is rarely addressed. As you read the previous material, did you feel some inkling of fear or despair? Did you scan the material, thinking to yourself that you already knew it? Did you find yourself growing irritated or frustrated? Were you feeling overwhelmed? Or did you wonder what any of this has to do with you? These reactions are important because they mediate how we understand problems and what we are willing to do about them.

One way reactions differ is basic optimism versus pessimism. You might have read the above material and felt growing hopelessness, whereas others might have read it thinking that although the picture seems gloomy, surely the creative spirit of human beings will enable us to invent and adopt solutions to solve our problems. These two views have been called the "doomster" and "boomster" responses (Bailey, 1993).

Such reactions demonstrate the important role that psychology plays in discussions about environmental problems. The boomster view (also called the "cornucopian view") was exemplified by Simon (1981; Simon & Kahn, 1984), an economist who argued that population growth is good because people eventually produce more than they consume. Human beings are not limited by the carrying capacity of an ecosystem, he argued, because unlike other animals, humans have the intelligence to redesign their habitat by inventing technology. Therefore, human ingenuity is likely to produce technological solutions that will solve problems in ways we cannot imagine at present. As resources are depleted, their market costs will begin to rise, slowing use and encouraging alternative technologies to develop. Human beings are (as in the title of Simon's book) "the ultimate resource." The free market will allow human ingenuity to flourish, and therefore human products and human well-being will continue to boom.

Although the boomster view remains a minority one, it is worth taking seriously because of its psychological implications. Boomsters argue that a headline-hungry media that needs to create bad news in order to assure public attention, sufficient Nielsen ratings, and advertising budgets, has exaggerated environmental problems. For example, despite graphic television pictures of the Exxon Valdez oil spill in 1989 showing oil-drenched wildlife and blackened beaches, and suggesting that Prince William Sound was hopelessly contaminated, Bailey (1993) argued that U.S. surface water quality *improved* since 1960. He cited examples, such as Lake Erie along with other waterways, that were cleaned up because of pollution control measures. Similarly, U.S. air quality has improved since 1970, as has air in cities around the world where the average per capita income surpasses $4,000–$5,000. Boomsters argue that as capital wealth accumulates, countries can afford better pollution control measures. Further, as humans depleted resources, they developed alternative technologies, such as the use of iron to replace bronze in 700 B.C., and optic fibers to replace copper in the 1980s.

In *The Skeptical Environmentalist*, Lomborg (2001) also argued that things are getting better, not worsening. Life expectancy has increased, infant mortality is declining, and human prosperity has improved overall. Acknowledging that starvation, poverty, and pollution represent real challenges, Lomborg argued that although "being overly optimistic is not without costs . . . *being too pessimistic also carries a hefty price tag* [italics in original]. If we do not believe in the future, we will become more apathetic, indifferent and scared—hiding within ourselves. And even if we choose to fight for the planet it will very probably be as part of a project that is born not of reasonable analysis but of increasing fear" (p. 351). Lomborg wrote that scientists and environmental groups have exaggerated or even falsified information about global environmental problems, which is exactly what many scientists and review committees have accused him of doing (Revkin, 2003; Union of Concerned Scientists, 2002).

In light of public anxiety about environmental issues, one would expect the boomster view to become quite popular, because it would relieve discomfort about an uncertain future. Yet both Simon and Lomborg bemoaned the fact the public has steadily increased its endorsement of the doomster view over the last few decades. Public opinion polls show a continuous rising of concern about environmental issues, surging membership in national environmental organizations, and soaring donations to environmental causes.

How, then, do boomsters explain the popularity of the alternative doomster vision? In addition to the irresponsible muckraking of the media, Bailey suggested that doomsters speak to some deep psychological, even religious, needs of the public. Doomsters, he argued, are the modern-day versions of the fire-and-brimstone preachers of previous centuries. While describing the coming environmental hell in graphic detail, they scare their audience with dreadful prophecies, then promise salvation through conversion to a new ecological worldview. Boomsters also see environmentalists' concerns about social justice and inequities in distribution of wealth as only the most current version of the Marxist vision of a world collapsing because of evil capitalism. A secular society that has lost the psychological services of the church still has deep-seated needs to be saved by somebody, and the environmentalists dish out a very successful version of apocalyptic visions with moral imperatives. In contrast, boomsters suffer the problem of having only the status quo to offer.

As psychologists, we find this debate intriguing because it demonstrates that perceptions of, and responses to, information about the environment depend on psychological needs. Boomsters and doomsters argue their cases with numbers and data, but obviously their conclusions are based on more than "facts"—they are also based on assumptions and values. The invocation of religious needs to explain environmental attitudes explains the counterintuitive reality that most people are willing to take a more pessimistic viewpoint, even though a more optimistic one would make them feel better. This explanation also implicates the role of the press in affecting beliefs, forcing us to consider how information is presented to us, what assumptions we carry to it, and how we construct conclusions. Whatever else the boomster position does, it makes a good case for the importance of psychology as an environmental science. We will discuss both the informational and spiritual dimensions of environmental concern in the following chapters as we examine more fully the ways in which people perceive and believe messages about environmental problems, and how they respond to them.

As the majority, doomsters show variations on their basic theme of pessimism, and do not always agree with each other, especially with respect to solutions. Some suggest that our problems can only be solved by massive governmental regulations, whereas others argue that only transformation of our deepest spiritual values will extricate us. Disagreement over solutions is inevitable, but giving up on them altogether is one risk of the doomster position. Lomborg had a good point: The complete "gloom and doom" picture can lead us to conclude there is no hope for warding off environmental catastrophes. The problems seem too huge, too complex, and too expensive for human beings to manage, and government control seems as unlikely as spiritual transformation. In light of inevitable collapse, the best way of coping would seemingly be to ignore these issues, as their damaging effects will occur regardless of understanding or efforts to delay them. Thus, many people assume that the only thing they can do is to live the best they can in the present, and try not to worry about a dismal future.

Whether one takes a boomster or a doomster reaction depends on one's assumptions about the future, and the future, of course, has not yet happened. Therefore, no one can say which one is more correct; instead, both are guesses. Arguments about specific data on particular environmental threats usually evolve to the conclusion that the past is not a sure guide for the future. For example, doomsters would say that even though technology has bailed us out so far, we cannot know that it will always do so. Boomsters would say that just because some resources are running out and pollution is accumulating, an as-yet unimagined human ingenuity will surely solve these problems.

These predictions about the future are contradictory and both cannot be totally true at the same time. Our guess is that something in each view is partially correct. That is, although environmental difficulties are grave, some aspects can be and have been addressed by human effort. In any case, we propose that while pessimism may be understandable, and may even be inevitable, it is also unaffordable if it leads us to ignore ecological threats. Allowing ourselves the luxury of slipping into despair is to bet against the future of our children and perhaps against all the life systems on the planet. As Kates (1994) put it, "Hope is simply a necessity if we as a species, now conscious of the improbable and extraordinary journey taken by life in the universe, are to survive" (p. 122).

THE PSYCHOLOGY OF OVERCONSUMPTION

An equally passive response to these issues would be to assume "they are not my problems because I am not personally causing them." For example, most readers have two or fewer children, so you might assume that you are not contributing directly to population growth. Similarly, most of us are not directly working on third world development, so we are not adding to the exponential growth rates of energy consumption and pollution there, nor are we logging forests, producing CFCs, or dumping wastes in the ocean. What, then, are *we* doing to deplete the carrying capacity of the planet to sustain human life? The most obvious answer lies in the extravagant use and misuse of the world's natural resources, especially energy and land.

North Americans are by far the biggest users and biggest wasters of the world's commercial energy. Less than 5% of the planet's popula-

tion lives in the United States, but this small group uses 24% of the total commercial supply. Amazingly, 84% of this huge expenditure of
commercial energy is wasted (G. T. Miller, 2002). Some of this waste is
inevitable: As energy is converted to various forms of food, fuel, shelter, and living organisms, waste heat is always lost. However, human
beings waste energy through inefficient behaviors, and Americans
waste over 40% in completely avoidable actions: by selecting energy-
inefficient home heating systems, appliances, water heaters, and automobiles when more efficient choices are available. A. Lovins (2002)
claimed that we could *quadruple* the energy efficiency of the United
States with current technology and without lifestyle changes or new
power plants simply by utilizing super-efficient lighting, motors, appliances, and building components.

North Americans literally throw their wealth out the window by
heating rooms with poor insulation. Most of us live in houses with
enough energy leaks to equal a large window-sized hole in the wall
(G. T. Miller, 2002). Most of us realize that we misuse our share of energy, yet we continue to do so. Deborah provides a good, although troubling, example. When she wrote the first edition of this chapter, she
observed that a tremendous amount of heat was escaping through the
beautiful windows in her home office. It was March, and the electric
heater had been on for several hours, warming her workspace. She and
her husband talked about converting over to gas heat (which is much
more efficient) but they do not have gas lines available. They also
talked about retrofitting their windows, but still have not replaced the
double panes with windows that would be more efficient than insu-
lated walls. Why not? Retrofitting would be expensive and laborious,
and they would have to throw out the very expensive double panes
they chose 15 years ago. But retrofitting would probably pay for itself
in saved energy within 5 years. Although Deborah cannot think of a
good reason for not having undertaken this action, they haven't done
it yet. Is it because electricity is still so cheap that they don't notice the
waste? Is it because they don't give a hoot about the world's carrying
capacity, but only their own comforts? Is it because they believe that
their own little waste doesn't really make that much of a difference?

These are psychological questions, requiring psychological inquiry.
Finding answers is crucial to solving global carrying capacity problems,
for unless we better understand our own behavior and how to change
it, we will not use sophisticated technological solutions when and if
they become available.

Everyday behaviors of people in industrialized countries also result
in dangerous pollution. North Americans generate almost 5 pounds of
garbage per person per day, about 10 times their body weight every

year (G. T. Miller, 2002). About 2.5 million nonreturnable plastic bottles are thrown away *every hour*. But even careful household recycling will not change the biggest solid waste problem—that produced by commercial and industrial activities, which generate 98% of the waste. North Americans sponsor this enormous waste production by buying products manufactured, packaged, and distributed through commercial operations. In fact, overconsumption is the biggest drain on the Earth's carrying capacity. North Americans consume, either directly or indirectly, over 100 pounds of raw materials a day (Durning, 1992), considerably more than those in developing countries, and even more than people in other developed nations. For example, an average North American uses more than 30 times the amount of gasoline, and consumes more than 4 times the amount of meat as the average person in a developing country (World Resources Institute, 2001). Further, a North American "uses 19 times more paper than the average person in a developing country, and most of it becomes trash: less than half of the paper used in the U.S. gets recycled" (Gardner, 2002, p. 9). Such voracious depletion occurs because, in the last century, we have transformed households from places that produced necessary objects to places that consume convenience objects. The commercial sector now provides markets, packaged food, clothing, entertainment, and services, which are commodities that were once produced in the home. And the things we buy—the fast food burger and soda, the jacket, the compact disc, the kitchen gadget—are produced from materials that leave a long trail of pollution in many third world countries, pollution that is invisible to the North American consumer. A pair of pants made of polyester and sold in a North American department store may be sewn in a sweatshop in Indonesia, from synthetic material manufactured in Singapore, which comes from oil refined in Mexico. And our consumer culture is spreading quickly, so that people in developing countries are aiming for "the good life" of North Americans, hurrying to develop the same extravagant lifestyles we model through movies, television, advertising, and tourism. Opening up trade barriers via efforts like the North American Free Trade Agreement and the World Trade Organization has only exacerbated that trend.

Yet, there is good reason to believe that overconsumption is not delivering the "goods." Empirical studies of people's happiness shows that it is not how much stuff people own, but the condition of their social relations, their work, and their leisure time that determines how much fulfillment people experience (D. G. Myers, 2002). We will discuss these studies in more detail in chapter 3, but the main point is that overconsumption does not lead to happiness. In fact, the race to pay for material possessions is more likely to detract from the quality of relationships, the creativity of our work, and the quantity of leisure time, the primary predictors of happiness. Attempting to meet psychological needs through overconsumption jeopardizes not only our physical habitat, but also our psyches (Kasser & Kanner, 2004).

CULTURAL VERSUS BIOLOGICAL CARRYING CAPACITY

The issue of overconsumption brings us back to the problem of carrying capacity. Biologists have defined carrying capacity as the maximum number an ecosystem can support, which means that the maximum number would be living at the lowest possible standard. Some biologists have estimated that the Earth could support 50 billion people, but of course, that would mean they would exist at a very meager standard of living. Supporting more people would require giving up most standard luxuries, including lighting, recreation, cars, fine arts, and (horrors of all horrors!) higher education. Most of us would probably prefer to see fewer people living at a higher standard, but which cultural amenities would we see as basic? And who should decide? From a biological point of view, carrying capacity can be estimated numerically, but when it comes to human populations, **cultural carrying capacity** is always much less than the maximum number because human beings use more resources than is absolutely necessary. Determining which requirements are basic necessitates a debate of values (Hardin, 2002). Undoubtedly, many people in developing countries would have different and more conservative answers about minimum luxuries than people in industrialized countries.

A more formal way of conceptualizing cultural carrying capacity is to consider the formula for environmental impact given by population scientists P. Ehrlich and A. Ehrlich (1991; the formula was first introduced by P. A. Ehrlich & Holdren, 1971).

$I = P \times A \times T$

where I is the impact of any group or nation

P is the population size

A is the per-capita affluence, as measured by consumption

T is the technology employed in supplying that consumption

OZONE SHIELD

GLOBAL CLIMATE

OLD-GROWTH FOREST

AIR QUALITY

HABITAT

SPECIES DIVERSITY

NATURAL SCENERY

TOPSOIL

WATER QUALITY

AQUIFERS

The Other Infrastructure

THINK OF IT AS AN INVESTMENT. —

Source: Toles © 1992 The Washington Post. Reprinted with permission of Universal Press Syndicate. All rights reserved.

With this formula, one can see that doubling a population will double its environmental impact if affluence and technology remain constant. Of course, impact is not as simple as this, because these terms are not completely independent. For example, as population and affluence grow, so does technological impact because it becomes more difficult to extract resources the more they are used (mines must be mined deeper, forests will be harvested earlier).

What this formula does illustrate, however, is that the United States is the world's most overpopulated nation. To see population as only a third world problem is a fallacy that many people, including a lot of environmentalists, still hold. Population in the United States and in other industrialized countries must continue to decrease if the affluence we enjoy is to be sustained. Or if population does not decrease, affluence will fall, either systematically with planning, or suddenly through ecological collapse.

Giving up comforts and conveniences may be more than we can fathom, and reverting to preindustrial culture is probably impossible anyway. Even if we could scale down consumption to preindustrial levels, most people would not want to. However, many preindustrial cultures have sustained themselves for centuries, demonstrating that sustainable culture is possible. While copying preindustrial cultures may not be feasible, selecting certain features might be useful. In addition, sustainable cultures may offer some benefits to human psychological needs that are not well provided for by industrialized cultures. The modern Western tradition of emphasizing the individual has given us both unsustainable technology and increasing social alienation. Embedded in the modern Western worldview, we try to use the former to mitigate the latter.

It may not even be necessary to "give anything up" in order to accomplish a reduction or reversal of environmental degradation. Improving efficiency or productivity is typically much more effective than significantly reducing overall use, and much relevant technology is already available. For example, it would be far easier to find an automobile with twice the fuel efficiency of our present cars than to cut our driving in half, and buying an efficient water heater is a lot easier than reducing our use of hot water (Stern, 2000).

CONCLUSIONS

It would be naïve to suggest that any one academic discipline will provide the solution to such a complex interplay of issues as those that underlie current ecological conditions. However, psychology has a lot to offer for understanding how our environmental predicament developed, and the psychological forces maintaining it. As a science, psychology can illuminate the empirical dimensions of behaviors that contribute to and result from environmental threats. Psychology can help us examine our thoughts, feelings, and behaviors, and to question our Western worldview, and understanding our patterns enables us to change them. As individuals, we have the power to make choices that do not exacerbate environmental problems. Feeling empowered on one level often inspires people to work at a more global level, and thus provides hope for more widespread social change.

Bringing psychology to speak to the unspoken pessimism most of us share about the future on an overcrowded and overburdened planet will make psychological theory personally and intellectually meaningful, and provide insight into how we might design a sustainable future. We start by examining the role of unconscious mechanisms underlying these issues, as we look at one of psychology's most important and controversial theorists: Sigmund Freud.

KEY CONCEPTS

Boomster versus Doomster perspectives

Carrying capacity: cultural vs. biological

Cultural evolution

Environmental problems: deforestation, global warming, overpopulation, ozone hole, overconsumption, water pollution, resource
depletion, species extinction

Evolutionary perspective

Exponential growth

Green Revolution

Impact = Population × Affluence × Technology

Psychological processes: behaviors, feelings, reactions, thoughts,
values, worldviews

Western worldview

World Scientists' Warning to Humanity

2

Freudian Psychology

*H*ow can people "know" so much about our environmental predicament and yet continue on with business as usual? How can we go on
destroying our resource base while realizing that we are doing it? Why
does the public so often relegate matters of the environment, which is
the basis of our existence and survival as a species, to the periphery, as
though the environment is the special interest of a group of folks called
"environmentalists" (Nicholsen, 2002)? Somehow, we must split off
our awareness so that we "understand" our environmental problems,
and yet "forget" them at the same time. Apparently, we are not as conscious as we like to think. These considerations lead us to consider the
enormous contributions of Sigmund Freud, who was the first and most
important psychologist to theorize about the unconscious.

Although Freud (1856–1939) is often dismissed or ignored by academic psychologists because they find his work unscientific, we believe
his contributions are crucial for our discussion of environmental problems because his views are so relevant, his ideas so useful, and his impact so enormous. Whereas little of his theory has been tested with

controlled experiments, it has had huge impact on our culture, as well as the practice of clinical psychology. Furthermore, recent work in cognitive neuroscience validates his more general claim that most of what we do is unconscious, as we will see (e.g., Bilder & LeFever, 1998; Gazzaniga, Ivry, & Mangun, 2002).

In this chapter we examine the main outlines of Freud's work in order to extract his most applicable concepts for understanding our ecological predicament. We apply his ideas to environmentally relevant contexts to illustrate the power of his insights. We then move on to an update of Freudian theory (called object relations theory) because it goes further than Freud did in helping us understand our impaired relationship with the environment. Finally, we end by examining what is useful about both Freudian and object relations theory for changing our environmentally relevant behavior. Paradoxically, Freud's emphasis on the unconscious elements of our functioning helps us see how to increase our awareness about how we have gotten into our mess and how we might extricate ourselves from it.

THE DIFFICULTY OF FREUD

It is ironic that Freud, who was trained as a physician, and only tangentially regarded as a psychologist by most academic psychologists, is often regarded by the public as one of psychology's most well-known figures. Because of Freud's work, our popular culture has become "psychologized": His ideas are common household terms, even if they are not well understood. Before Freud, we in the West had no notion of neurosis, of the unconscious, of defenses, of psychotherapy, or of clinical psychology. Even the idea that emotional problems could be treated as a mental illness was not conceptualized, much less widely accepted.

Looking back on Freud's work, we can now see the most spectacularly insightful concepts alongside the most spectacularly misguided. Of course, our judgments as to which is which proceed from our own assumptions about human nature, born from our most personal experiences of ourselves. As you read through this chapter, keep track of which ideas you find reasonable, and which seem outlandish. Regardless of your analysis, in all of psychology's 100-year history, no other psychologist surpasses Freud's productivity, genius, or influence on Western thought.

One reason that Freud's views are often difficult to accept is that they do not paint a pretty picture of human beings. In Freud's eyes, our basic core is weak, irrational, selfish, and rigidly determined. In the words of one of his most compassionate biographers,

Freud's estimate of the human animal is far from flattering, and his message is sobering in the extreme. To expose oneself to the full gravity of Freud's thought is therefore risky and unsettling, and many have found it more soothing by far to soak up fragments of that thought through bland popularizations, or to rely on the doubtful wisdom of common discourse. Freud took some pride in disturbing the sleep of mankind [sic], and mankind has responded by trivializing him, watering him down or finding reasons—whether by denouncing his theories or denigrating his character—for disregarding him altogether. (Gay, 1989, pp. xiii–xiv)

But although his ideas are often dismissed, many thinkers, including the immodest Freud himself, have described his contribution as equivalent to that of Copernicus and Darwin, because all three have systematically dislodged human beings from thinking of themselves as the center and pinnacle of the universe (Burtt, 1954; Butterfield, 1960; Koyre, 1968). Copernicus informed us that the planets do not revolve around the planet Earth, but instead around the sun; Darwin helped us realize that humans are not categorically different from other animals, but instead share common ancestry; and Freud showed how irrational and biologically determined we are, thereby helping us see that our behavior is less intelligent and God-like than we previously thought.

Nowhere is human frailty more saliently observed in Freud's work than in his thinking about our struggle against the environment. Freud believed that although we construct impressive technologies to ward off nature's destructive powers, our efforts are only temporarily successful. Consider his words from *The Future of an Illusion* (1927):

The principal task of civilization, its actual *raison d'etre*, is to defend us against nature. We all know that in many ways civilization does this fairly well already, and clearly as time goes on it will do it much better. But no one is under the illusion that nature has already been vanquished; and few dare hope that *she* will ever be entirely subjected to *man*. There are the elements which seem to mock at all human control: the earth, which quakes and is torn apart and buries all human life and its works; water, which deluges and drowns everything in turmoil; storms, which blow everything before them. . . . With these forces nature rises up against us, majestic, cruel and inexorable; *she* brings to our mind once more our weakness and helplessness, which we thought to escape through the work of civilization. (p. 693, italics added)

In this passage we see Freud's vision that human beings stand in opposition to nature. (Notice his gendered understanding of this conflict by his reference to humans as male, and nature as female; we will examine the implications of this distinction in chap. 3.) Freud viewed humans as weak and helpless, subjected to the brutal forces of nature. For Freud, both the natural world and the inner psychological world of the human being are untamable and unmasterable. The best we could hope for was temporary, fragile, uneasy, anxiety-based truces and compromises between the competing forces both within and outside the individual psyche. As we read Freud, we may feel belittled and diminished. Understandably, we may have defensive reactions to his views, the same sort of defensive reactions that might occur when we read about the seriousness of our ecological plight that we discussed in chapter 1. In fact, the notion of defense is one of Freud's main contributions, as we shall see shortly.

THE BASIS AND BASICS OF FREUD'S THEORY

Because Freud's writing filled 24 volumes produced over a 50-year career (Strachey & Freud, 1964), his work is impossible to thoroughly describe in one chapter. Nonetheless, there are three main principles to Freud's thought that underlie the many particular concepts and case studies comprising the bulk of his writing. If you grasp these three principles, you will have a good foundation from which to apply Freudian thought to ecological issues:

1. Much of our behavior is a result of unconscious motivations.
2. Conflict is universal, chronic, and inevitable.
3. In order to function effectively, we split off our awareness of unwanted thoughts, feelings, and wishes, and use defenses to disguise and contain them.

We will examine each of these principles, explaining what Freud meant by them as well as how he came to believe them. In order to properly comprehend Freud's theory, however, we must first understand something about the *Zeitgeist* (the implicit values and beliefs at work in a culture during a particular period of time) that nurtured his ideas.

Freud helped formulate our modernist worldview, ushered in by the Enlightenment, a worldview that assumes both the environment and human behavior are determined by material, physical events. In the latter half of the 19th century, Europe's increasingly materialist culture was supported by an industrial revolution in full gear. Freud learned from his brilliant and world-famous mentors, Ernst Brucke and Hermann Helmholtz, that mental life is the result of activity of the central nervous system, and that all psychological events should be understood as physical energy that circulates through the brain and nerves. Such a view seems obvious now, but in the late 1900s it was a progressive idea, which contradicted the then more popular notion that psychological events emanate from some vital force, such as a soul. Instead, Freud was an utter materialist: All of our psychological life can be understood as a product of physical forces. To buttress this newfound materialism, Freud and his teachers enthusiastically embraced the newly published work of Charles Darwin. Natural selection dispensed with any need for God, a soul, or for any other spiritual/religious entity or explanation. A new worldview emerged in which the entire universe became a set of physical elements.

This burgeoning materialism fed the industrial revolution as people came to believe that the primary goal of human beings is to convert natural resources to products and profit. As industrialism and capitalism fed each other, the older ecological worldview faded, a worldview shared by most preindustrial cultures, and included a picture of humans as a small part of a spiritualized nature who should pay respect to their natural environments.

Freud was caught up in the new openness and vitality of enlightenment thinking, but he also worked in a sexually repressive society that forbade his patients, mostly women, opportunities for expressing their sexual desires. Impressed by the bizarre symptoms that he treated in his patients, Freud came to believe that psychological functioning is a creative outcome of the interplay between physical, instinctually based drives and the social, cultural, and moral pressures to tame, channel, subdue, or repress them. He came to see **sexual instincts** in particular, which Freud called **Eros**, fundamental in shaping the personality of the adult. For Freud, Eros included not only sexual desire, but also drives for physical pleasure, pleasure from eating, and touching. Freud also watched, with horror, the unfolding of World War I in Europe, and concluded that the horrific killing he witnessed could only be explained by an unconscious, **inborn**, **irrational need for destruction**, which he called **Thanatos**. The fact that three of his sons fought in the war only increased his dismay.

UNCONSCIOUS MOTIVATIONS

How does the unconscious help us understand our ecological predicament? From the Freudian perspective, our planet is populated by a species systematically destroying its own habitat. Although they think of themselves as intelligent and rational, the creatures, driven by Eros, are destroying themselves through overconsumption and overpopulation. Rushing through existence in order to procure more and more appetitive satisfaction, the animals instead enjoy less and less. Filled with Thanotos, they unconsciously destroy their environment, at the same time building weapons of mass destruction that threaten to destroy the whole of their species. From a Freudian perspective, environmental destruction is the result of instinctual urges that drive human behavior.

Thus, the strong unconscious drives of Eros (sexual pleasure and reproduction) and Thanatos (aggression, violence, and destruction) rule our actions, despite our most sophisticated attempts to deny and conceal them. Becoming aware of our environmental problems does not mean that we can easily stop ourselves from ruining our habitat, and it should be no surprise that we continue to proceed even while we become conscious of our environmental crises. Because behavior results from deeply buried instinctual drives, it is not easy to change. Freud might say, if he were alive today, that our environmental predicament is inevitable.

Like an iceberg that has 80% of its mass below the surface, the human psyche, Freud believed, is predominantly unconscious and unobservable. Freud posited that if we became aware of our unconscious sexual and aggressive motivations, we would be greatly disturbed. Instead, our psyches expend energy to keep impulses below the surface so that we can fool ourselves into thinking that we behave for rational or moral reasons, when in fact much of our behavior is driven by subversive needs, wishes, fears, and impulses that are quite selfish and unacknowledged.

The view that human behavior is primarily unconscious is supported by recent work in cognitive neuroscience (T. D. Wilson, 2002). For example, Gazzaniga (1998; Gazzaniga et al., 2002) demonstrated that we behave, and *then* we explain why we did what we did. A behavior like throwing something in the trash occurs unconsciously and automatically, like a reflex. If someone asks why you threw it out, rather than recycled it, you would invent a reason (e.g., "Oh, the trash can was more convenient."). Our conscious brain interprets and explains our unconscious actions.

CONFLICT

As a materialist who believed that our psychological functioning comes from the physical actions of the nervous system, Freud had other important materialist thinkers to build on, none more important than Sir

Isaac Newton. Newton's principle of the conservation of energy served as a pivotal organizing feature to Freud's theory about the psychological life of human beings. All energy is supplied by the nervous system and must be divided up between three psychological structures: the **id** (consisting of the appetitive desires, seeking pleasure), the **ego** (a reality-oriented mechanism that considers realistic constraints on impulse expression), and the **superego** (the moral principles that are internalized from parents and society). If energy is given to one structure, then it must necessarily be reduced in another.

For example, consider the conflict one might experience when buying a fast-food hamburger. The id experiences hunger; the ego considers price, convenience, and nutrition; the superego might ask about the moral implications of contributing to environmental and social damage (hamburger is usually produced in conditions horrific to cattle, meat packers, and tropical rain forests). As one structure grows stronger, the other structures weaken. Concerns about rainforest habitat might dwindle with intense hunger (the superego might be overpowered by a very strong id); or one might not be hungry enough to wait in a long line (a weak id might be overpowered by a pragmatically oriented ego). Many of our environmental choices involve conflicts of just this sort. We are able and willing to enact environmentally beneficial behaviors as long as inconvenience, high prices, and strong appetites are not in our way. At the other extreme, superego guilt or shame normally nag at us when id appetites go unchecked, producing unresolved anxiety.

Thus, our environmentally destructive behavior may be understood as the outcome of the distribution of physical energy to these competing psychological structures. In Freud's view, the same conflict over the allocation of physical energy is mirrored in our relationship to society and to nature. As individuals, we compete against others for energy, just as our inner psychological structures compete against each other for energy. This view that we compete with other humans for a finite amount of energy in the physical system is congruent with our problem of planetary carrying capacity, which we discussed in chapter 1.

DEFENSES

Finally, we come to a crucial Freudian principle for understanding ecological problems. Freud postulated that we defend ourselves from anxiety by "splitting" our awareness, so that we can remain essentially unconscious about our instincts without entirely ignoring them. This part

in–part out compromise allows us to give allegiance to both the instinct
and its denial. Here are Freud's own words to describe this process:

> Let us suppose, then, that a child's ego is under the sway of a powerful in-
> stinctual demand which it is accustomed to satisfy and that it is suddenly
> frightened by an experience which teaches it that the continuance of this
> satisfaction will result in an almost intolerable real danger. It must now
> decide either to recognize the real danger, give way to it and renounce the
> instinctual satisfaction, or to disavow reality and make itself believe that
> there is no reason for fear, so that it may be able to retain the satisfaction.
> Thus there is a conflict between the demand by the instinct and the prohi-
> bition by reality. But in fact the child takes neither course, or rather he
> [*sic*] takes both simultaneously, which comes to the same thing. He replies
> to the conflict with two contrary reactions, both of which are valid and ef-
> fective. On the one hand, with the help of certain mechanisms he rejects
> reality and refuses to accept any prohibition; on the other hand, in the
> same breath he recognizes the danger of reality, takes over the fear of that
> danger as a pathological symptom and tries subsequently to divest himself
> of the fear. It must be confessed that this is a very ingenious solution of
> the difficulty. Both of the parties to the dispute obtain their share: the in-
> stinct is allowed to retain its satisfaction and proper respect is shown to
> reality. But everything has to be paid for in one way or another, and this
> success is achieved at the price of a rift in the ego which never heals but
> which increases as time goes on. The two contrary reactions to the conflict
> persist as the center-point of a splitting of the ego. (Freud, 1938/1964, pp.
> 275–276)

Freud went on to describe a particular case in which a child was fright-
ened by his father's punishing him for masturbating. Let us drop the
sexual dimension, and consider the more general question of prohib-
ited instinctual drives, and more specifically, our own instinctual,
appetitive desires in the face of impending ecological disaster.

Here is our problem: We seek comfortable housing, delicious food,
stimulating entertainment, personal mobility, and successful careers.
Each of these desires leads us to behaviors that we know contribute to
an impending ecological collapse, an event so dire and overwhelming
that we cannot fully fathom its consequences. As with the case of the
child, wouldn't splitting our awareness be an ingenious solution, allowing us to both maintain our behavior and still retain our knowledge of
reality? This is precisely the state that most of us live in—a split-off,
fragmented, dissonant state in which we continue on with our destructive behaviors while paying some, although not full, heed to the
mounting threats to our ecosystem.

How do we manage such ingenuous and effective splits? Freud suggested that we construct our partitions through a variety of **defense**

mechanisms. As we shall see in the following list of examples, defense mechanisms protect us from our discomfort, enabling us to believe that we are behaving quite reasonably. Defenses are actually quite irrational: They hide reality from us. But they are also functional, by shielding us from our discomfort, so we don't like to give them up. Very much like the principle of cognitive dissonance, which we will discuss in the next chapter on social psychology, defenses demonstrate the illogic of our behavior while also illustrating the vulnerability of our self-concepts.

For example, most of us rationalize frequently. **Rationalization**, one of the most common defense mechanisms, occurs when we create an attractive but untrue explanation for our behavior. For example, Deborah rationalizes when she tells herself that she bought a sweater because it was on sale. Because she really didn't need another sweater, her purchase, however small, contributes to the collapse of the planet's ecosystem by enhancing the market for unnecessary goods. Unnecessary consumption depletes resources and increases pollution by encouraging additional manufacturing and distribution of more unnecessary goods. Like most middle-class North Americans, Deborah finds it too uncomfortable to recognize that fact, so she supplies a more attractive explanation for her behavior and claims that she bought it because it was cheap. Unnecessary purchases are never really cheap—they are very costly from an environmental and social perspective, but rationalization keeps anxiety at bay.

Similarly, most of us **intellectualize** our environmental predicament by failing to recognize our own hand in creating it or the implications it has on our own future. **Intellectualization** occurs when we distance ourselves emotionally from the problem by describing it in abstract, intellectual terms. It is often easier to talk about the general principles of resource depletion than to recognize our personal contributions to it. And frequently we can allow ourselves to notice more general threats, rather than experiencing how they directly endanger us. For example, many people believe that toxic waste is a problem in general, or for *that* community, not *mine* (which may be why so many people use the NIMBY principle—Not In My Back Yard—when responding to environmental threats. NIMBY helps us keep the threat more distant). Topsoil loss affects farmers, not me. Extinction is a problem for other species, not our own. Intellectualizing helps us stay defended by allowing us to superficially address the issue without experiencing anxiety about its impact.

A similar kind of distancing is achieved by the defense mechanism called **displacement**. Freud suggested that displacement occurs when we express our feeling to a different, less threatening target. For example, instead of yelling at the stranger driving a gas-guzzling car or

Source: Toles © 1994. The Washington Post. Reprinted with permission of Universal Press Syndicate. All rights reserved.

sport utility vehicle (SUV), Sue yells at her partner for missing a turn, and having to drive a few extra blocks out of the way. We often express our environmental concerns through indirect and ineffective, but more comfortable, routes. Consider, for example, buying a t-shirt with a picture of a whale on it. The t-shirt does not help the environment, although the picture of a whale leads us to think that it does. To use an even more uncomfortable example, recycling gives us the feeling that we are doing something good for the planet, and of course, we are. However, recycling is a much less direct action than cutting our consumption in the first place. Reducing consumption is much more difficult, so recycling serves as a displacement for our anxiety. It allows us to express our concern, without having to endure the more anxiety-provoking challenge of curbing consumption. Although we certainly agree that recycling is better than nothing, and it is an important function to undertake, it will not solve our problems, and we use it as a defense when we think it will.

Sometimes we are aware of our anxiety, but actively try to think about something else. **Suppression** involves the conscious attempt to put the anxiety-provoking thought out of one's mind. Most of us use suppression quite regularly, when we walk past a homeless person, hear a disturbing newscast about nuclear waste, or contemplate the effects of driving our cars. We begin to experience anxiety, and we intentionally try to change our awareness to reduce it. We shift our attention away from the homeless person we are passing or the carbon dioxide our car is emitting, and change the radio station or our thoughts to avoid discomfort about nuclear waste.

Whereas suppression is a conscious defense, **repression** is unconscious. When we use repression, we do not realize we are doing it. We don't try to put the anxiety-provoking material out of our mind—it just happens. A good example of repression is Deborah's surprise at "finding out" about the nuclear waste problem at a nuclear production site (Hanford) just a few miles from where she lives. Even though information about Hanford had been in the news on and off for 20 years, she only recently "discovered" the problem. She had read about the Chernobyl and Three Mile Island accidents, but never bothered to learn about the giant nuclear reservation not far from her home, which is really much more troubling. She unconsciously repressed not only the waste, but the entire operation, somehow not hearing the news stories or seeing them in the newspaper. She had driven past the reservation many times but (with the government's help) did not see or think about its existence. Repression just occurred naturally without any conscious attempt on her part (although the government's insistence on tight security helped set up an environment in which repression is easy). When a citizens' action group succeeded in getting 19,000 pages of previously classified documents released, her (and many other people's) repression ended, and anxiety replaced it instead.

Repression is certainly the most effective defense, but it is not easy to maintain, especially when information from the world around us threatens to lift its protective force. When stimuli from the outside jeopardize our defenses, we often use **denial**, a mechanism that allows us to insist that the anxiety-provoking material does not exist, while simultaneously expressing our anxiety in the form of impatience, irritation, or even anger. For example, we think that some of our colleagues are in denial about our environmental predicament. While refusing to see or acknowledge the ecosystem's fragility, they express anger and irritation at the very idea. They use sarcasm and humor to reject threats, or mutter the phrase "politically correct" ("p.c.") to dismiss uncomfortable thoughts about not only the environment, but also racial inequalities and other social injustices. When denial is used as a defense, there is a subtext of emotional frustration or hostility. Anxiety is "leaked" alongside the mechanism of repression, which gives denial its own special flavor of tension.

Maxine

Reprinted by permission of the artist.

This flavor of tension is also a part of two other mechanisms, reaction formation, and projection. In **reaction formation**, a person denies the impulse, and *also* gives intense energy to expressing its opposite. For example, the great vehemence with which some environmentalists proclaim self-denying, holier-than-thou, judgmental attitudes about "yuppies" or American comforts suggests that they haven't thoroughly dropped their own instinctual drives toward creature comforts themselves. Likewise, the sneering hostility with which Arnold (1993) described environmentalists as "pathological fools" (p. 42) who buy into "spiritual crap" (p. 30) makes us wonder about his former role as a Sierra Club official. In these cases, it is not the belief or attitude that is questionable, it is the hostility with which it is expressed that suggests underlying emotional conflict.

Like denial and reaction formation, projection also leaks anxiety. **Projection** occurs when we perceive in others what we fail to perceive in ourselves. Most of our judgments and criticisms of others involve some degree of projection, especially when our criticisms are particularly heated or derisive. After all, it is much easier to recognize weaknesses in others than in ourselves. For example, perhaps you have been irritated at someone for being a bad listener, when in fact your own listening skills could use work. Deborah gets irritated by the Wise Use Movement's staunch insistence that what is good for the farmer, rancher, or miner must be good for everybody. Yet, it is painful for Deborah to recognize that she too overgeneralizes her values onto others, assuming that what she thinks is important is ultimately important for everyone. Judgments based on projection have a special flavor of irritation or hostility. Like Deborah, you can learn about your own projections by considering your own irritations about others' behavior.

Finally, Freud proposed that the best defense mechanism we can employ is **sublimation**. Sublimation occurs when we channel our unconscious anxiety into socially acceptable projects, which we do when we go to work or in some way contribute to society. Expressing pain through creative poetry and painting or expressing anxiety by writing a book (!) are popular forms of sublimation. Joining an environmental organization, working to reduce pollution in your community, and modifying your own consumption habits are all examples of sublimation. The full extent of the feeling is not experienced because it is channeled into a culturally useful creation, thereby protecting the individual while contributing something of value. Freud, himself a disciplined and arduous worker, continually sublimated his own impulses into writing, thinking, and communicating with colleagues.

Freud believed that defense mechanisms are inevitable and necessary; indeed, he argued that civilization depends on the inhibition of our basic impulses, and thus on the defenses that prevent their direct expression. Without them we would inappropriately display all sorts of dangerous libidinal or aggressive behavior. Defenses allow for the normal functioning of the individual in a society that requires us to behave, conform, cooperate, and adapt despite our biological drives. But defenses also extract their cost. It takes energy, that limited physical commodity, for which various psychic structures compete. To the extent that energy is tied up by defense mechanisms, less is available for creativity, spontaneity, or realistic problem solving. The extreme case of a completely defended person is the textbook neurotic who spends so much time warding off unacceptable impulses that little else is possible. Surely you have met a few people like this in your lifetime, people who are so afraid of experiencing anything new that all that is possible is a rigidly maintained series of familiar behaviors. These people are shut off from others, as well as from their own creative potential.

Yet we will need this creative potential to solve our environmental problems. Thus, from a Freudian point of view, we must gradually confront our defenses, loosening them slowly so that we may go beyond them without being overwhelmed by the anxiety they help manage. To do this, we must be willing to experience gradually increasing states of discomfort. For example, we cannot begin the difficult problem of environmental clean-up until we allow ourselves to feel the anger, disgust, or guilt that confronting our waste sites might elicit. We must be willing to acknowledge dismay, sadness, and fear about our environmental predicament in order to free up the psychic energy now used by the defenses to be used in more creative problem solving. From a psychoanalytic perspective, being willing to experience discomfort is the first step toward a solution to our problems. We will say more about this principle later in the chapter.

CRITIQUE OF FREUD AND PSYCHOANALYSIS

Much of Freud's theory about specific sexual functions, symbolic expressions, and therapeutic interventions has been reworked or abandoned by psychoanalysts who followed him. The importance of Freud's contribution has been matched by the vehemence with which his ideas have been attacked. As psychologists who are basically more appreciative than critical of his views, we are often impressed by the hostility with which his ideas are criticized (and we wonder about the defense mechanisms that might be at work!). Nevertheless, there are important flaws in Freud's theory that we need to address.

First, Freud's work is criticized most often because there are few empirical studies to support it. Freud claimed to be a scientist, but as he admitted, he did not have the means to test his ideas scientifically (Bilder & LeFever, 1998). Most of his major principles do not easily translate into measurable observations. A related problem is that quite opposite behaviors are explained by the same mechanism, making it difficult to test whether the mechanism is present or absent. For example, if you violently object to Freud's theory, he might say you are defending against your anxiety; because his theory is so accurate, you find it threatening. Here Freud's theory is untestable because there is no way for it to be contradicted. Whether or not you approve of his theory, his theory is supported. A proposition that cannot be empirically contradicted cannot be empirically supported.

Others criticize Freud for his biased, culturally relative ideas about sexuality and gender roles. In particular, feminists have attacked his distorted view of women, and his inability to take them seriously. His concept of "penis envy" is particularly objectionable. On the other hand, feminist psychoanalysis has abandoned some of his concepts while centrally relying on others. In this regard, we must mention Chodorow (1978, 1989), whose focus on parenting relationships (and object relations theory to be discussed shortly) gave rise to a theory of gender differences that has been widely influential. Chodorow formulated a psychoanalytic explanation for the female ethic of care (as in Carol Gilligan's work on female morality, which we will talk more about in chap. 3). Because the daughter separates from the mother later than the son does, females stay in a relationship with the primary caretaker longer, and consequently have greater needs for maintaining connection. Boys have relatively greater needs for building and maintaining separation.

Despite the tremendous controversy surrounding Freud's work, it is worth underscoring his extraordinary contributions. Freud launched clinical psychology by addressing, defining, and treating the neurotic patterns in his patients as psychological disorders. His revealing self-analysis helped us see that normal people use defenses and display character patterns that are simply more obvious in the neurotic patient, but not qualitatively different from normal functioning. His careful scrutinizing, theorizing, and prodigious writing gave us a theory of the unconscious, the notion of defenses, and the concept of conflict in everyday behavior. Although specifics of his treatment techniques and interpretations have been largely discarded, his theorizing about defenses has withstood the test of time, research, and empirical test (R. L. Atkinson, R. C. Atkinson, Smith, & Bem, 1993). The many studies of cognitive dissonance theory described in the next chapter, for example, can be considered empirical demonstrations of rationalization. In sum, Freud's contributions are undeniable.

OBJECT RELATIONS THEORY: RE-EXPERIENCING THE MOTHER

Examining some of the features of object relations theory (ORT) will help us understand how our deepest attitudes toward the environment can be shaped by our earliest experiences with our caretaker. ORT helps us think about why some people care so passionately about the condition of our ecosystem, the well-being of other species, future generations, and other people in far-off lands, while other people seem to be oblivious.

ORT explains how we come to experience our sense of self in relation to the world, especially to other people in the world. The central premise of ORT is that we construct our sense of self from our interactions with others, particularly the person who was our primary caretaker (either a biological or adoptive mother or father, or other caretaker). Our interaction with that important first person lays a template on which we organize and interpret later experiences. The self is not a given, but a complicated psychological project that takes several years to be constructed.

From an ORT perspective, the phrase "Mother Earth" makes tremendous sense: We experience our relationship with the planet in terms of our experience with our mother. Our earliest encounter with

Over the Hedge © Reprinted by permission of United Feature Syndicate.

our first object—the caretaker or mother—becomes a foundation for our relationship with all other objects, including the Earth. Although we do not know of any experimental test of this claim, it makes conceptual sense that we project our earliest relationship on to our sense of the world. The popularity of the phrase "Mother Earth," and its frequent appearance in Native American worldviews (Merchant, 1983) also supports this assertion.

The term *object* may seem an unfortunate one to denote other people, implying that we treat them as objects rather than human beings. The term clearly comes from Freud, who wrote repeatedly about how the child learns to channel biological drives from the target of the mother to other "love-objects." In his words,

> the child's first erotic object is the mother's breast that nourishes it; love has its origin in attachment to the satisfied need for nourishment. There is no doubt that to begin with, the child does not distinguish between the breast and its own body. . . . This first object is later completed into the person of the child's mother, who not only nourishes it, but also looks after it and thus arouses in it a number of other physical sensations, pleasurable and unpleasurable. . . . [Herein] lies the root of a mother's importance, unique, without parallel, established unalterably for a whole lifetime as the first and strongest love-object and as the prototype of all later love relations. . . . (Freud, 1949, p. 56)

There are many variations of ORT and consequently important disagreements, especially regarding the relative power of biological drives versus social experiences as the root explanation for our sense of self (Greenberg & Mitchell, 1983). However, all object relations theorists agree that our sense of self is constructed over time, in interaction with our earliest caretakers. Empirical research has validated the central view that attachment processes occurring early in life affect later emotional functioning (Bowlby, 1989).

Most object relations theorists would endorse the general pattern of development laid out by Mahler (e.g., 1972). According to Mahler, the developmental process takes place over 3 to 4 years, and proceeds from "normal autism," in which the baby experiences an undifferentiated and disorganized set of sensations having to do with need gratification. As the baby and caretaker learn to read each other's cues, they bond together and experience "symbiotic unity." Although this unity is illusory, it is crucial for the child in order for it to trust the world. If the caretaker is unresponsive to the infant's needs, or places too many demands on the infant in return, attachment will be impaired and a host of personality impairments would affect the child's sense of the environment. At about the fourth or fifth year, the "separation/individuation" process begins. While learning to separate itself from the caretaker, the child frequently returns for affirmation and comfort. Finally, the child learns "constancy of self and object," coming to see itself in relationship to other separate beings. Healthy development makes it possible for us to experience ourselves as integrated, multidimensional beings, who, like other people, possess both gifts and faults. Healthy object relations development gives rise to adults who can appreciate themselves while being able to appreciate and bond with others, without either compulsive dependency or fear of intimacy.

The ability to experience one's separateness and yet bondedness with others is a delicate process and many factors can interrupt its optimal conduct in the critical days and years after birth. There are at least two ways in which the self–other split can be damaged that will produce later impairment in our relationship with other people and the environment: excessive early demands and attention withdrawn too early.

Excessive Early Demands

If the caretaker puts excessive demands on the baby, failing to read its cues, but instead inflicting the caretaker's needs, then the child will learn to build a "false self" in which the requirements of others are taken as his or her central being. The attachment formed with the caretaker does not involve the infant's authentic self, but instead an expected or attempted self. Such an individual is incapable of true creativity because life is lived in a state of exacted conformity.

If the caretaker forces the child to feed when it is not hungry, wakes the child when it would prefer to sleep, or otherwise inflicts environmental pressures on the infant that do not fit its internal needs, an orientation to the external world is created before the child organizes its internal one. For example, the rigid feeding schedules popular with parents during the 1940s and early 1950s would produce too many demands too early. The result would be a child who builds a "false self," responding too often to outside demands without being sufficiently tuned to one's internal reality. The baby would develop into an adult who is constantly focused on satisfying the norms of the social group, without adequate self-insight or direction.

Much of the irrationality of our environmentally unsustainable behavior could be attributed to a "false self" system. Without a firmly rooted internal organization, we are likely to use external objects to express who we are. Thus we pursue material pleasures that really function as symbols of our self in relation to others. Automobiles would be an example of a material luxury that do much more than move us from one location to the next: Cars also make a statement to others about who we are. Some people feel personally embarrassed or belittled by driving one style of car rather than another. Clothes are another case of the use of material possession to express the externalized self. Most of us own many more clothes than we really need. Most of our clothes are chosen for "style," and many people feel uncomfortable if they are not properly dressed for a certain occasion, or diminished if their clothes do not feel attractive for one reason or another. Thus, most luxury items function to fulfill pleasure as well as status; we enjoy not only what the object gives us, but also what it says about us. Much of our overconsumption may be driven by a "false self" system.

Even if we do not get caught up in conspicuous consumption, the "false self" system would drive environmentally destructive behaviors by propelling people to take up careers that do not satisfy deeper values or commitments. Many (perhaps most) jobs are done because they are available, rather than because people deeply believe that doing them will make the world a better place. No matter what work one does, the person is healthier psychologically if the work is chosen out of a belief that it is important work that needs to be done in order for society to function effectively. Pride in one's work, and a sense of its value, are signs of a healthy internal organization. Regardless of one's choice, questions about right livelihood eventually surface, often in painful ways during midlife or old age, when people are likely to assess their contribution to the world. Less reliance on the "false self" would make it easier to choose right livelihood earlier in life.

Attention Withdrawn Too Early

At some point, the caretaker must withdraw attention, but if it is done too early or abruptly, trust in the outer world will be damaged. Most of us are fortunate to have had enough good caretaking to bond with our caretaker and then tolerate well enough the inevitable separation/individuation that ensues. Yet because initial interaction with the caretaker is so delicate and so primordial, it rarely is perfect. Whatever small inadequacies it delivers, it lays the foundation for our experience of all other objects in our psychological reality: the crib, toy, the rest of the family, and eventually, the group, the work unit, and finally, the sense of the world. Healthy functioning requires that we have faith that our needs will be met in the future; without this confidence, our trust in the world is damaged. Damaged trust can lead to four neurotic reactions that are likely to impact environmental behavior: narcissism, depression, paranoia, and compulsion.

Narcissism.   First, if an infant suffers a prolonged state of unmet needs, its orientation can become fixated on need gratification, producing a chronic state of **narcissism**. The child learns it cannot depend on the world to satisfy its desires. Such a child will have difficulty recognizing or respecting objects and people that do not offer to alleviate its needs.

From this perspective, a large part of our difficulty could be understood as a kind of massive narcissism, in which we have assumed that nature exists for our need gratification. Our inability to appreciate nature for its own complexity and beauty signals a deeply seated narcissism whereby we see the natural world only as resources, which should be extracted and used for the comfort and convenience of human beings alone. At best, other species are considered irrelevant; more likely their well-being is jeopardized because we consider them either useful for our purposes or noxious to our comfort.

From an object relations point of view, our human anthropocentrism indicates limited psychological development. By positing that we are "on top" of the biological spectrum, humans portray their immaturity and narcissism. We are not suggesting here that humans should be forbidden to use other species or elements of the ecosphere; all species feed on one another, and life in general would be impossible without the food chain that subjects one species to another's biological needs. What we are suggesting, however, is that our Western tendency to regard all of the natural world as simply a storehouse of natural resources awaiting our use, misuse, and waste is narcissistic.

Narcissism can prevent recognition of our responsibilities to members of our own species. For example, we live for the present, and try to suppress our fears about the well-being of the next generation. We focus on the safety of our own family and try to suppress our concerns about those in our neighborhoods, or those in the third world. Recognizing and concerning ourselves with the needs of others requires that we go beyond our own need gratification, to enlarge our scope of justice (to use vocabulary introduced in the next chapter).

Compulsion.   Narcissism can also set up the personality for compulsive behaviors such as addiction. According to Freud, a **compulsion** is any repetitive action that a person feels driven to make and is unable to resist. As a defense mechanism, compulsions help us manage anxiety. For example, many of us have had the experience of ameliorating a bad mood or experience by purchasing something new. In fact, there are many women's jokes about it, such as the greeting card that says "I'm depressed" on the cover, and on the inside it says "Wanna go shopping?" For many Americans, shopping is an addiction. The person may know somehow that it is not appropriate, and some people even do it in private, hoping that their friends will not see them (a key signal of addictive behavior). Consumer goods offer a temporary substitute for the loss of a nurturing environment we experienced early in life, but no longer can. Addictions can also involve drug or substance abuse, compulsive eating or gambling, or sexual activity. In all cases, the individual's experience is organized around need satisfaction; the world is simply a place that offers or denies the opportunities to satisfy one's needs. Unfortunately, however, addictive needs and narcissistic impulses are never satisfied, because the target objects cannot feed the deeper psychological need for self-definition. (We discuss this idea of a deeper self in more detail in chap. 7.)

Depression.   If the baby experiences too sudden a withdrawal, unmet needs can lead it to chronic despair. The child would become vulnerable to **depression**, suffering a primal loss of confidence in the outside world and its own ability to affect it. A chronic sense of loss, hopelessness, or grief would pervade the personality, and the individual would become depressed, especially whenever real losses are incurred. The ability to "keep the faith" would be difficult for such individuals.

Depression is a serious psychological problem that often leads to suicide and suicide attempts. In 2000, almost 30,000 people in the United States died from suicide, and it is now the third leading cause of death among persons from age 10 to 24 (Center for Disease Control, 2002b). From an ORT viewpoint, high rates of suicide are understandable in light of the large number of babies who are born to parents who are either physically or emotionally unavailable to them, either through overwork, divorce, teenage pregnancy, or substance abuse. Empirical evidence demonstrates that adults who are prone to depression are more likely than average to have lost a parent early in life (Barnes & Prosen, 1985).

Adult reactions toward environmental difficulties can easily lead to despair, especially as the complexity and the enormity of the problems become clearer to us. Understanding our environmental predicament can shrink our trust that the world will provide for us, and in some ways diminished trust seems appropriate. On the other hand, our need to find active and creative solutions to a deteriorating physical world also requires that we stay hopeful, if not always confident. We will say more about how to maintain emotional fortitude in light of our environmental problems at the end of this chapter and in chapter 8.

Paranoia.   Finally, the child could translate lack of trust into chronic **paranoia**, in which it experiences the world as an antagonistic place where only bad things happen. Such a person lives in a chronic state of fear and suspicion, fearful that at any moment someone may turn against her or him. Full-scale paranoia is an unusual pathology, but more subtle versions are quite common. Consider, for example, Freud's view that nature stands in opposition to human existence, and must be tamed by technology so that its nefarious effects are reduced. From an ORT perspective, his view of a separate and threatening universe illustrates a cultural pattern of diminished trust projected onto nature.

By now, you might be thinking that this is a lot to blame on early caretakers. Other schools in psychology (like the behaviorists, who are the focus of chap. 4) put more attention into investigating present causes of behavior, rather than an individual's early history. Focusing on the present can make it easier to see what and how to change. However, considering how difficult it is to alter habitual behaviors, it seems plausible to us that deeply patterned experiences of the self in relation to the world provide an important template on which the rest of the adult personality is built. The important contribution of ORT is the proposition that the self is a construction based on many experiences, which occur early in life and lay down character patterns that are often difficult to change.

Difficult, but not impossible. Although becoming conscious of our character patterns is not easy, awareness of them offers the opportunity to make choices outside of the patterns. A paranoid person may become aware of the paranoid pattern, and with the help and experience of more trustworthy relationships, choose to trust instead, knowing that the trust response is awkward and difficult. Similarly, a compulsive shopper may become aware that shopping is an addiction, and choose to satisfy needs for connection through some other method, even though unconscious impulse would still lead the person in the direction of the shopping mall. Choosing to contradict the pattern will not happen until the person becomes conscious of the pattern, and the myriad ways in which it unconsciously drives behavior. When a person comes to recognize the pattern, then alternative choices can be made. The important insight is that our sense of self and our relationship to the world, as well as the defenses that we use to manage our anxieties, are all psychological constructions. Becoming aware of our deeply set patterns and habitual defenses offers us the opportunity to see their constraints and to begin to act outside of them.

USING FREUD'S IDEAS

To approach our difficulty from an analytic framework, we have to talk about the psychotherapy Freud developed, called **psychoanalysis**. From this perspective, because behavior is controlled by deeply unconscious forces and maintained by an active defense structure, we must learn to experience unconscious feelings in order for anything to heal. Consequently, Freud believed that emotional material must be allowed to surface and be expressed. This expression he called **catharsis**, a term he borrowed from Aristotle. Catharsis is a spontaneous and powerful emotional expression that slips past the defenses. Freud viewed psychic energy as analogous to the energy of a steam engine; if the energy is not expressed somewhere, then the system will eventually explode. Emotional discharge frees us from this tightly organized system of defenses, releasing the energy that was tied up in keeping the unacceptable feelings unconscious.

Although catharsis is not a popular idea in experimental psychology, it still carries import in psychoanalytic circles where it refers to the expression of emotional energy. From this viewpoint, we will not be able to creatively develop solutions to our predicament until we allow ourselves to experience and express the uncomfortable feelings our environmental problems cause us. Thus, the first step in solving environmental problems is to allow ourselves to *feel*. The feelings we defend against will not be pleasant to experience: anger, sadness, disappointment, shame, fear. These feelings are legitimate reactions to our situation, and attempts to block them only stand in our way of true healing. Without the direct experience and expression of such feelings, part of our psyche must be allocated toward arranging a defense of them, thus robbing our full intelligence for finding creative solutions.

But how are we to experience these feelings without being overwhelmed by them? Psychoanalytic theorists such as Nicholsen (2002) argued that we need to experience them in the safety of "holding environments" that is, the psychological safety of a loving bond. Originally, the loving bond was with the person who mothered us, but as adults we must find trusted allies who can be present with our strong feelings without themselves being overwhelmed by them. These allies can be therapists, mentors, teachers, and in some cases, close friends or partners.

Working with holding environments, Macy developed "despair and empowerment work" to free up psychic energy for more adaptive behaviors. For Macy, despair rests just under the surface of our psyches, embedded in a feeling of powerlessness and meaninglessness. Expressing the despair often leads to concomitant expression of fear and anger. Such catharsis, however, then frees up the psyche to redirect energy toward adaptive solutions.

> Repression is physically, mentally and emotionally expensive: it drains the body, dulls the mind and muffles emotional responses. When repressed material is brought to the surface and released, energy is released as well; life comes into clearer focus. Art, ritual, and play have ever played a cathartic role in our history—just as, in our time, psychotherapy does too. By this process the cognitive system appropriates elements of its experience, and by integrating them gains a measure of both control and freedom. (Macy, 1983, p. 23)

Even without hiring a therapist to do such work, however, you can profit from this approach by taking a moment to visualize a trashed world, clogged by pollution, with starving or greedy people depleting its last resources. Imagine you and your family, even your own children, forced to drink unsafe water, exposed to air pollutants that destroy lungs and immune systems, and malnourished by inadequate food.

What feelings surface in you? Your appreciation and understanding of the Freudian approach will be enhanced if you write down your reactions. Allow yourself to "climb into" even the most fleeting of sensations, so that you can further identify and "own" those feelings. The more fully you allow yourself to experience your feelings, the more your energy will be available for redirection toward creative solutions.

A Freudian perspective would predict that as we begin to sense the seriousness of our planetary predicament, many of us will feel anxiety,

Time Magazine © Time Inc./TIMEPIX. Reprinted by permission.

sadness, or helplessness. Working with these emotions for a few moments will help you experience them more fully. It will probably also
help you experience how automatic and habitual the defense system is.
We do not *want* to feel our painful feelings, and we use myriad defenses to stay away from them. Track not only your feelings, but the
ways in which you minimize, distort, deny, or intellectualize them. A
despair/empowerment therapist would help you to exaggerate your
feelings, allowing the expression of them to become fuller and fuller,
until the whole of you is immersed in them. This holistic response
would enable a temporary cessation of the splitting we ordinarily use
to maintain our functioning. Once the splitting is interrupted, the full
power of the person can be experienced. Much of our resistance to full
experience is the fear that as soon as we allow it to occur, we will be

immobilized. "If I allow myself to experience any sadness, I will be overcome by chronic despair." Just the opposite happens, however. Once I allow myself to experience the fullest degree of sadness, energy is lined up and available for redirection.

From a Freudian perspective, our deeply set instinctual drives will be difficult to change (although not impossible). Adult character is built on an infantile pattern of neediness, and the accoutrements of adult society function as symbolic expressions of those needs. Although we do not really need the luxury car, we *do* need the sense of self-edification and validation that such a car provides. Until we change the social meanings of luxury items in a consumer culture, we will be unlikely to change our behavior patterns. Unless, that is, we develop insight into the ways in which our behaviors are irrational expressions of deeper needs that can be satisfied in more direct ways. When we do the necessary emotional work of confronting and experiencing our deeper feelings, behavioral changes will be sustained, rather than superficial and fleeting.

Let us consider the problem of overconsumption from a Freudian and ORT perspective. Knowing that those of us in the United States constitute less than 5% of the globe's population but consume over 30% of its resources, and knowing what a problematic chain of events such overconsumption creates in the global system, our superegos should create moral injunctions against unnecessary material purchases. Yet from an object relations viewpoint, purchases represent an unconscious expression of self; we will not be able to sustain any meaningful behavior change until we become conscious of the deeper reasons for our overconsumption. What would this mean in terms of our daily behavior? We might decide not to go to the shopping mall because we recognize the temptations that meet us there. We might even decide out of moral responsibility to forgo a particular purchase that we would normally enjoy making.

Unfortunately, psychoanalytic theory would predict that verbal resolutions will eventually fail. Our resolutions are likely to deteriorate, and our unresolved issues will express themselves eventually, either through more binge shopping, harsh criticism about somebody else's consumption behavior, or other substituted forms of consumption. It is not until we experience and integrate the deeper unconscious feelings that we will be able to permanently reduce our consumption.

For example, when Deborah recognizes that her interest in buying a new stereo system is probably coming from an old feeling of being deprived or feeling powerless, she can choose to notice all the ways in which she is currently not deprived, or is really powerful. When such feelings are made conscious, recognized, and integrated into the adult world, the new purchase looks and feels obscene, and ceases to interest her. Changing instinctually driven behavior is difficult, but this does not mean that we should not start trying immediately. What it does mean is that our initial efforts are likely to be inconsistent. Moreover, it means that we should try to stay in touch with the *feelings* that motivate the purchase, which facilitate or deny the purchase, and with alternative means for expressing our sense of self. The key point is that from a psychoanalytic perspective, consciousness is crucial. Eventually, with several years of steady practice, our consumption patterns will change. But they will not change before we confront and become conscious of our deeper feelings for self-validation, pleasure, and aggression, finding other ways to sublimate those needs instead of through environmentally destructive behaviors.

From a Freudian perspective, you can begin to create a sustainable world in the following ways:

1. Being willing to experience your own despair, anxiety, sadness, or anger over a faltering physical world and the enormity of the global dimensions that drive its environmental crises; expressing those feelings fully in a safe place so that energy ordinarily used by your defenses can be freed up and redirected to creative solutions.

2. Recognizing your own defenses and working gently with them; seeking out troubling information and noticing how uncomfortable it makes you; noticing your reactions that help you avoid discomfort, and gently choosing alternative behaviors.

3. Recognizing your own unconscious needs to express personal identity through material consumption; finding alternative ways to direct your energy and your needs for self-fulfillment.

4. Choosing a specific project for helping create a sustainable world and allowing yourself the latitude to be inconsistent, ambivalent, anxious, or inefficient as you complete it.

CONCLUSIONS

The psychoanalytic tradition gives us a rich set of ideas with which to consider our ecological predicament. Freud formulated important understandings of the role of the unconscious, of defense mechanisms, and of the bodily basis of our unconscious motivations. ORT extended his work to focus on the construction of the self and a way of thinking about variations in the self–world experience. In general, the Freudian tradition suggests that changing our sense of ourselves in the world and our relationship to nature will not be an easy task. We have deeply rooted reasons to believe that we are separate beings, competing for the resources of nature. But the Freudian tradition helps us to reconsider our views by demonstrating the unconscious and irrational mechanisms that support them.

Noticing how deep-seated our impulses are for environmentally inappropriate behavior also suggests that we should be compassionate with ourselves and with others, realizing that we are facing a monumental task. We are likely to experience disappointment and frustration with our inability to change a lot all at once. But over time, in safe emotional relationships, we can free up our psychic energy for the crucial task of changing our behavior and building a sustainable world.

We value the Freudian approach for leading us to compassion. Compassion is crucial for ourselves (forgiving ourselves for our errors) as well as for others (especially those who do not agree with us). One of Sue's students provides a good example of this point. After taking Sue's class on environmental psychology, the student interacted differently with her father, who was very adamant in his anti-environmental opinions. She practiced really hearing his views, and gently offering alternate viewpoints. Ultimately, he shifted some of his environmentally destructive behaviors. When we feel heard, understood, and cared for, it's a lot easier to consider changing long-standing patterns.

Freud himself was more pessimistic. As a determinist, Freud saw little hope for the ability of human beings to survive and transcend the incontrovertible forces of nature that ply against us at every turn. Freud well understood human efforts to fend against nature, and even glimpsed the destructive potential that our successful attempts might bring. By suggesting that we "have gained control over the forces of nature to such an extent that [we] would have no difficulty in exterminating one another to the last [hu]man" (Freud, 1930/1961, pp. 39, 92) Freud recognized the anxiety that our control of nature elicits, even 20 years before the creation of the atomic bomb. Because it is no easier to control our own natures than it is to control the outer physical world, our illusion of technological control is both dangerous and frightening.

Yet we do not have to adopt either Freud's determinism or his pessimism to use and profit from his theories. To the extent we are willing to experience some discomfort, we can begin to examine our own defense structure, and the underlying object relation pattern it supports. Have you ever noticed that it is the more mature, self-aware, and insightful people who are able to note their limitations without being devastated by them? By noticing our own shortcuts in thinking, our own attempts to justify our actions and ward off discomfort, our

chronic orientation to the world around us, and our habitual attempts
to soothe our vulnerable self-concept, we may become more mature,
more conscious, and ultimately more likely to survive. Thus, in order
to become conscious, we must learn about the ways in which we are
unconscious. Such learning is not easy, but if you have managed to
sense a defense or two, or an ego pattern that you use, you are well on
your way.

KEY CONCEPTS

Anxiety

Catharsis

Damaged object relations: compulsion, depression, narcissism,
paranoia

Defense mechanisms: denial, displacement, intellectualization, projection, rationalization, reaction formation, repression, sublimation, suppression

Ego

Id

Instinct

Object relations theory

Psychoanalysis

Splitting

Superego

Unconscious

3

Social Psychology

I magine that you are at a party with some friends. One of them is talking about the Environmental Issues Club she belongs to and its work on the Endangered Species Act (ESA). The ESA, a federal regulation adopted in 1973, makes it illegal to engage in any practice that threatens the extinction of a species, like the Northern Spotted Owl or Chinook Salmon. Since its adoption, lawmakers have continuously discussed revising or dropping the ESA because efforts to protect certain species hinder some industries, such as timber and aluminum companies. Your friend explains that her group is collecting signatures to send to Congress to urge them not to change the ESA. You don't know much about the issue one way or another, but you like your friend a lot, and decide, along with the rest of the people standing there, to sign her petition. After all, it does seem reasonable to try to protect species from extinction. Her argument that we humans shouldn't have the right to let other species perish because of our human actions makes sense.

A few days later she calls you to thank you for your support, and she tells you there is a meeting next week to learn more about the legislation and the grassroots efforts to save the ESA. As she is talking, you start thinking about a letter you read earlier that morning in the newspaper. It was written by a prominent community businessman and it argued that the ESA is a threat to American freedoms and the free market system. You thought the letter was well written and you see his point about government interference with business opportunities. Now you feel torn. What do you tell your friend? Will you go to the meeting? Are you more likely to go to the meeting because you previously signed the petition? How does your liking for your friend stack up against your respect for the businessman in influencing your decision? Are you likely to weigh his opinion more because he is male? Does the fact that he is a male affect his attitudes about environmental issues?

In this example we see some important topics of **social psychology**, which is the scientific study of social influence. How does our attraction to and respect for others determine what we think and do? Does gender sway our responses? How about education, age, and political affiliation? How do you come to decide whether human beings have the right to knowingly extinguish other species?

Although we like to think our attitudes and behaviors are based on rational and logical assessment of facts, a brief glimpse at social psychology reveals the enormously powerful (although usually unconscious) influences that other people have on us, our reasoning, beliefs and values, and behavior. From a social psychological perspective, our understanding and actions about environmental issues are largely social phenomena.

In this chapter, we survey some of social psychology's most important concepts, as they can be applied to environmental issues. After examining a few classic studies in the field, we will look at how they can help us think about ways to increase environmentally appropriate behavior. By the end of the chapter, we hope you will agree that what we do and what we believe arise from an intriguing composite of socially determined rules, beliefs, and explanations, making our environmentally relevant behavior very much about social influence.

OUR IRRATIONAL ATTEMPTS TO LOOK RATIONAL: COGNITIVE DISSONANCE THEORY

Leon Festinger (1919–1989) inspired an enormous amount of research, debate, and insight into the way social influence works. Festinger began his career with an interest in how people explain away their anxieties by making up explanations. To find out, he and two of his students infiltrated a religious cult, whose leader had professed the end of the world. Under secret cover, the researchers studied how cult members experienced and coped with their crisis (as phrased in Festinger, Schachter, & Reicken's book title *When Prophecy Fails*, 1956). Assuming the world would go on, Festinger was curious as to how the cult members would deal with the "unequivocal and undeniable evidence that [their] belief is wrong" (p. 3). What impressed the researchers was that the most ardent believers emerged from the experience more, rather than less, convinced of their accuracy. When faced with the painful contradiction between their beliefs and reality, the true believers found a new explanation: Because of their prayer and goodness, God had decided to save the world.

Festinger's work on failed prophecy is reminiscent of the boomster/doomster debate we discussed in chapter 1. When beliefs are strong, people are unlikely to change their minds simply because new information is available. Instead, contradictory "facts" are discounted, distorted, or disregarded so that the more vigorous opinion remains undiminished. (That's probably why many people try to avoid discussions of religion or politics at the dinner table—we're more likely to change our opinion of our dinner partner than we are our strongly held positions.)

In more general terms, Festinger posited that whenever we experience a discrepancy between two thoughts, cognitive dissonance exists. **Cognitive dissonance** produces an uncomfortable state of tension, which motivates us to take whatever steps we can to reduce it, including changing beliefs or behaviors in order to appear consistent. However, we don't need such an extreme illustration of a religious cult to understand how dissonance reduction works. To go back to our opening example, Festinger would predict that your friend's telephone call would create cognitive dissonance and you would be uncomfortable until you reduced it. Her request to attend the meeting would elicit two contradictory cognitions: On the one hand, you feel allegiance toward your friend, some agreement with her view about the importance of saving the ESA, and an urge to appear consistent with your recent signing of her petition; but, on the other hand, you also respect the importance of American freedoms, the articulate nature of the anti-ESA letter, and the businessman himself, so you feel some sentiment against the ESA. Festinger would predict that your motivation to resolve this conflict will lead you to diminish the importance of one viewpoint and elevate the importance of the other. For example, if you do agree to go to the Environmental Club meeting, you will be likely to find some reason why the businessman is not very convincing (perhaps you'll decide that business people are myopic about environmental problems); or if you refuse to go to the meeting, the letter will seem more convincing (what else is more important to protect than American freedom?). Festinger emphasized the importance of postdecision shifts in our reasoning: Once committed to a decision, we line up and rearrange our conflicting cognitions to fit it.

Most of us reduce our cognitive dissonance over environmental problems by creating plausible but untrue explanations for our behavior. For example, unsure whether Deborah should contribute money to an environmental cause presented to her in an umpteenth mass mailing appeal, she discards the plea, picturing the director in a fancy limousine and thinking to herself that "they probably spend way too much on overhead." Likewise, if you decide not to go to the ESA meeting, you're likely to prop up your decision by finding additional reasons: You don't have the time, or you have a competing commitment, or you might be coming down with a cold. These are not necessarily lies, but they are reasons that might not occur to you unless you needed them to justify your decision.

Of course, dissonance can also be used to increase environmentally appropriate behavior. One way this has been demonstrated is through the **foot-in-the-door technique**. If someone gets us to agree to a small action, they can often get us to undertake a bigger one. The foot-in-the-door technique would lead to the prediction that you'll be more likely to go to the ESA meeting (a big action) because you previously signed the petition (a little action). Researchers have successfully used this technique to increase energy conservation behaviors. For example, one study (Pallack, Cook, & Sullivan, 1980) observed families who had volunteered to participate in conservation projects and randomly assigned them to two different groups. The first group was asked to have their name published in the newspaper (they all agreed); the second group was not asked. Even though none of the names were ever published, the group that agreed to the public commitment showed a 15% greater reduction of gas use and a 20% greater reduction of electricity use than did the group that was not asked. Apparently, the intent to go public was enough to induce behavior change; people try to live up to their public image. Similarly, other research (Werner et al., 1995) demonstrated that simply signing one's name indicating one's interest in curbside recycling, increased participation beyond that of other persuasion techniques, like a face-to-face visit or receiving a flyer. Other research (Cobern, Porter, Leeming, & Dwyer, 1995) showed more recycling of grass clippings by those people the researchers asked to speak to their neighbors about it, than those they didn't ask. Finally, Hornik, Cherian, Madansky, and Narayana (1995) demonstrated that commitment to recycling is a much stronger predictor of recycling behaviors than monetary rewards, or other personal factors like perceived satisfaction or locus of control.

Foot-in-the-door effects can be accomplished in other ways. For example, Hutton (1982) randomly selected sets of households and mailed water-flow restrictors to them, together with information about conserving water; another set of households received only the information and not the devices. The group that got the devices used less water. More importantly, however, this group also showed a variety of other conservation behaviors, such as turning down their hot water heaters, cleaning their furnaces, and installing automatic thermostats. As long as you start conserving in one area, you might as well do it in others. Likewise, Arbuthnot and his colleagues (1977) were able to increase recycling behavior by simply asking people to complete a survey about recycling or to send a pro-recycling postcard to the city council. Getting people to adopt a small pro-environment behavior can lead them to adopt other pro-environment behaviors, presumably because behaviors are changed to maintain consistency with publicly expressed attitudes.

Although these techniques are useful, there are a few caveats. First, foot-in-the-door and commitment techniques work with behaviors of similar domain. In other words, getting people to sign a petition about recycling, or make a promise to recycle, might increase their recycling behaviors, but it will not necessarily do much for other environmentally relevant behaviors (like bicycle riding). Second, although weak forms of public commitment can have an effect, the strength of a person's commitment is central for sustaining long-term behavior change. People who make strong written commitments (Pardini & Katzev, 1983–1984) or individual commitment (Wang & Katzev, 1990) are more likely to continue recycling than those who make weaker verbal ones or none at all.

Thus, our motive to look consistent is a powerful form of social control. Dissonance reduction can even produce a stronger effect than reinforcers such as money: Katzev and Johnson (1984) compared the energy use of homeowners who signed a written commitment to reduce energy with another group that had been offered money to do so. Those who signed the pledge showed more reduction.

ATTITUDES VERSUS BEHAVIOR

Certainly we like to think our behavior is consistent with our attitudes, but we usually think attitudes cause behavior: We think we recycle cans because we believe it is important to save resources; if someone told us we think it is important to save resources because we recycle cans, we would think that explanation was bizarre. Most attempts to influence social behavior, including advertising and marketing, work on the commonsense model: Change what people believe and that will change their behavior. Environmental education seems like the first step to increasing environmentally responsible actions.

Yet social psychologists have learned a lot about attitudes that make this simple rule insufficient. As we discussed in chapter 1, many people have pro-environment attitudes that are incongruent with environmentally relevant behaviors, but it isn't just in our environmental actions where we are hypocritical. Morally relevant attitudes fail to match individual behavior in a host of other arenas. For example, most people claim they are not racist, even though racist behaviors are universal, especially in the most intimate situations (e.g., marriage or sex) (D. G. Myers, 2002). Similarly, people's attitudes about cheating have little to do with whether or not they actually cheat (Wickler, 1969).

Not surprisingly, then, research on the relation between environmental attitudes and behaviors has shown inconsistent results. Sometimes pro-environmental attitudes correlate with pro-environment behavior (e.g., people who think recycling is important are more likely to recycle). Sometimes pro-environmental attitudes are unrelated to behavior (e.g., people who think use of fossil fuels should be reduced do not necessarily drive less than others). When different studies show contradictory results, it is often useful to do what social scientists call a meta-analysis. A **meta-analysis** looks for patterns across various studies in order to make sense of contradictory data.

Hines, Hungerford, and Tomera (1986/1987) did a meta-analysis on environmental attitudes and behavior. By aggregating 128 different studies, they showed that the correlation between attitudes and behavior is positive, although not very strong. Attitudes and behavior are more tightly related when actual behavior, rather than self-reported behavior, is measured. For example, your attitudes about recycling say more about how much you *actually* recycle than how much you *say* you recycle. This might be because when people self-report, they overestimate the amount of environmentally responsible behaviors they do. Attitude–behavior consistency is also stronger when people belong to environmental organizations, when they feel personally responsible, and when they verbally express their intentions to engage in responsible behaviors. In addition, the more specific the behavior and the attitude statement, the more the consistency (Vining & Ebreo, 2002). For example, an attitude about recycling cans correlates with the behavior of recycling cans better than a general concern about environmental problems correlates with a variety of conservation behaviors.

WHO CARES ABOUT THE ENVIRONMENT?

It's worth noting that interest in environmental problems is not randomly distributed across the population. Demographic variables show predictable association with environmental concern. A few decades ago, environmental sociologists Van Liere and Dunlap (1980) showed that environmental concern is more prevalent among people with more education and in higher social classes. There are at least two possible explanations for a relation between class and attitude: (a) Education could enhance environmental concern through information and socialization; or (b) default: Those with less socioeconomic standing may have more immediate concerns (e.g., crime, disease, and hunger) than long-range environmental ones. On the other hand, concern is not completely determined by wealth. Dunlap, Gallup, and Gallup (1992) also demonstrated that public concern about environmental problems is high, even in poorer countries like Mexico, Poland, and Chile.

Second, pro-environmental attitudes are more prevalent among younger than older people. Perhaps young people are less integrated into the American economic system or dominant social paradigm (see later discussion), so it is easier for them to hold pro-environmental attitudes because they are less likely to be family wage-earners. Or per-

When asked by Gallup International, people around the world are critical of their governments' protection of the environment. In the world's largest opinion poll, two thirds of the 1.25 billion respondents said their government has done too little to address the environmental issues in their country. In only 5 of the 60 participating countries did a majority agree that their government had done the right amount to address environmental issues.

Has your government done enough?

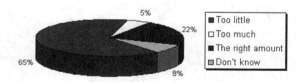

And only in 3 countries (Armenia, Cameroon, and Hong Kong) did a majority think that economic growth is more important than protection of the environment. In all other countries the protection of the environment was viewed as more important than economic growth.

Figures and text from the Gallup International Millennium Survey, retrieved online from http://www.gallup-international.com/survey11.htm. Reprinted with permission from Gallup International Association, London, England.

FIG. 3.1. Environmental concern is global.

haps younger people are more affected by environmental disasters such as the oil spill off the coast of Spain in 2002, because they have had less experience with the robustness of nature relative to its fragility. Perhaps, because more of their lifetime experience has been filled with smoggy skies, overcrowding, and falling fish yields, they are more disturbed about environmental damage.

Third, urban residents are more concerned about environmental problems than rural residents. Urbanites may have experienced more environmental problems directly, and/or may be less dependent on extractive resource use than small town residents. Rural residents may be less likely to romanticize nature and think of it as a pretty painting because they live in closer contact with wilderness spaces. Fourth, political affiliation is correlated with environmentalism. Environmentalists are more likely to be Democrats than Republicans, possibly because of their greater comfort with regulation and reforms and their weaker alignment with business and industry. Finally, for reasons to be discussed shortly, women tend to have more environmental concerns than men, especially when it comes to hazards that impact the local community or health of the family (Mohai, 1992; Stern, Dietz, & Kalof, 1993; Zelezny, Chua, & Aldrich, 2000).

Toles © 1994. The Washington Post. Reprinted with permission of Universal Press Syndicate. All rights reserved.

Concern about environmental problems implicates a larger worldview. To get a feel for our claim here, try responding to the following questions by circling how much you agree or disagree:

1. We are approaching the limit of the number of people the earth can support.
   Strongly Agree
   Mildly Agree
   Mildly Disagree
   Strongly Disagree

2. The earth has plenty of natural resources if we just learn how to develop them.
   Strongly Agree
   Mildly Agree
   Mildly Disagree
   Strongly Disagree

3. If things continue on their present course, we will soon experience a major ecological catastrophe.
   Strongly Agree
   Mildly Agree
   Mildly Disagree
   Strongly Disagree

4. Humans were meant to rule over the rest of nature.
   Strongly Agree
   Mildly Agree
   Mildly Disagree
   Strongly Disagree

These statements illustrate the way researchers measure environmental beliefs with the New Ecological Paradigm Scale (Dunlap, Van Liere, Mertig, & Jones, 2000). If you agree with the second and fourth statements more than you agree with the first and third, you probably hold what Pirages and P. R. Ehrlich (1974) called a dominant social paradigm (DSP). The DSP reflects a belief in "abundance and progress, growth and prosperity, faith in science and technology, and commitment to a laissez-faire economy, limited governmental planning and private property rights" (Dunlap & Van Liere, 1978, p. 10). Pirages and P. R. Ehrlich (1974) called these views dominant because they illustrate the modern Western worldview that people in the industrialized world have held for many generations. These assumptions accompany beliefs that land not used for economic gain is wasted, that individuals have the freedom and right to develop land for economic profit, and that human beings should convert however much of the natural world they can procure to support their private well-being. Faith in science mitigates concern about approaching limits or destruction of the ecosphere.

The most coherent version of this viewpoint was expressed in the "Wise Use Movement" of the 1990s. Supported by extractive industries, and comprised of ranchers, farmers, miners, and other landowners who believe they have a right to use the land as they see fit, this movement pushed for county ordinances restricting federal environmental regulations. For example, a county plan approved by Ontonagon County, Michigan asserted that:

> All natural resource decisions affecting Ontonagon County shall be guided by the principles of protecting private property rights, protecting local custom and culture, maintaining traditional economic structures through self-determination, and opening new economic opportunities through reliance on free markets. ("Wishful Thinking," 1994, p. 40)

Such a statement upholds traditional American values while subtly elevating local county regulations over federal law.

People who think environmental problems are unimportant show strong agreement with DSP items such as:

- support for the status quo ("We should know if something new will work before taking a chance on it.")
- distrust of government ("Regulation of business by government usually does more harm than good.")
- support for private property rights ("Property owners have an inherent right to use their land as they see fit.")
- faith in science and technology ("Most problems can be solved by applying more and better technology.")
- support for economic growth ("The positive benefits of economic growth far outweigh any negative consequences.")

People who have high DSP scores show less concern about environmental problems, such as population control, pollution control, resource conservation, environmental funding, and environmental regulations (Dunlap & Van Liere, 1984; Pierce, Dalton, & Zaitsev, 1999; Widegren, 1998).

If you agreed more with items 1 and 3, you hold a New Ecological Paradigm (NEP) (Dunlap et al., 2000); NEP scores are correlated positively with more concern about environmental problems. That is, people who believe that world ecological issues are pressing, who support pro-environmental policies, and who believe community air and water pollution are serious problems are likely to agree with NEP statements such as:

- "We are approaching the limit of the number of people the Earth can support."
- "If things continue on their present course, we will soon experience a major ecological catastrophe."
- "The balance of nature is very delicate and easily upset."

Research with the NEP scale between 1976 and 1990 showed significant increases in public endorsement of the NEP. For example, Item 3 ("If things continue on their present course, we will soon experience a major ecological catastrophe") had 60% agreement in 1978 and 78% agreement in 1990. In line with data we described in chapter 1, the public appears to be increasing its support for the NEP and reducing its support for the DSP. Dunlap also documented widespread environmental concerns in 22 other countries and recently demonstrated that people around the world believe that their governments should do more to address environmental problems (see Fig. 3.1).

One of the items on the NEP scale is "Plants and animals have as much right as humans to exist." This statement gets us back to our problem of the Endangered Species Act (ESA). How do you come to decide whether or not other species have a right to exist? Dunlap's research shows that your opinion on this question relates to a whole host of other beliefs about environmental limits, the delicacy of nature, the threat of ecological catastrophe, and your worldview in general (Hodgkinson & Innes, 2000). From a social psychological perspective, that's because we spend a lot of our cognitive energy constructing coherent meaning in a social context.

ATTRIBUTION THEORY: MAKING UP MEANING

Worldviews are a coherent picture of reality, and one example of our attempt to figure out the world. Other attempts at making meaning give rise to explanations for other people's behaviors. Social psychologists call the act of creating explanations for behavior the **attribution process**. We rarely see the social world strictly in terms of overt behaviors. Instead, we are continuously attributing those behaviors to our constructed explanations. He smiles when he is hiking in the wilderness because he's happy. She throws paper in the trash, rather than recycles, because she doesn't care. Attributions help us make sense of our social world, create a sense of order and consistency, and provide convenient shortcuts for interacting with others. But sometimes attributions get in our way.

For example, most of us make the **fundamental attribution error** on a regular basis. We overestimate the degree to which other people's behaviors are due to their personal traits, and underestimate the degree to which they are caused by the situation. For example, when Deborah sees a colleague drive his car two blocks to the library, she explains that behavior as laziness and lack of awareness about environmental issues; she's less likely to attribute it to the possibility that he has to carry 14 books back. But when *she* drives her car around the campus to the library, it's obviously due to the situational demand of returning so many books. "I'm not lazy, but he is." Most of our attribution problems come from these kinds of **self-serving biases**: We like to think of ourselves in favorable ways, and resist uncomplimentary explanations.

For example, most people like to think of themselves as well informed. However, when Archer and colleagues surveyed California residents, they found huge discrepancies between how much people claimed they knew about energy conservation and how much they really knew. After taking objective tests to measure their knowledge, people were asked to predict how well they performed. They assumed they knew from one half to two thirds of the answers; instead their actual scores ranged from 1.4% to 41% (Archer et al., 1983). Similarly, most people like to think that they are not wasting energy and will go to impressive lengths to explain away evidence showing they are. For example, Hackett (1984) demonstrated how people like to believe their energy consumption is normal, and use creative attributions to maintain that view, as the following explanation from a utility user illustrates:

> I had gotten my PG&E bill and said out loud about how awful it was and she (a little old lady) looked at me and said "oh, I don't pay anything like that." It turned out her apartment is the same size as mine but she said she paid only about $20 a month for heat. I couldn't believe it. I've thought about that so much. She was really tiny, real small, though, not like me. I think maybe these real little old ladies just don't have much meat on their bones, so they don't need much heat to get warmed up. (quoted by Hacket, 1984, p. 298)

THE RATIONALITY OF IRRATIONAL BEHAVIOR

From the outside, explaining away the end of the world or a higher energy bill all looks pretty irrational, as does a lot of other behavior social psychologists have observed in the laboratory. The frequency and ease with which social psychologists have been able to induce illogical behavior has led Aronson (1994) to conclude that "people who do crazy things are not necessarily crazy" (p. 9). Instead of attributing our behavior to personal characteristics of the individual, social psychologists instead look to the situation to examine the social forces that induce us to behave irrationally. For example, Milgram (1974) showed that two thirds of his participants pushed levers that they believed would inflict shocks that could seriously hurt or kill another human being. Because they followed such instructions given by a research scientist, social psychologists emphasized the power of the situation to induce obedience.

Instead of looking for internal explanations like evil, social psychological explanations focus on the situation instead, specifically, the norms and roles these situations support. A **norm** is an implicit rule, an expectation about what kind of behavior is appropriate in a given situation. A **role** is a set of norms that accompany any particular relationship to other people in that situation. In the Milgram simulation, obedience to the experimenter was maintained by norms communicated by the professional appearance of the laboratory, by the explicit orders given by the experimenter, and by the lack of any social support for disobedience.

Whereas Milgram's laboratory experiments were extreme (and so controversial on ethical grounds that they could not be conducted today), norms and role expectations continually shape our behavior, whether or not we are aware of them. We constantly "read" a social setting for what is appropriate language, manner, gestures, and behavior. We become so dependent on these cues that we only notice their importance when we have trouble deciphering them. For example, you are much more likely to sign the ESA petition if everyone else at the party is signing it because others communicate a norm that is easy to read. In the absence of knowing what is expected, our behavior is more uncertain (when you receive a telephone call, it's not as easy to read the norm, because other people are not present to demonstrate their reactions). This is not to say that everyone conforms in all situations, but that when we are uncertain about an action, we look to situational cues to help us decide what to do.

FROM NORMS TO ENVIRONMENTALLY APPROPRIATE BEHAVIOR

A good example of how norms get communicated for littering behavior was observed by Cialdini and his colleagues (Cialdini, Kallgren, & Reno, 1991). They placed handbills on the windshields of cars parked in a parking garage. Drivers approaching their cars from the garage elevator experienced one of two conditions: Either the garage was littered with handbills, or the garage was clean and litter-free. The experimenters observed what the drivers did with the handbill on their windshield. Knowing something about norms and how they are communicated, what would you predict? Drivers were far more likely to throw their handbill on the ground in the already littered garage.

This experiment explains something Deborah could never figure out about the neighborhood where she once lived in south London. The streets were constantly blowing with litter, and she often observed Londoners contributing even more to it. She was revolted by such behavior, and thought her fellow neighbors crass and insensitive. A more social psychological explanation would be that the litter continued by virtue of the norm it expressed. Analogously, Deborah recently attended a convention of the American Psychological Association in Chicago, where she noticed recycling containers placed in some hallways, but not in others. Notably, there were no containers at the convention registration desk, as there had been at previous conventions, so people weeding out their folders had no place to recycle. Many looked for bins with what appeared to her to be frustration and annoyance. Previous placement of the containers had communicated a norm for recycling behaviors, but when the containers were no longer available, the norm persisted and produced dissonance.

Finding ways to communicate behavioral norms through changing cues in the environment is an important social psychological approach to solving environmental problems. Some behaviors will be difficult to change through norms because they are typically not done in public. For example, backyard composting is usually unobservable to neighbors. That is why McKenzie-Mohr (2000b) asked householders to post decals that demonstrated their participation in a composting program. When they did so, backyard composting increased. Laws and regulations contribute greatly to norms by requiring environmentally appropriate behavior. Federal laws regulating Corporate Average Fuel Economy (CAFÉ) standards that limit emissions of automobiles would communicate acceptable maximum levels of pollution and fuel efficiency, just as seat belt laws have greatly increased buckling up behaviors. Unfortunately, the 2002 U.S. Congress voted against increasing CAFÉ standards.

Norms can be transmitted by the particular features of a situation, or by hearing about what other people are doing. **Social diffusion** occurs when people change their behavior to be in line with what others do. Like a fashion that spreads throughout a group, environmentally appropriate behavior can be induced through interactions with one's acquaintances. Your personal relationship with your ESA friend, as well as the ESA-relevant attitudes of your other friends, are going to be important determinants of your response to her request. Likewise, research has shown that the best predictor of whether or not people purchase solar equipment is the number of acquaintances they have who currently own solar equipment (Leonard-Barton, 1981). Similarly, a strong predictor of recycling behavior is having friends and neighbors who recycle (Oskamp et al., 1991). Other studies have shown that environmentally responsible consumer choices are influenced by high status people who know about and choose environmentally friendly products (Flynn & Goldsmith, 1994), and that energy conservation is influenced by social networks (Weenig, 1993). Thus, the more people you know that support the ESA, the more likely you are to support it yourself.

When we conform to our friends and neighbors, we use them as a **reference group**: a constellation of people who portray standards with which to evaluate our attitudes, abilities, or current situation. A reference group is made up of people we like or respect, and by the power of normative influence, they can have big effects on our environmentally relevant behavior. For example, Deborah has noticed that she is much less likely to order meat when dining out with her vegetarian friends than with her meat-eating friends, and more likely to bring used paper to write on when she goes to her campus Conservation and Recycling Committee meetings than other committee meetings! But reference groups don't have to be present to be powerful. Simply making norms salient to the group is enough to change environmentally relevant behavior:

> The Washington Energy Office enlisted high-profile architects and builders and used highly publicized meetings between the governor, the builders, and the building owners in designing its Energy Edge program. . . . The Energy Edge program made energy-efficient design prestigious and a status symbol for new buildings. Smaller, lesser-known developers indirectly disseminated the technology by imitating the program's features. (Dennis, Soderstrom, Koncinski, & Cavanaugh, 1990, p. 1115)

Obviously, people do not just pay attention to the facts. They pay attention to a host of other variables, including the social status of the person communicating the message. We are much more likely to imitate or be persuaded by someone of a higher status than of a lower status. One of the earliest findings in social psychology is that the **credibility of the source** makes a difference. If two different people present exactly the same information, we will be more persuaded by the one we believe has more credibility. That is why New York City residents cut their electricity use by 7% when asked in a letter with New York State Public Service Commission letterhead. The plea had no effect when the same letter was sent on Con Edison stationery. Apparently, people trusted or respected the Public Service Commission more than Con Edison (Craig & McCann, 1978).

When norms are not written into law, many people do not comply. Have you ever heard people say that they *know* they are supposed to recycle, but it just isn't convenient? The distinction between personal and social norms can help us here. **Personal norms** are feelings of obligation to act in a particular way, whereas social norms are sets of beliefs about the behavior of others (Cialdini, Reno, & Kallgren, 1990). For example, Deborah feels guilty when she forgets to take her portable cup to the coffee shop because of her personal norm about wasting paper cups, even though she rarely sees others bringing their own cups, which would communicate a social norm.

As you might expect, activating personal norms is often more powerful than activating social norms, although both kinds of norms are more effective for changing behavior than information or pleas. To test these ideas, Schultz (1998) designed a clever study of recycling behavior that compared the effects of different kinds of messages placed on green door hangers that the experimenters hung on front doors. Five different experimental groups received different kinds of messages: (a) a plea to recycle, (b) a plea plus written feedback on individual recycling, (c) plea plus written feedback on the neighborhood's recycling, (d) plea plus information about recycling in general terms, and (e) a control group that received nothing. Households in the individual feedback group got messages about the amount of material they recycled over a 9-week period, and the group feedback condition received information about the recycling rates of the neighborhood.

As shown in Fig. 3.2, the individual feedback condition had an immediate effect, although it tended to diminish over time, relative to the group feedback group. The slower but steadier effect of group feedback may again underscore the power of group norms: An idea about what others are doing may continue to affect us, as our personal norms change in line with them.

NORMS, ALTRUISM, AND JUSTICE

Personal norms guide our sense of right and wrong. We feel guilty when we break them, as Deborah does when she fails to bring her shopping bag to the grocery store or her personal cup to the coffee

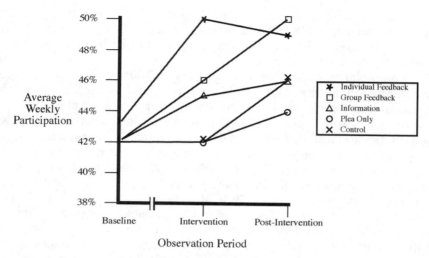

FIG. 3.2. Enhancing group norms through feedback sustains recycling. From Schultz, P. W. (1998). Changing behavior with normative feedback interventions. In Basic and Applied Social Psychology, 2(1), p. 30. © Lawrence Erlbaum Assoc. Reprinted with permission.

shop. Although stores give small (3–10 cent) rebates for bringing bags or cups, her own guilt is not about financial loss, but her sense of responsibility to future generations and her sense of betraying her caring about the environment. Because the rewards for recycling are more personal than social, most people think of recycling as a behavior in the moral domain (Thogersen, 1996). Thus, feelings of environmental responsibility are important predictors of ecological behavior (Kaiser, Ranney, Hartig, & Bowler, 1999). (By the way, the fact that we are more motivated by guilt than by money could be used to argue that social psychological approaches are more potent than behavioral ones emphasizing external reinforcers. However, behaviorists would come back and say that guilt is a function of one's history of reinforcement. We will look at the behavioral approaches more closely in chap. 4.)

Do personal norms correlate with behavior? In general, yes, although all of us break our own personal norms now and then. Studying German adults, Kals, Schumacher, and Montada (1999) found that a personal sense of environmental responsibility predicts energy conservation and political activities (e.g., signing petitions and supporting environmental organizations). These researchers also demonstrated that one's environmental responsibility is correlated with an emotional affinity toward nature, as well as indignation about insufficient protection of it. People who spent time in nature, especially with significant others, had emotional feelings about the health of the environment. In other words, past experience in natural settings is a powerful predictor of emotionally caring about the environment, and Geller (1995) argued that caring about the environment is a crucial predictor of environmentally responsible behavior.

Emotional experiences frame our sense of fairness, and give rise to environmental justice. The field of environmental justice has grown in national importance and is a natural outgrowth of the civil rights and environmental movements (Bullard, 1994). Bullard wrote extensively regarding clear and disturbing patterns of unjust environmental policies that place populations of color and lower income at greater risk for environmental pollution (Bullard, 1983, 1990, 1993, 1994, 1996; Bullard & Johnson, 2000). Bullard's main work used U.S. populations, but the same picture is increasingly true globally, as industrialized countries export toxic waste and build environmentally hazardous industrial sites in developing nations (Newton, 1996). In 1994, President Bill Clinton established the Office of Environmental Justice located in the Environmental Protection Agency (EPA). The EPA defines **environmental justice** as the "fair treatment and meaningful involvement of all people, regardless of race, color, national origin or income, with respect to the development, implementation and enforcement of environmental laws, regulations, and policies" (Web site: http:/es.epa.gov/oeca/main/ej/index.html). The Office of Environmental Justice ensures that projects receiving federal funds include consultation with affected populations about environmental and health effects to screen for environmental injustice.

How are we, as psychologists, to respond to the call for environmental justice? You'd probably agree that all people should have a voice in environmental decisions, regardless of race, color, or income. However, the term *environmental justice* is tricky because both environmentalists and anti-environmentalists use similar moral claims to justify their opposing positions. For example, like environmentalists, anti-environmentalists appeal to claims of equal access by different groups, and responsibility to less powerful people. Anti-environmentalists argue that environmentalists are immoral when they try to ban use of public lands to farmers and ranchers because of the importance of equal access, and immoral when they promote regulations that eliminate jobs or harm communities (Clayton, 1994).

More recently, Clayton (2000) posited that environmental justice as it is used by the EPA and most others is a form of **distributive justice**, that is, environmental resources and problems ought to be distributed equally between different groups. Distributive justice contrasts with **procedural justice**, the fairness with which environmental decisions are made. Whereas environmental and anti-environmental groups differ on their assessment of distributive justice, all groups greatly value procedural justice. There are multiple definitions of justice, even though when we are invested in a situation, we assume that our point of view is more fair, right, and just than our opponent's, whose view we see as expedient, greedy, or selfish. Again, we are prone to make attribution errors about those who disagree with us.

Distributive justice brings up the problem of responsibilities to more distant interests, such as future generations and nonhuman species. According to the **norm activation theory of altruism** (Schwartz, 1977), we help (or, in this case, practice environmentally responsible behaviors) when we feel a sense of moral obligation, and when personal norms are accompanied by awareness of harmful consequences of not doing so. Many studies (Black, Stern, & Elsworth, 1985) have shown that environmental behaviors like recycling (Vining & Ebreo, 1992), yard burning (Van Liere & Dunlap, 1978), energy use, and pro-environmental attitudes (Thogersen, 1996) are predictable from activating personal norms about harmful consequences.

But harmful consequences to whom? Are we talking about other people or other species? Do future generations and nonhuman species have moral standing in questions of environmental justice? Or is it enough to concern ourselves with the underprivileged human beings who are currently alive, which is a big number in and of itself? Here our question about the ESA is directly at stake. How wide is our net of moral responsibility, and what psychological mechanisms determine to whom we feel responsible?

Opotow (1990, 1994, 2001; Opotow & Weiss, 2000) argued that nobody has an infinitely wide **scope of justice**, and those who fall outside it will be seen as expendable, undeserving, or irrelevant. We deny responsibility to those who are excluded from our scope in three ways (Opotow, 2001):

- We deny outcome severity (use double standards, conceal harmful outcomes).
- We deny stakeholder inclusion (practice outgroup prejudice, dehumanization).
- We deny self-involvement (diffuse responsibility, use self-righteous comparisons).

Thus, when Deborah smashes a carpenter ant in her kitchen, she rarely feels guilty because those ants fall outside her scope of justice. As she kills them, she frequently thinks about how annoying they are (they actually eat her log cabin house and sometimes they bite her), and she denies their stakeholder inclusion. Obviously her house and its other inhabitants (e.g., her husband, dog, and cat) are inside, and the ants are outside, her scope of justice.

Why do we draw this arbitrary line? Deep ecologists (Devall & Sessions, 1985) argue that we shouldn't, that other species have just as much right to their place on the planet as human beings. We will revisit this idea in chapter 7 as we look at holistic psychology. For now, let us just say that we believe the work of both Clayton and Opotow should humble us. It is not easy to notice environmental injustice, but once we do, our job is not done. If we cannot hear the moral claims of those who disagree with us, or those who lay outside our scope of justice, and cannot notice the ways in which our own moral judgments rest on denial and moral exclusion, we will be unlikely to resolve environmental conflicts.

Environmental conflict rests on differing views of environmental justice, and resolution will require that we work collaboratively with players who hold different models than our own. Actively participating in group discussion and taking alternative perspectives is crucial for constructive resolution of differences (Gregory, 2000). Hard as it may be to resolve disagreements about environmental problems, we will need to build positive relationships with opponents and proceed with respect, humility, and open hearts, while remaining focused on our responsibility to pursue justice.

Is this asking too much? S. Kaplan (2000) argued that conceptualizing environmental behavior as altruism, and depending on people's sense of moral responsibility is problematic. Because the definition of altruism includes a component of self-sacrifice, it communicates a dour future of discomfort as we confront environmental problems. To the extent that environmentalists call on self-sacrifice, they can promote feelings of helplessness and futility (Roszak, 1994). Indeed, K. R. Lord (1994) showed that people are more likely to recycle when messages are framed in positive, rather than negative, terms. The role of emotional responses in mediating changes in environmental behaviors has not received much empirical attention yet (Vining & Ebreo, 2002), although it seems plausible that emotions can facilitate as well as get in the way of our solving problems (Vining & Ebreo, 1992).

To offset helplessness and despair, S. Kaplan (2000) suggested participating in problem-solving groups. In other words, an alternative to the altruism and morality framework is to arrange conditions so that people feel empowered by their successes. From a social psychological perspective, the norms of hope and vision that groups can supply are important sources of support for environmentally responsible behavior. We will have more to say about this point in our last chapter.

GENDER AND ENVIRONMENTALISM

Whether or not environmentalism is best conceptualized as altruism, a large body of empirical work now exists demonstrating that women have more environmental concern and undertake more environmentally responsible actions than men (Zelezny, Chua, & Aldrich, 2000). This difference holds up across cultures and age groups. Females show more environmental concern on the NEP scale (described earlier), more concern about the consequences of environmental problems on personal well-being, the well-being of others, and the well-being of the biosphere (Stern, Dietz, & Kalof, 1993). To put it in terms of our previous discussion, women show a larger scope of justice with respect to the well-being of other species. Why would this be so?

Before answering this question, let us make a few disclaimers. We are not saying that all women are more environmentally responsible than men. In fact the size of the sex difference in environmental concern and responsibility is small. As shown in Fig. 3.3, even though there are group differences between men and women, there is a lot of overlap between the groups, so many men feel more environmental responsibility than women. Secondly, in discussing sex differences, we are not implying that environmental problems are the fault of men. Clearly women play a large role in contributing to environmental devastation, as they contribute to overconsumption, overpopulation (reproduction), and pollution. To solve our environmental problems, we will need the best efforts of both men and women alike to find ways to change the behavior of *both* sexes.

Now back to the question of why, as a group, women might show more environmental responsibility and behavior than men. One answer is suggested by Stern et al. (1993), who found that women are more likely to see the link between environmental conditions and harm to others. Their analysis draws on the work of Carol Gilligan, who argued that women evaluate social dilemmas using an **ethic of**

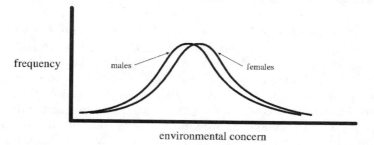

FIG. 3.3. Gender differences are small but consistent.

care. Because women are more likely to see a world of inherent inter-connections they are more accepting than men of messages that connect environmental conditions to potential harm to themselves, others, and other species or the biosphere.

The view that women have a special relationship with the environment is called **ecofeminism**, a movement that emerged in the 1970s as the women's movement and ecology movements developed simultaneously in industrialized countries (Diamond & Orenstein, 1990; Spretnak, 1990). Ecofeminists argue that patriarchy oppresses both women and nature, as it promotes a worldview valuing dominance, hierarchy, dualistic thinking, and power-based relationships. Some ecofeminists go further and posit that women's reproductive systems, their menstrual cycles, and their capacity to give birth organically place them closer to the physical world, the lunar cycles, and the rhythms of nature. Others would simply claim that women's roles as family caretakers means they have to be more concerned about, and in touch with, the natural environment because the health of their families depend on it. Ecofeminists recognize differences of race, class, and culture, but focus on the common experience of women in the world. For example, at a meeting of the Global Assembly of Women for a Healthy Planet, Antrobus, an environmental activist, emphasized:

> the commonalities that we all share as women—a consciousness that many of us have, if we allow ourselves to have it, of the exploitation of our time and labor in unremunerated housework, subsistence agriculture and voluntary work. Our commonality lies in the often conflicting demands of our multiple roles as caretakers, as workers, as community organizers. Our commonalities lie in our *primary responsibility for taking care of others*. Our commonality lies in our concern about relationships; the commonality that we share is the exploitation of our sexuality by men, by the media, and by the economy. The commonality that we share is in our vulnerability to violence. Our commonality finally lies in our otherness, in our alienation and exclusion from decision-making at all levels. (Antrobus, 1993, pp. 269–270, italics added)

It seems reasonable to us that women are drawn into environmental concerns because, as family caretakers, they are first to notice the damaging effects of polluted water, food, and air on their family's health. Rachel Carson's *Silent Spring* (1962) serves as an example of the way in which women have catalyzed concern about environmental problems. Grassroots resistance to male-run environmentally destructive projects are legendary throughout the world: In India, women have hugged trees to prevent logging; in Kenya, women have planted trees throughout the "Green Belt"; in Japan, women have demanded accurate labeling of dangerous chemicals; in New York, Lois Gibbs (who was often dismissed as "a hysterical housewife") organized a Clearinghouse for Hazardous Waste following her efforts to uncover the infamous Love Canal dump. Male scientific experts have been quick to characterize the environmental movement as hysteria (a female problem, related to the word *hystero*, or uterus).

Gender differences in environmental concerns have wide-ranging implications. Throughout the world, in both developed and developing nations, women are primarily responsible for child care, housework, food preparation, and family clothing. In rural subsistence economies, women are the main providers of fuel, food, and water, and they depend heavily on community-owned waterways, forests, grasslands, and croplands for accomplishing these chores. When international development efforts convert community resources to privately owned farms, women must go farther and work harder to provide fuel, food, and water. As a result, resources are more quickly depleted because more people are forced to forage on smaller community spaces. In southern Zimbabwe, for example, forests were cut in order to install mines and mining towns to support a cash economy. This forced women to gather their fuel from leftover forests, and severe deforestation resulted (Jacobson, 1992). Women (like men) who are desperate to provide for their families will deplete available resources, but when development efforts pay attention to the crucial roles that women fulfill, they are less likely to cause environmental devastation (Kabeer, 2001).

Although rarely articulated, development projects that leave women out stem from a stereotypic belief about men and women: the assumption that men are wage earners and women are dependents (Winter, 2002). This erroneous view of women as dependents translates into projects that focus on men and their access to jobs, despite data showing that the nutrition of children is more closely tied to the income of women than men (Jacobson, 1992). In the developing world, poverty, overpopulation, and environmental destruction coincide. Poverty drives overpopulation because there is no other form of social security than children who will take care of their parents in old age; gender bias requires that women continue to have babies until enough sons are born to take care of them and perform sacred funeral rites. For these reasons, development that ignores women increases both environmental destruction and overpopulation by increasing poverty. The gender bias of international development demonstrates the important role of psychology in what seem like nonpsychological issues: economics, foreign policy, and agriculture.

Finally, our gendered notions of nature can contribute to environmental destruction. What does it mean to call unexplored land "virgin territory" or our planet "Mother Earth"? Consider the words of an Exxon senior vice-president describing the aftermath of the Valdez accident: "Water in the [Prince William] Sound replaces itself every 20 days. The Sound flushes itself out every 20 days. Mother Nature cleans up and does quite a cleaning job" (Sitter, 1993, p. 221). The view that "Mom will pick up after us" seems plausible because it is women, rather than men, who do the vast majority of housework, cleaning, laundry, and tidying. Although understandable in terms of object relations theory (chap. 2) the idea of Mother Earth is problematic, and likely to hinder our responsibility for solving our environmental problems. In Seager's (1993) words:

> The earth is not our mother. There is no warm, nurturing, anthropomorphized earth that will take care of us if only we treat her nicely. The complex, emotion-laden, conflict-laden, quasi-sexualized, quasi-dependent mother relationship . . . is not an effective metaphor for environmental action. . . . It is not an effective political organizing tool: if the earth is really our mother, then we are children, and cannot be held truly accountable for our actions. (p. 219)

THE SOCIAL PSYCHOLOGY OF OVERCONSUMPTION

Embracing an ethic of care could help us critically address overconsumption, a pivotal source point for most other dangerous planetary problems. In the West, consumer culture is facilitated in part by applied social psychologists who go to work in the advertising industry, designing messages to persuade their audiences to buy products they otherwise would not purchase. As the chairman of President Eisenhower's Council of Economic Advisers once said, the American economy's "ultimate purpose is to produce more consumer goods" (quoted by Seager, 1993, p. 120).

Today, the most frequent and explicit messages we receive are sales pitches. Advertising, an enormously powerful form of applied social psychology, explicitly urges us to see ourselves deprived until a particular product is purchased, unfulfilled until a new gadget is owned, hungry until that next burger is consumed. And advertisers are especially likely to focus on the self-doubt and personal insecurities of women. As one chief executive put it 40 years ago, "It's our job to make women unhappy with what they have" (quoted by Seager, 1993, p. 120). Total global advertising is a truly colossal enterprise, rising from $103 billion in 1992 to $256 billion in 2001 (Agency Income Report, 2002).

The result is that in the industrialized countries, an average person consumes 3 times as much fresh water, 10 times as much energy, 14 times as much paper, and 19 times as much aluminum as someone in a developing country (Durning, 1992). Per capita, per day, people in the United States use energy equivalent to that of 3 Germans, 6 Mexicans, 14 Chinese, 28 Indians, or 168 Bangladeshis (Whole Terrain, 2001/2002). Our voracious appetites are fed by the natural resources of the developing countries that typically export to us their raw materials in exchange for some of our manufactured ones. Our disproportional use and abuse of the planet's resources not only pollutes and depletes our own country, but fuels a global trade system that feeds us as other countries fall into debt and disintegration. Our consumer culture sponsors much of our own dangerous behavior, and also encourages developing nations to abandon their cultural traditions and adopt ours. As Durning asked in the title of his 1992 book analyzing overconsumption, we must also ask: *How Much is Enough?*

We believe this is a crucial question each individual must examine on a continual basis. Yet there is little reason to believe that very many people are asking it. Consumerism is spreading in our country as well as throughout the world. For example, in 1970, 39% of entering college students in the United States indicated they believe that it is essential to be "very well off financially"; in 1998, 74% said so. The proportion reporting they are going to college "to make more money" rose from 50% to 75%. Meanwhile, those who said they believed it essential to develop a meaningful philosophy of life fell from 83% to 43%. By 1998, financial wealth became first priority, ranked higher than meaningful philosophy, helping others, becoming an authority in one's field, or raising a family. "For today's young Americans, money matters" (D. Myers, 2000, p. 58). Meanwhile, in the last 5 years, the savings rate of U.S. citizens has gone negative, so that we now spend around $35 billion more than we earn. United States credit card debt is $1.5 trillion, and one million bankruptcies are filed annually (Schumaker, 2001). Undoubtedly, these numbers reflect the success of the intentionally designed consumer culture articulated just after World War II.

Yet, increased consumption does not deliver the really important goods: Research shows that people are not happier when they own more things. Above a minimal poverty level, reports of personal happiness are completely unrelated to financial income or material possessions. Since 1950, the purchasing power of Americans has doubled, yet their reports of personal happiness has remained essentially constant (see Fig. 3.4). Instead of contributing to our happiness, consumerism is more likely to detract from it because it reduces our potential for building personal happiness. Again, to quote Durning (1991):

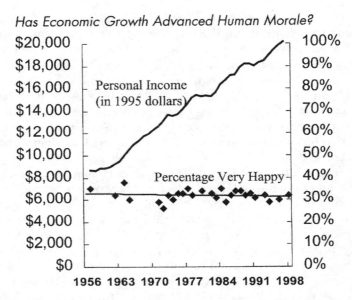

Has Economic Growth Advanced Human Morale?

FIG. 3.4. While inflation-adjusted income has risen, self-reported happiness has not. From Myers, D. G. (2000). The funds, friends, and faith of happy people. *American Psychologist*, 55, p. 61. © American Psychological Association. Reprinted with permission.

The tragic irony is that while the consumer society has been stunningly effective in harming the environment, it has failed to provide us with a sense of fulfillment. Consumerism has hoodwinked us into gorging on material things because we suffer from social, psychological, and spiritual hungers. . . . Fulfillment . . . has to do with the timeless virtues of discipline, hope, allegiance to principle, and character. Consumption itself has little part in the playful camaraderie that inspires the young, the bonds of love and friendship that nourish adults, the golden memories that sustain the elderly. The very things that make life worth living, that give depth and bounty to human existence, are infinitely sustainable. (p. 169)

Empirical research on happiness supports Durning's claims. When asked "what makes you happy?" the vast majority of people mention, before anything else, satisfying close relationships with friends, family, and romantic partners (D. Myers, 1992). Well-being also comes from active hobbies pursued during leisure time, along with meaningful work (Csikszentmihalyi, 1999), and a sense of personal control over one's life and circumstances (Langer, 1983). Leisure time, meaningful work, and personal control tend to become scarce in the mad rush to work harder and own more. Moreover, college graduates with "yuppie values"—who preferred a high income and occupational success over close friends and happy marriage, reported much more unhappiness (Perkins, 1991). Thus consumerism is threatening not only our environment, but also our psyches.

Maintaining an environmentally responsible lifestyle in the midst of commercial culture is not easy. However, there are alternatives to buying unnecessary goods that damage the planet. One important form of resistance is the growing "Voluntary Simplicity" movement (Elgin, 1993) in which people intentionally downsize their jobs, homes, and personal possessions in order to live a more balanced and harmonious life. Voluntary simplicity in the United States has grown steadily in the last decade as people discover that their frenzied lives surrounded by myriad material possessions do not deliver the fulfillment for which they yearn. We will say more about this issue in the last chapter and in the appendix.

As we consider purchasing habits, it is important to remember that reducing consumption is far more important than recycling or reusing. Our global trade patterns make overconsumption the single most important change that we in the developed nations can make. Carrying a cloth grocery bag to the market is important, but it will not change the global pattern of industrialized nations gulping the planet's resources, while simultaneously causing more and more poverty throughout the world. However, when we shop, there are greener choices of products that inflict less harm on the environment.

GREEN CONSUMERISM

In line with past research (Mainieri, Barnett, Valdero, Unipan, & Oskamp, 1997), we define **buying green** as purchasing and consuming products that are benign toward the environment (e.g., products with postconsumer recycled materials, with minimal or reusable packaging, and made from biodegradable ingredients). As one would expect, people who have stronger pro-environmental beliefs about the importance of buying green are more likely to buy products boasting environmental claims. Once again, women are more environmentally concerned and make more environmentally friendly purchases (Ebreo, Hershey, & Vining, 1999). Age, income, and education are not related to purchasing patterns.

Purchasing food is one of the most continuous and significant environmental choices we make. Food habits are socially induced behaviors that have important environmental repercussions:

> Americans eat oysters but not snails. The French eat snails but not locusts. The Zulus eat locusts but not fish. The Jews eat fish but not pork.

> The Hindus eat pork but not beef. The Russians eat beef but not snakes. The Chinese eat snakes but not people. The Jale of New Guinea find people delicious. (I. Robertson, 1987, quoted by Myers, 1992, p. 187)

People who want to make environmentally appropriate food choices must consider the issue of meat eating. Because livestock eat grain and soybeans, meat is an energy-inefficient food form. Twenty vegetarians could be fed by the same amount of land needed to feed one meat-eating person (Hollender, 1990). Although meat could be produced in environmentally sustainable ways, currently it is not. Land degradation from grazing now constitutes one of the planet's most serious environmental problems: 90% of harmful organic waste-water pollution is attributable to U.S. livestock, and livestock produces 250,000 pounds of excrement per second. Such pollution destroys fish and shellfish in rivers subjected to livestock runoff. Because feedlots are so unhealthy, 55% of antibiotics in the United States are given to livestock, posing health risks for humans who eat them (Hollender, 1990).

Part of the difficulty in changing our food consumption habits arises from social diffusion: With everyone else making these inappropriate food choices, it is easy for us to make them too. Furthermore, resisting them can be socially awkward. When Deborah's parents visited her a few years ago, she took them to a local restaurant that served her father's favorite: barbecued spare ribs. She thought about asking where the beef was produced, but felt that such a question would be socially awkward. Soon Deborah was thinking about what a special treat this was, in an effort to reduce her cognitive dissonance about feeding her parents an environmentally destructive food. Ironically, they were busy applying similar dissonance reduction strategies, as her father had recently had heart bypass surgery and knew that eating red meat can be dangerous. (The risk of a meat-eating American male having a heart attack is 50%; the risk to a vegetarian American male is 4%; Hollender, 1990.)

Walking into any American supermarket presents norms that easily lead us to globally destructive choices. Food appears plentiful and cheap; plastic bags appear free; thoughtful placement and advertising of items makes it easy to select unneeded products; other people comb the aisles filling their baskets with environmentally destructive choices. Given such strong norms, social psychologists would predict that changing behavior will be difficult. Choosing to shop in alternative settings would be wise from a social psychological point of view. Food stores offering items in bulk (enabling the consumer to reduce unnecessary packaging), farms selling direct to customers (enabling the reduction of fossil fuels used to ship food all over the country), and

Source: Reprinted with permission of Chris Suddick.

stores offering a good selection of healthful fresh organic foods instead of chemically treated, processed foods, all provide situations in which good choices are easier to make.

Making environmentally responsible consumer choices will require some thoughtfulness, but is not so difficult once you start. For example, when Deborah first drafted this chapter during the early weeks of December, she also contemplated her Christmas gift list. She attempted to make choices with less environmental impact than those she had chosen the previous year. Some of her gift items were a set of music lessons for her husband, a membership at the YWCA for her best friend, and for her niece a hand-crocheted vest she had purchased 20 years ago in Greece. To the extent that she purchased new objects, she did so primarily through mail order, because going shopping provides too many norms for environmentally irresponsible buying. Deborah enjoyed her time away from the shopping mall, where the advertisements, strategically placed sale items, and other busy shoppers purchasing large amounts communicate a norm of buy, buy, buy, and buy some more. Christmas, the biggest shopping season of the year, has become a consumer (and environmental) nightmare.

Once we make small changes, other changes become easier. Deborah remembers switching over to a brand of nonpolluting household cleaners (sold widely under the name of Shaklee products). Realizing that these cleaners were cheaper and just as effective, she examined other household items, like fabric softener, which really seemed unnecessary. In this way, the foot-in-the-door technique can facilitate a larger series of changes, once the initial changes are made. Asking our grocers about local and organic products, registering our desire for them, and talking to our friends about having similar conversations, can start a self-attribution process that results in bigger changes than we might first expect. When we explain our actions to ourselves as environmentally responsible, and begin to see ourselves as global citi-

zens, we become more conscious of other choices, and changes become easier and easier.

Switching from a consumer to a sustainable lifestyle will be healthy not only for our environment, but also for ourselves, as we will see in chapter 5 on physiological and health psychology. In the last chapter, we will say more about what a sustainable culture might look like, and how the various subfields of psychology could contribute to it. For now, however, let us close by summarizing our ecological problem from a social psychological perspective.

CONCLUSIONS

From a social psychological perspective, environmentally relevant behavior is a function of a complex interaction of social influences. Norms and roles affect our choices by influencing what we think of as appropriate behavior in any given situation. When choices become more difficult, we try to reduce dissonance by justifying our actions. We explain our own behavior by attributing it to various features of the situation, but we are more likely to attribute other people's behavior to their personalities. We imitate and are influenced by people who are in our reference group. We care about those inside our scope of justice. Relative to men, women care more about the environment, its impact on others, and the well-being of the biosphere. This gender difference most likely arises out of women's differing roles, and gives rise to different levels of moral responsibility. Finally, although we are materially better off than ever before, research shows that we are not happier. Overconsumption, facilitated by a form of applied social psychology known as advertising, is depleting the planet's resources as well as our own psyches.

From this perspective, insights from social psychology can help us redesign situations to include more norms, roles, and social influence mechanisms that induce environmentally responsible behavior, and fewer norms, roles, and social influence mechanisms that lead us toward overconsumption. Deliberately avoiding situations with environmentally destructive norms, while simultaneously joining groups, cultivating activities, friendships, and commitments that support environmentally responsible behavior, makes a lot of sense from a social psychological point of view.

If there is any single message from social psychology, it is that changes are much easier to make and keep if we put ourselves in social situations that support them. Our immediate reference groups of friends, relatives, and colleagues are enormously powerful social influence agents. As Lewin (1959) observed at the outset of social psychology, "It is easier to change individuals formed into a group than to change any of them separately. As long as group values are unchanged the individual will resist changes. . . . If the group standard itself is changed, the resistance which is due to the relation between the individual and the group is eliminated" (p. 228).

Social psychology is limited, as well. Not all of our behavior is a product of group influence. If it were, everyone in any given situation or group would respond exactly the same way. Instead, individual behavior is enormously variable. Resisting the group, experiencing conflict with its norms, and acting on the basis of more deeply seated personal norms also occur in our daily experience. While emphasizing the power of the situation, social psychology ignores individual differences between people. In its endeavor to illuminate the principle that "people who do crazy things are not necessarily crazy," social psychology does not look at the internal (perhaps eternal) ways in which human beings respond to factors beyond the group.

Finally, social psychology's emphasis on making meaning focuses researchers' attention on the way people think about and perceive social situations. Behavioral psychologists would argue that this focus is unnecessary, and that we should just cut to the chase by studying features of the immediate situation. For this approach, we now turn to chapter 4.

KEY CONCEPTS

Altruism
Attitudes versus behavior
Attribution

Cognitive dissonance
Dominant social paradigm
Ecofeminism
Environmental justice
Factors influencing environmental concern: age, education, gender,
    political affiliation, social class, urban vs. rural residence
Foot-in-the-door technique
Fundamental attribution error
Gender differences in environmental concern
Green consumerism
Justice (distributive, environmental, procedural, scope of)
New ecological paradigm
Norm activation theory of altruism
Norms (personal, social)
Obedience to authority
Reference group
Role
Self-serving bias
Social diffusion
Voluntary simplicity

4

CHAPTER

Behavioral Psychology

Most thoughtful people agree that the world is in serious trouble. . . . That many people have begun to find a recital of [the] dangers tiresome is perhaps an even greater threat. . . . Traditional explanations of why we are doing so little are familiar. It is said that we lack responsibility for those who will follow us, that we do not have a clear perception of the problem, that we are not using our intelligence, that we are suffering from a failure of will, that we lack moral strength, and so on. Unfortunately, explanations of that sort simply replace one question with another. Why are we not more responsible or more intelligent? Why are we suffering from a failure of will? A better strategy is to look at our behavior and at the *environmental conditions* of which it is a function. There we shall find at least some of the reasons why we do as we do. (Skinner, 1991, pp. 19–20; italics added)

From a behaviorist's perspective, current global threats result from environmental conditions, or **contingencies**, that maintain destructive human behavior. If we are to extricate ourselves from our ecological predicament, we must change the environmental conditions so that our behavior can change. The wizardry of technological solutions might be impressive, but if we do not develop a *behavioral* technology to change what people actually do, we will not be successful.

How can human behavior be changed? Most of us would probably think first of educating people, changing their attitudes and beliefs, so they could then choose more appropriate behavior. We assume that people choose to behave in line with their beliefs. Surprisingly, however, as we discussed in the last chapter, our beliefs and attitudes are only indirectly related to behavior. Trying to change people's behavior by changing their beliefs is generally unsuccessful. In fact, behaviorists would not be surprised by the claims made in the opening pages of this book that we suffer from *knowing* about environmental problems, but not knowing what to *do* about them. Behaviorists have always argued that it is more effective and efficient to target efforts directly on behavior change. Getting distracted by trying to change hypothetical inner events like feelings or attitudes is a waste of precious time.

Instead, **behaviorism** focuses on the ways in which behavior is controlled by the environment. When we say "environment" here, we mean the total physical, social, political, and economic situation in which a person behaves. This is a wider use of the term than has been employed up to now in this book. Previously, our use of the word has referred to the more physical dimensions of our habitat, such as resources and pollution, water and wilderness. But from a behavioral perspective, our total environment cues certain behaviors, which then are followed by rewards or punishers. Our behavior changes when environmental stimuli vary; conversely, we can modify behavior by changing relevant stimuli.

Organisms also "operate" on the environment thereby generating consequences, as Skinner (1953) noted when he coined the terms **operant behavior** and **operant conditioning**. Because of this two-way relationship, we exist in a *behavior–environment interactive system*. Because of this system, we cannot define who we are, or what we do, without examining the environment in which we behave. This idea of a functional unity between the person and the environment is a crucial contribution to which we will return at end of this chapter. Behavioral theory also provides many useful concepts and principles with which we might redesign the environment to maximize environmentally appropriate behavior.

Although the behavioral approach in psychology is not as popular as it was several decades ago, we believe that its insights can significantly enhance our understanding of both our environmental problems and their solutions. In fact, its influence has been so strong that it may have been too successful for its own good: Important elements of the behavioral viewpoint have been so thoroughly assimilated into mainstream psychology that they are not even discussed anymore. Measuring observable behavior is so common a feature of good research that we no longer call it behaviorism (Boring, 1957).

Behaviorism grew out of the **functionalist** school of psychology, which sought to understand the ways that behavior serves an adaptive function in its environment, and thus reflected the influence of Darwin's theory of evolution by natural selection. For example, **classical** (also known as **Pavlovian** for its founder, Ivan Pavlov) and **operant** forms of **conditioning** depend on the fact that animals form associations between stimuli in their environment (classical) and between the animal's behavior and its consequences (operant). These adaptive mechanisms for associative learning can be useful in understanding current environmental issues. We will briefly review the relevance of classical conditioning, and then focus on operant conditioning as it has many direct applications in fostering more environmentally responsible behaviors.

CLASSICAL CONDITIONING

A contemporary example of classical conditioning is the public fear about nuclear accidents. News reports of the Chernobyl accident, and footage from the bombing of Hiroshima and Nagasaki during World War II, depict horrendous suffering that people endured from radiation sickness. In this case, radiation is an **unconditioned stimulus** (US), and images associated with the effects of radiation (**conditioned stimuli**, CS) produce **conditioned responses** (CR) of anxiety and concern in viewers. These emotional responses can generalize to other sources of radiation, such as all nuclear power plants.

Nuclear engineers are fond of calling this fear "irrational" and point out that many more people have died in accidents from hydropower and coal plants than nuclear plants (M. R. Fox, 1987; J. A. L. Robertson, 2000). However, statistics cannot attenuate the very strong conditioned response to nuclear power plants. If the nuclear industry better understood the process of classical conditioning, it might have a clearer idea about the genesis of public fears. As it is, many people feel patronized when they hear nuclear officials call the public irrational or paranoid, and this reaction further exacerbates the problem of public trust in the nuclear industry. We will further discuss the discrepancies between public and expert assessment of risks, including nuclear power, in the cognitive psychology chapter. For now, this example echoes a major theme of this book, which is that information alone (e.g., regarding the relative safety of nuclear power) does not change behavior (e.g., motivating people to support its use).

OPERANT CONDITIONING

Although classical conditioning is relevant to current ecological issues, many Skinnerian analyses of operant principles have been applied directly (e.g., Nevin, 1985; Skinner, 1985, 1991). In fact, Skinner was one of the first psychologists to repeatedly relate the issues of resource depletion, pollution, and overpopulation to human survival. His best-selling novel *Walden Two* (1948) explored the question of utopia from a behavioral perspective, and is a thoughtful and provocative look at how behavioral principles can be used to design a healthier and more effective society. A more serious discussion of the behavioral approach to human problems appeared in his later book *Beyond Freedom and Dignity* (1971). In both works, he examined the problem of designing a sustainable culture, proposing that impending ecological disasters stem from inappropriate human behavior. He argued that we must redesign culture to shape more appropriate behavior; that is, we need a technology of behavior focusing on maintaining the health of the environment in which behavior occurs.

Before we describe its applications, let us review the terminology and basic components of Skinner's theory. Operant conditioning procedures build on Thorndike's (1898, as cited in Skinner, 1953) **Law of Effect**, which stated that behavior followed by a favorable consequence would be "stamped in" (**positive reinforcement**, in Skinner's terminology), whereas behavior followed by an unfavorable consequence would be "stamped out" (**punishment**). Reinforcement refers literally to strengthening, or increasing the likelihood of behavior, while punishment decreases the probability of the particular behavior. Skinner elaborated by noting that removing a stimulus can also reduce a behavior (termed **negative punishment**; e.g., removing privileges, charging a fine), and removing some stimuli **negatively reinforces** or increases the associated behavior (e.g., curing a headache negatively reinforces taking aspirin). The term "negative" refers to removal of the stimulus; there is a negative (inverse) association between the behavior and stimulus (see Table 4.1). Moreover, Skinner determined that it is more effective to control behavior through positive reinforce-

*"Oh, not bad. The light comes on, I press the bar, they write me a check.
How about you?"*

ment than by punishment because punishment often produces undesirable behavioral side effects, such as aggression.

Some examples might be helpful here. The grocery store where Sue shops offers 5 cents for every bag she brings with her to carry groceries. This rebate represents positive reinforcement, as the nickel reinforces the behavior of bringing her own bags. In addition, Oregon and several other states have a "bottle bill," where the purchase price of products in glass bottles and aluminum cans includes a 5-cent deposit, refundable upon return of the bottles and cans. If Sue fails to return a bottle, she loses a nickel. This is negative punishment, as she is missing out on a refund, so we might say that laziness is punished. On the other hand, if Sue returns the bottles and gets a refund, the refund

TABLE 4.1
Reinforcement and Punishment: Four Types of Operant Relationships

	Effect on Behavior	
	Increases Behavior	Decreases Behavior
Stimulus Added	Positive Reinforcement (Bring grocery bag, get 5¢)	(Positive) Punishment (Waste water, get yelled at)
Stimulus Taken Away	Negative Reinforcement (Conserve, avoid getting yelled at and feeling guilty)	Negative Punishment (Litter, pay fine)

serves as a positive reinforcer. Both explanations are valid in this case; the key point is which behavior is the focus of the analysis (i.e., laziness or returning the bottles).

A similar examination can be brought to bear on Sue's behavior concerning water use. She grew up hearing the phrase, "waste not, want not" and was taught to use water sparingly while brushing her teeth or washing dishes. As an adult, Sue lived for several years in a home with a well (rather than city water) and took conservation even more seriously out of fear the well would run dry—an outcome that would punish wasteful behavior. For example, she and her partner adopted the phrase "if it's yellow, let it mellow; if it's brown, flush it down" for toilet flushing conservation. More recently, it occurred to her that the water with which most toilets are flushed is cleaner than the water many people have to drink. More than 1 billion people (or one out of every six people on this planet) do not have safe drinking water, and about half of all people in the world do not have sufficient water for basic sanitation and hygiene (Gardner, 2002). For all of these reasons, Sue continues to be very conscientious about water use, and hates to see waste (e.g., leaky faucets; people's wasteful behaviors). From her perspective, waste has been punished (e.g., by her mother yelling at Sue when she was a child), and avoiding waste is negatively reinforced (avoiding punishers like being yelled at, or running out of a scarce resource).

Feelings are important in maintaining many behaviors shaped by operant conditioning. This statement may come as a surprise to readers who think that behaviorists discount feelings and other internal events. That is a common misconception of behaviorism. Rather, behaviorists argue that internal events like feelings cannot *cause* behavior; the causes of behavior lie in the external environment. Emotions and cognitions are simply other *behaviors* that also result from environmental events. Thus, when Sue was punished for wasting water, her behavior changed and she also experienced certain emotions, such as shame. Feeling ashamed became associated with waste, and now when Sue has been or is tempted to be wasteful, that same feeling occurs. Avoiding shame or guilt continues to negatively reinforce her conservation behaviors.

Not only does behavior change because of its relation to consequences, but the **schedule of reinforcement** makes a difference in the strength and durability (persistence) of the behavior. We should note that schedule of reinforcement really means "schedule of consequences," as it refers to both reinforcement and punishment and includes positive and negative (inverse) relationships with the behavior. Behavior tends to change most quickly when the consequences are consistently administered (a continuous reinforcement schedule). How-

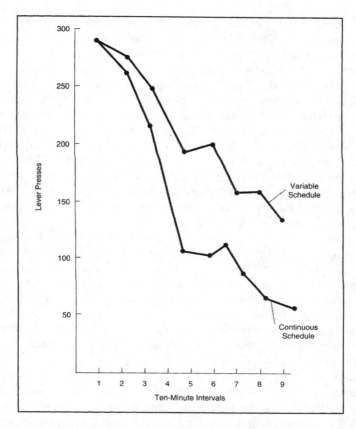

FIG. 4.1. Variable reinforcement schedules produce behavior that is more resistant to extinction than continuous reinforcement schedules.

ever, if the reinforcement schedule is intermittent rather than continuous, some behaviors will last longer when the reinforcers are withdrawn (in operant terminology, behavior will **extinguish** more slowly; see Fig. 4.1). For example, the Coast Guard inspects industrial wastes from processing plants on inland waterways on a random schedule (Cone & Hayes, 1980). Companies do not know when the inspection will take place, just as we do not know when a patrol car will be checking our speed as we drive. These random schedules are powerful forms of behavioral control. The industrial chemical company and highways where we regularly drive may not be patrolled for months, but because the schedule is intermittent, our transgressions are controlled for a longer time than if we had noticed the continuous presence of, and then the sudden disappearance of, the patrol boat or car.

There are several kinds of **intermittent reinforcement** schedules and they produce different behavioral results. For example, most people recycle their bottles on a **variable ratio schedule**, a schedule in which the number of responses varies for each reinforcer. When Deborah brings a box of bottles to the recycling center and gets the rebates for her effort, many separate behaviors of rinsing and saving bottles have accumulated to result in the monetary reinforcement. Sometimes she brings in 40 bottles, sometimes 42, sometimes 48, depending on the size of the bottles and the degree to which the box is overflowing (often related to the amount of entertaining she has done, and for how long she has put off the task). If Deborah recycled bottles every Saturday, her behavior would be on a **fixed interval** schedule. Conservation of electricity is controlled by a kind of fixed interval schedule. Once a month (a fixed time interval) you receive a bill for the amount of energy you have used, no matter how many times you have turned off the light switches. Fixed schedules tend to produce slow rates of responding right after the reinforcer, and then higher rates as the next reinforcement opportunity approaches. For example, you probably do not study the textbook immediately after taking a test in a course. Biweekly classroom tests are an example of fixed interval reinforcement schedule; they produce lots of studying just before the event, and not very much directly afterward. On the other hand, **variable interval** and **variable ratio** schedules produce steady and high rates of responding.

Behaviors developed under optimal reinforcement schedules can become habitual and thus very durable. An example from Deborah's experience illustrates the power of both continuous and variable schedules. A few years ago she lived in Denmark for 7 months, a country in which people usually brought their own cloth shopping bags to the grocery store because the plastic bags at the counter cost almost $1.00 a piece. It was easy for her behavior to change in Denmark because the reinforcement for doing so (saving $1.00) was continuous, as well as sizable. When Deborah returned to her home in the Pacific Northwest of the United States, shopping bags were free, but deforestation was also visible. Not only were stories about forest issues continually in the news, but driving across the state she was shocked to see huge patches of clearcuts in what had been a rich forest cover when she left. Even though there were no monetary reinforcers for bringing her own bag, this seemed a more appropriate behavior because so much of our forest is lost to unnecessary paper use. In fact, through a community volunteer group, Deborah helped set up a cloth bag project, making cloth shopping bags available in supermarkets, and trying to persuade friends to use them instead of the paper and plastic bags given at the counter (she became known as "the bag lady"!).

Here's where the variable reinforcement schedule came in. After having become known to friends as a person committed to cloth grocery bags, it was embarrassing to meet one of them in a supermarket without having her cloth bags. Deborah never knew when she would see one of her friends, but the chance of meeting one helped maintain the habit of bringing a bag every time she entered the store, or returning to the car to get one if initially she forgot it. After a while, bringing the bag became automatic, and Deborah no longer thinks about whether or not she will meet a friend. The intermittent schedule helped keep the rate of responding so high for such a long time that the behavior became habitual, and will be very resistant to extinction. Unfortunately for others, no strong continuous rate of reward is available to shape the behavior in the first place, so intermittent schedules are not very useful. Grocers still give free paper and plastic bags, and even the rebate once offered for customers' bags has been dropped in many stores. Consequently, use of cloth bags has not been established in the general public. Even though many people bought the bags, they find it difficult to remember to use them. A behaviorist would say that effective reinforcement schedules are not yet available for changing this behavior.

Like other animals, humans **discriminate** between stimuli by learning to respond only to stimuli that signal when reinforcement will follow, and not to respond when behavior will not be reinforced. For example, humans discriminate between bottles that are marked for rebate (soda and beer bottles stating "5¢ deposit redemption value") and those that are not (juice or wine bottles). The discrimination occurs because bringing in the former will be reinforced, while bringing in the latter will not and may even be punished as the clerk laughs at us.

Thus, behavior is controlled by **discriminative stimuli**, denoted as S^Ds. Our environment is filled with S^Ds, including signals, prompts, and models, which we will discuss more fully later. For now, however, the point is that behavior is embedded in two different kinds of stimuli, those that cue the behavior, called S^Ds, and those that follow the behavior, called S^Rs, for **reinforcing stimuli**. Because of the operation of discriminative stimuli and the consequences of our behavior, Skinner said that behavior is under **stimulus control**. Conceptually then, behaviorists look at behavior as a series of responses (R), each with its own discriminative and reinforcing stimuli. The units of behavior may be indicated by

$$S^D \rightarrow R \rightarrow S^R$$

where a discriminative stimulus (S^D) sets the context in which a particular behavior (R) will be reinforced or punished.

Before we examine some of the specific ways in which behaviorists are developing a technology of environmentally appropriate human behaviors, let us raise a question about how a behaviorist might explain our environmental mess in the first place. How can our ecological troubles be due to inappropriate behavior, if actions are simply products of stimulus control at work in the environment? In other words, behaviorists argue that our behavior is a result of the environment, not of some inner events like conflicts or values. In that case, behavior cannot be right or wrong because it simply reflects what is occurring in the situation in which we behave (as Skinner once said, "The organism is always right"). If that is true, then how can it be so maladaptive?

Behaviorists would argue that maladaptive behaviors result when short-term consequences differ from long-term consequences. Our behavior is under the control of short-term reinforcers, even if it brings delayed aversive consequences. Driving may ultimately be bad for our health (as we get less exercise) and for the planet (as we contribute to pollution and global warming), but the immediate reinforcement is so powerful (getting to where we need to go quickly and conveniently) that we do it anyway. In other words, we are caught in a **contingency trap** (W. M. Baum, 1994). Many "bad" habits, including environmentally destructive behaviors, are very difficult to change because breaking habitual behavior usually involves a short-term cost. Sometimes, we must deliberately change the short-term consequences to bring them in line with long-term outcomes. For example, Sue refuses to purchase a parking permit at Willamette University where she works so she is not tempted to drive. If Sue succumbs to the short-term convenience of driving, her behavior will result in immediate punishment (a parking ticket). She has intentionally altered the contingencies to control her behavior so it is more in line with her long-term concerns about global warming and pollution.

Another way to look at our inappropriate behavior is to consider the effects of culture. Skinner (1990) argued that culture changes faster than adaptive behavior. Culture, a complex conglomeration of reinforcement schedules, changes faster than behavior because behavior is often slow to extinguish; that is, it outlasts changes in environmental contingencies. For centuries, reproductive behavior was highly rewarded by societies with small populations. Now, however, reproductive behavior is producing dangerous overpopulation. In most cultures, the threat of material scarcity encouraged families to accumulate extra wealth; now overconsumption pollutes and depletes resources. For several centuries, Americans were reinforced for settling wilderness and "conquering nature"; as of 2003, there is very little wilderness left. Eventually, behavior that is not reinforced will extinguish, and the culture will discontinue the reinforcers (e.g., parents of large families may not enjoy as much social support as they once did). But the natural evolution of behavior can take decades, if not lifetimes.

For these reasons, behaviorists believe that humans can and should facilitate behavior change by redesigning the environments in which environmentally relevant behaviors take place. The natural process of behavioral adaptation will be too slow. We can appreciate this point by remembering the exponential growth of our environmental difficulties; we simply may not have time to wait for the slower form of behavioral evolution to take place. The same point can be made about the consequences of economic behavior. As we will discuss later in this chapter, market forces may be too slow to change our purchasing behavior, and we may require additional price regulations for expedient adjustment.

How then can we use the principles of behavioral psychology to change our behavior? Obviously, we must change features of the environment in which our behavior takes place. In the words of Geller (1992a), we must change behavior through "modification or removal of contingencies currently reinforcing behaviors detrimental to the environment" and establish "new response-consequence contingencies to motivate the occurrence of behaviors beneficial to the environment" (pp. 814–815). This approach, called behavioral engineering (Geller, 1987), consists of two main strategies: (a) those focusing on the stimuli that signal behavior (S^{D}s), called **stimulus control**; and (b) those focusing on the reinforcers that follow behavior (S^{R}s), termed **contingency management**. Both the reinforcers and the reinforcement schedule are important issues in contingency management. Sometimes these approaches are called **antecedent** and **consequence strategies** because they specify on what comes before and what comes after behavior.

ANTECEDENT STRATEGIES: CHANGING THE S^{D}s

Culturally sustainable behavior cannot be reinforced before it has occurred, so we must design an environment that is likely to signal appropriate behavior. This involves manipulating the S^{D}s. Behaviorists have looked at three types of S^{D}s: **prompts**, **information**, and **modeling,** and have shown that each can have some effect on enhancing appropriate behavior. Prompts are signals that communicate what actions are appropriate. Often, they are verbal stimuli providing instructional control. For example, signs placed over lightswitches, reminding users to turn off the light when they leave a room, have reduced energy use. Research has shown that the more specific the prompt, the greater its effectiveness. A sign saying, "Faculty and students—please turn off lights after 5 p.m." is more effective than one that says "Conserve Electricity." Prompts that are polite are more effective than those that are demanding (the word "please" can make a difference), and the closer the prompt to the behavior point, the better (a sign over a lightswitch is more effective than a sign across the room). Thus, polite, salient, and specific reminders can change behavior (Geller, 1987).

Delivering more general information is less effective than specific prompts. The mere presentation of information through instructions, slogans, pamphlets, or articles is typically ineffective, even though huge amounts of money and paper are spent on such endeavors. Although common sense suggests that we need to educate people about environmental problems, education by itself does very little to change behavior. Such an outcome is not surprising to behaviorists, who have argued all along that attitudes and awareness do not necessarily indicate much about actions. To a behaviorist, attitudes are forms of verbal behavior that may or may not be correlated with other behaviors. Thus, there is no reason to believe that education alone would change what people actually do, a view supported by many studies (see review by Gardner & Stern, 2002). For example, Hirst and colleagues demonstrated that millions of dollars spent on information dissemination resulted in only 2% to 3% energy conservation in the state of California (Hirst, Berry, & Soderstrom, 1981).

Information that is especially vivid and focused on outward behavior, however, is more effective. For example, in one study, information about energy conservation was shown on a video demonstrating a person turning down a thermostat, wearing warmer clothes, and using heavy blankets. With this treatment, viewers reduced their energy use by 28% (Winett et al., 1982). Demonstrating appropriate behavior is called modeling, and modeling works better than simply describing. Aronson and O'Leary (1982–1983) provided a wonderful example of the power of modeling in a study of the men's shower at the University of California Santa Cruz field house. Although most students at U.C. Santa Cruz would describe themselves as "environmentalists," very few conserved water in the shower. Even when Aronson and O'Leary put up a sign asking users to "1) Wet down 2) Turn water off 3) Soap up 4) Rinse off," only 6% of users followed these water conserving instructions. However, when the researchers asked a confederate to demonstrate the appropriate behavior whenever a user entered the shower room, compliance with the instructions rose to 49%. When two models were used, 67% of users imitated the models. Live modeling is undoubtedly (at least in this study) a powerful form of stimulus control, much more powerful than mere information or instructions. Sue has frequently experienced this phenomenon during walks with friends: When she bends down to pick up litter during the walk, her friends will do so as well.

CONSEQUENCE STRATEGIES: CHANGING THE S^{R}S

Although manipulating S^{D}s can have some effect, especially via modeling, most behaviorists are more interested in the **consequence strategies**, called contingency management. If behavior is not reinforced, then it will not be strengthened or selected. The most important priority for changing behavior, then, is to make sure that environmentally appropriate behaviors are rewarded by changing the S^{R}s that follow them. Unfortunately, most of our current environmentally *in*appropriate behaviors are rewarded (through convenience, social status, comfort, and pleasure) and our environmentally appropriate behaviors are not. From a behavioral perspective, we must rearrange these contingencies.

The most obvious way is to begin rewarding behavior we want to see increased. For example, if people in the United States were to use public transportation instead of driving their own cars, fossil fuel consumption could be reduced enormously. With less than 5% of the population, U.S. citizens drive as many miles each year as the rest of the world combined, and 80% of us drive to work alone (G. T. Miller, 2002). Everett and his colleagues (1974) were able to greatly increase bus ridership by directly rewarding bus riding. These researchers set up two specially marked buses that gave tokens to passengers upon boarding. The tokens were redeemable for food, entertainment, or another bus ride. Not surprisingly, when tokens were given, bus ridership increased by 150%. Similar kinds of strategies have been used to get people to clean up litter. When adults were given raffle tickets for picking up trash, they quickly picked up more, at least in recreational areas (Powers, Osborne, & Anderson, 1973). Children will clean up litter more quickly and cheaply than a professional maintenance staff if the kids are given tickets for amusement rides when bringing in litter (Casey & Lloyd, 1977). Children also learned to clean up nearly 100% of their trash when offered a dime for turning in a bag of litter in the theater lobby of a Saturday children's matinee movie (Baltes & Hayward, 1976).

Feedback as S^{R}s

Although reinforcing specific behaviors may be very effective, it can also be very difficult. Even if we could arrange for reinforcement to be given for every environmentally relevant behavior a person makes, it would become very expensive to do so. Furthermore, political problems often prevent arranging contingent rewards. For example, 11 states have implemented bottle bills (consumer rebates for returning empty containers), increasing recycling of bottles and cans by as much as 97% in some states.[1] In most other states, however, manufacturers have successfully lobbied against the passage of these bills because of the inconvenience posed to those involved in the manufacturing and distribution process. Similarly, cities have often reduced vehicular traffic and single passenger automobiles on freeways by allowing cars with two or more passengers to travel in special lanes. Such programs, however, have also been canceled because other drivers have been irritated about the loss of lane privileges and traffic delays in regular lanes. Whereas positive reinforcement of specific, environmentally friendly behaviors may be highly effective, substantial political difficulties often impede its use.

For these reasons, it is often easier to reward the results of behavior, rather than the behavior itself. Simply giving people feedback about their behavior is often enough to reinforce it, so there is no need to give them money or raffle tickets as well. Many researchers have investigated the power of feedback, most notably on energy consumption (for reviews, see Cone & Hayes, 1980; Gardner & Stern, 1996; Geller, Winett, & Everett, 1982). In general, giving consumers more information about their energy use helps them reduce it. This effect has been accomplished in many ways: more frequent billing and usage information, including graphs that demonstrate energy use over the past year, devices that signal consumers to turn off their air conditioners when outside temperatures drop below a certain point, and home energy audits. Home energy audits can be helpful in getting participants to insulate, install weather stripping and storm windows, and reduce fuel consumption, although the number of people who ask for the free audit is surprisingly small (Yates & Aronson, 1983).

Even feedback informing the individual of a *group* behavior can be effective. When Van Houten, Nau, and Marini (1980) displayed a sign showing the percentage of drivers *not* speeding the day before, the number of speeding drivers was significantly reduced. And other researchers (Schnelle, Gendrich, Beagle, Thomas, & McNees, 1980) demonstrated that littering behavior is decreased when the previous day's litter count is displayed on the front page of the local newspaper. Feedback seems to be effective because it has both informational and moti-

---

[1]For more information, and for statistics from individual states, see http://www.bottlebill.org/

vational properties: It tells participants their progress toward a goal. Feedback also can be much cheaper than rebates and rewards, especially if it can be made relatively automatic.

As encouraging as some of these studies are, most of the research shows short-lived and small results, usually in the 10%–15% range, but often much smaller. For example, attempts to reduce electricity consumption through frequent feedback resulted in only 4.7% savings (Hayes & Cone, 1981). For the great majority of individuals, behavior does not change at all. For example, fewer than 6% of eligible households have requested a free energy audit (Harrigan, 1994), which the 1978 National Energy Conservation Policy Act mandated be offered to the public. Less than 20% of those receiving audits demonstrated significant behavioral changes, even when given free, personalized, specific feedback about the energy waste in their homes (Yates & Aronson, 1983). Online energy audits are available (e.g., Home Energy Magazine, 2001, http://www.homeenergy.org/webaudit.otheraudits. html) and although to our knowledge no research is available on their effectiveness, it is unlikely that they will prove much more successful than personal audits. Consumers see energy efficient actions and investments as punishing, or the reinforcers are not apparent to them. For example, Harrigan (1994) identified several reasons why people do not employ conservation measures in their homes. People find the actions:

- Unfamiliar and intimidating ("I've never touched my water heater, let alone adjusted it").
- Confusing, with too many choices ("There are 15 kinds of caulk on this shelf—which one should I get for my windows? For my dryer vent?").
- Difficult to do ("How do I change my showerhead to a low flow model?").
- Unpleasant ("My water heater is in the basement, and it's dark and dirty down there").
- Done in isolation ("My neighbors haven't told me that they turned down their water heater thermostat, so why should I do it?").
- Difficult to evaluate, results virtually invisible ("I turned down my water heater thermostat and wrapped the tank, but I can't tell whether doing so made any difference in my bill").
- Easy to ignore ("I think I have done everything I can to make my home more energy efficient").
- Expensive ("I know I should do something, but I don't have the money to invest in insulation right now").

Behavior changed by reinforcement contingencies over a short period of time often reverts back to its baseline level when the reinforcers are withdrawn (new behavior is easily extinguished), and most of the studies applying behavior analysis to environmentally related behaviors have been short term (Geller, 2002). Behaviorists have often purposely designed studies to demonstrate the nondurability of behavior so they could show that new behavior is tied to the reinforcement contingencies. For example, in the bus riding study described earlier, bus riding quickly fell off when the token program ceased. Behavior that returns to baseline levels when reinforcers are withdrawn is an important methodological observation, but it also shows the transitory nature of new behavior. In addition to changing behavior, then, behaviorists must also design programs for maintenance and generalization (as in the grocery bag example), but that is difficult and expensive.

These arguments constitute powerful barriers to action, and must be overcome by persuasive interventions rather than the solicitations and marketing typically provided by media or through the mail. McKenzie-Mohr (2000a, 2000b) outlined four steps for promoting sustainable behavior in his description of Community-Based Social Marketing: recognizing the barriers to environmentally appropriate behaviors, selecting particular behaviors to promote, specifically designing programs that effectively address the barriers, and following-up after the intervention to evaluate its success. Some techniques that have demonstrated success in overcoming obstacles include recognizing customers who get results or who promise to make the changes (positive reinforcement), providing individualized and personalized information to guide conservation efforts (e.g., antecedent stimuli), and giving direct feedback (Harrigan, 1994; McKenzie-Mohr, 2000b). It is also more important to promote one-time actions that represent significant increases in efficiency (purchasing a fuel-efficient vehicle or investing in solar power) than to focus on repetitive behaviors, which are likely to extinguish if not consistently reinforced (McKenzie-Mohr, 2000a; Stern, 2000). Stern noted that purchasing efficient appliances and technology will ultimately be more effective because it is has more potent effects and is also more "palatable" to consumers than most lifestyle "curtailment" strategies.

Prices as S^Rs

An important explanation for the relatively small effects of reinforcement on environmentally appropriate behavior is that the really powerful S^Rs remain unchanged. One obvious form of powerful S^Rs is price. Changing S^Rs in the way of prices and tax breaks would require government or social control on a much larger scale than that available to the lone behavioral researcher. For the most part, behavior analysts have not brought their principles to discussions of public policies, in part because they are seen, and see themselves, as scientists rather than policymakers (Geller, 1990, 2002). Yet, it is important to examine the ways in which financial incentives continue to reward environmentally inappropriate behavior.

For example, humans continue to deplete resources because the **real costs** of consumption are not yet contingent on our actions. When we pay artificially low prices that do not reflect the cost of resource replacement, or pollution clean up involved in production, we are rewarded for inappropriate behavior. Fossil fuel consumption is a classic example. Giving people a token to ride the bus is trivial compared to the real costs we should be charged to drive cars. Gasoline prices reflect short-term market availability, not costs incurred from air pollution, global warming, or ozone depletion, so we continue to drive cars that in reality we cannot afford. According to Hawken (1993), "The marketplace gives us the wrong information. It tells us that flying across the country on a discount airline ticket is cheap when it is not. It tells us that our food is inexpensive when its method of production destroys aquifers and soil, the viability of ecosystems, and workers' lives" (p. 56). From a behavioral perspective, an important way to confront the depleting carrying capacity of the planet is to begin calculating and then charging real costs. We need to implement a system that induces the public to pay as we go, rather than incur ecological debts to be paid by future generations. To do this, we must examine the monetary values of natural resource depletion and charge accordingly.

Calculating real costs involves a lot of guesswork, of course, but even approximate hunches can help us envision how we might better control environmentally appropriate behavior. For instance, Durning provided a good example of how to begin thinking about and calculating costs of deforestation. Since 1950, we have increased our demand for tropical lumber by a factor of 15 (Durning, 1993). Overall, almost one half of the forests that once existed on the planet are gone (G. T. Miller, 2002), and only about 6% of the original forests remain relatively undisturbed in the lower 48 United States (World Resources Institute, 2002a). The situation is getting worse: More tropical forests were lost in the 1990s than in the 1980s (World Resources Institute, 2000–2001).

Many factors contribute to accelerating rates of global deforestation, including corruption, slash and burn agriculture, and urban development. But the most powerful reasons are economic: We simply do not yet pay the real price for lumber. Most governments subsidize their lumber industries by awarding timber contracts on the basis of power and political ties rather than open bidding (Durning, 1993). In 2000, the timber industry's lobby contributed more than $2 million to U.S. political campaigns (Hogan, 2001). At least 150 legislators in 34 states reported financial connections to the timber industry, and the industry receives $1.3 billion annually in federal government subsidies (Knott, 2000). Yet the U.S. Forest Service has typically lost money while it seriously overcuts its forests, failing to replant sufficiently to insure sustainable yield (Durning, 1993).

Less than 3% of the world's forest timber is currently produced by sustainable procedures (sufficient replanting, selective cutting, and delayed harvesting) (Atyi & Simula, 2002, p. 10), making "good wood" (wood that is sustainably produced) very difficult to procure. (Difficult, but not impossible; www.certifiedwood.org is a Web site where you can find out where to buy wood grown sustainably.)

Current practices make sustainably produced wood seem expensive, even though in the long run, it is cheaper than wood extracted unsustainably. Unfortunately, we haven't begun to charge the real costs of destroying intact forest ecosystems in our pricing of forest products. Intact forests provide "climate regulation, erosion and flood control, habitat and watershed protection [and supply] non-wood forest products . . . and other significant economic benefits on an on-going basis. International trade in non-wood forest products alone is worth over $11 billion a year, not counting the even greater local value of these products and the millions of jobs created" (Worldwatch Institute, 2002b). Thus, wood that is extracted with unsustainable techniques is astronomically expensive. A mature forest tree in India, for example, is estimated to be worth $50,000. The real cost of a hamburger from cattle raised on cleared rainforest is $200. And a wild Chinook salmon from the Columbia River is estimated to be worth $2,150 to future sports and commercial fishers (Durning, 1993).

If calculating real costs is difficult, then charging them is even more problematic. Who can price their product in terms of real ecological costs and stay competitive against others who do not? Some would argue that nobody is able to do so without government intervention. Perhaps we need a series of graduated taxes, which would provide revenue to repair the damage caused by the most ecologically destructive products. For example, wood cleared from original intact forests or is clear cut could be taxed heavily; wood produced from secondary forests taxed less heavily; and wood produced from sustainable crops taxed least. Money collected from such fees could be used to replant forests. Obviously, tariffs would also have to be instituted so that ecological pricing would apply to international as well as domestic markets (Durning, 1993).

Manipulating prices to effect behavior change is based on the **rational economic model**, which states that consumers should act rationally in a way that reduces the costs while maximizing their purchases (this concept is discussed further in chap. 6). Most economic theory rests on this behavioral view of human nature. Although price regulations are consistent with a behavioral viewpoint, behaviorists rarely discuss price incentives, disincentives, and government regulations as an effective way to change behavior (Geller, 1992b). Geller suggested this reticence exists not only because these policies are cumbersome, but they often elicit negative attitudes. Controlling market forces through central regulation of prices is obviously difficult, as the collapse of the Soviet Union suggested. Further, as we shall see in chapter 6, there is very little evidence that the so-called rational model of human behavior is valid. Behaviorists argue that reinforcers control our actions, but in the complex world of human behavior, there are many different kinds of reinforcers in addition to monetary ones. Consequently, human behavior is under the control of more factors than simply prices. In the words of Stern (1992), environmentally appropriate behaviors are a product of

> the human dimension . . . the rich mixture of cultural practices, social interactions, and human feelings that influence the behavior of individuals, social groups, and institutions. . . . Instead of assuming that people invest in energy efficiency if and only if they expect to save money, [we should also] hypothesize that people invest because they have heard from people they trust that the investment will pay or because their friends have already made investments and are satisfied with the results. (pp. 1224–1225)

But perhaps prices are more important than Stern and others think. Both policy analysts and behavior analysts have questioned these conclusions, arguing that people in the United States have not yet been subjected to effective price controls (Geller, 1990; Zoumbaris & O'Brien, 1993). For U.S. citizens, even doubling the price of gas or electricity still makes energy relatively inexpensive in the face of their enormous wealth. Looking at data from other countries that have instituted stiff gasoline taxes, Zoumbaris and O'Brien concluded that consumption is reduced when gasoline becomes relatively expensive. Furthermore, taxes collected on energy expenditures could be used to reduce those collected on income or savings, thereby reinforcing nonconsumptive behaviors while discouraging consumptive ones. As it is, our current tax structure penalizes conservation (savings) while encouraging consumption.

The most obvious problem with a price incentive strategy is that it is difficult to change the reinforcement history of those who are responsible for *setting* prices. In order for political leaders to implement appropriate pricing, they must be willing to lose the financial support from industry and special interest groups that lobby to keep artificially low prices in place. Political leaders are on a short reinforcement schedule of 2 to 6 years, when they face the problem of financing their reelection campaigns. Disappointing their benefactors will end the opportunity to continue their careers. However, appropriate pricing requires a commitment to the effects of our collective behavior over a much larger time frame, perhaps the next 20 to 50 years. From a behavioral viewpoint, pricing mechanisms will not work because the reinforcement schedules of those who could implement them are inappropriate for the task. These considerations lead us to believe that U.S. campaign finance reform should be a high priority for solving environmental problems.

SOCIAL TRAPS AS REINFORCEMENT DILEMMAS

In addition to inadequate pricing structures, we are also caught in a global contingency trap (also known as a **social trap**), as mentioned earlier and defined as "an opposition between the highly motivating short-run reward or punishment, and the long run consequences" (Platt, 1973, p. 643). There are both individual and social versions of contingency traps. For example, individuals may experience a dilemma between enjoying the experience of smoking, while knowing that they might ultimately suffer from lung disease or realizing that the tobacco industry is not very environmentally friendly. Because the punishers are so far removed from the behavior, they do not exert much stimulus control. A similar phenomenon was examined on a societal scale by Hardin (1968). Hardin, an ecologist, described "the **tragedy of the commons**," using the example of farmers allowed to graze their cows on a limited piece of common land. If too many animals graze there, overgrazing will ruin the land, as each farmer

> will try to keep as many cattle as possible on the commons. . . . The rational herdsman concludes that the only sensible course for him [*sic*] to pursue is to add another animal to his herd. And another; and another. . . . But this is the conclusion reached by each and every rational herdsman sharing the commons. Therein is the tragedy. Each man is locked into a system that compels him to increase his herd without limit—in a world that is limited. . . . Freedom in a commons brings ruin to all. (p. 1244)

This phenomenon illuminates an evolutionary perspective, which presumes that any action promoting a relative advantage will be selected for. From an evolutionary perspective in the tragedy of the commons, herdsmen are compelled to do whatever is necessary to provide, for example, more milk and meat for their offspring in order to ensure the transmission of their genes to future generations (e.g., Nevin, 1991). In this and many other environmentally relevant situations, the adverse consequences of irresponsible behavior are often uncertain, and result from the behavior of many other people—not just one individual. And, as in most environmental problems, rewards to the individual are more immediate and compelling than the delayed costs to the population. The result is a damaged biosphere. In Skinner's (1991) words,

> we are not likely to take the advice we are now being offered [about changing environmentally destructive patterns] because the immediate consequences are punishing. The old susceptibilities to reinforcement are still with us, and the behavior they strengthen is naturally incompatible with any attempt to suppress it. It takes strong advice to induce most people to stop consuming irreplaceable resources, to moderate the joys of procreation and parenthood, and to destroy weapons that make them feel secure against their enemies. (p. 20)

Thus, we are often fighting evolution-based patterns in our attempts to behave in environmentally responsible ways, a theme explored further in chapter 6.

Using a behavioral perspective, Platt (1973) argued that environmentally inappropriate behavior regarding shared resources can be changed by altering the reinforcement contingencies that support it, for example by:

1. reducing the interval between short-term reward and long-term punishment (e.g., making the long-term costs clearer);
2. adding reinforcers for environmentally appropriate behavior (e.g., instituting tax breaks for conservation behavior); and
3. adding punishers for inappropriate behavior (e.g., taxing polluting behavior).

Follow-up research has shown the merit of Platt's analysis. Most of the work has been conducted through laboratory simulations in which undergraduates play a game with shared resources. For example, at Colorado State University, students played a "tree game" in which each player pretends to be managing 20 plots of trees with two other players. A player can choose to harvest up to three plots in any given year (round), and is told that the plots will double on even numbered rounds. The goal is to maximize one's own harvest. When given no other information, players will quickly exhaust the shared plots, failing to derive a policy of sustainable yield. However, when verbal reinforcement for conservative harvests are given by the experimenter ("Good harvest strategy, Player X"), players learned to minimize initial harvests and thereby maximize long-term yield (Birjulin, Smith, & Bell, 1993). Similarly, punishing overconsumption can reduce its occurrence (Bell, Petersen, & Hautaluoma, 1989).

Many studies have shown that people will forgo immediate reinforcers for longer term group goals, especially if they identify with the group and feel responsible toward it (Dawes, 1980; Gardner & Stern, 1996; Van Vugt, 2002). In other words, "cultural practices can oppose the evolutionary susceptibility to immediate reinforcement and the contingencies of individual experience" by making social approval contingent on behaviors that reflect group goals (Nevin, 1991, p. 43).

However, group identity is more difficult to define and measure than individual reinforcers like game points or praise. Geller (1994) formulated a model of environmental management that includes group goals, but this approach is unusual within the behavioral tradition. Thus, let us go back to the fundamental place to lodge a behavioral analysis: at the level of the individual.

BEHAVIORAL SELF-CONTROL

More congruent with a behavioral viewpoint than manipulating economic regulations or group identity is to focus on behavioral engineering that takes place at the individual, rather than the governmental, level. How can we as individuals use behavioral principles to change our behavior? Individual behavioral engineering can be implemented in three ways: (a) modeling appropriate behaviors so that others can copy them, as in the shower study described earlier; (b) intentionally reinforcing another person's behavior through compliments and appreciation; and (c) changing one's own behavior.

For example, when her father explained his ingenious system for saving water (recycling water from the sink, to tub, to toilet), Deborah expressed genuine admiration and approval to him directly. Such **social reinforcers** are powerful controls on our behavior, and provide the basis for entire cultural organization. Expressing our reactions to others' behavior can help change it. Unfortunately, such expressions can also "backfire" and cause the recipient to feel manipulated or nagged, depending on how the reinforcer is delivered. When one of Deborah's colleagues asked another to print memos on both sides of the paper, he received a nasty (one sided) note telling him to mind his own business!

Perhaps the most effective way to change individual behavior is to start by changing one's own. This approach, called **self-control**, occurs when individuals change reinforcing and discriminative stimuli in order to change their own behavior (Skinner, 1953). For example, Sue is hoping to maintain a certain level of writing output now that classes have started up again. When she finishes revising this section, she is going to take her dog, Phoebe, out for a walk. While generally enjoying working on this book, sometimes she has to discipline herself to get a certain number of pages finished each day that she has available for writing. In order to meet our deadline, Sue needs to make some pleasurable experiences contingent on her writing output.

If you have ever dieted or in some other way disciplined yourself to achieve some goal, then you have implemented a kind of self-control project. Athletes put themselves on training schedules, students on study schedules, Christmas shoppers on saving schedules. A self-control approach can also be used to change environmentally relevant behaviors. To see how it would work, let's take a closer look at the details of self-control and apply them to a behavior that has environmental repercussions.

Originally conceptualized by Skinner in 1953, several good resources are available for designing self-control projects (e.g., Watson & Tharp, 1989). One version by Martin and Pear (1988) offers a six-step procedure that can be easily conceptualized and applied. Let's work through a self-control project so you can see the procedure in enough detail to design your own.

The six steps Martin and Pear (2002) suggested are:

1. Define the problem.
2. Make a public commitment.
3. Observe baseline behavior.
4. Design stimulus control.
5. Formulate a contract.
6. Check on changed behavior.

Step 1

The behaviorist would approach the project systematically, starting with defining a specific behavioral goal. We must go further than the typical intention to, say, reduce consumption, by defining the goal in behavioral terms. To reduce consumption is too vague. Instead, defining the goal more specifically enhances the probability of success. The first step would be to choose a particular commodity or material of which you would like to reduce your use.

For many of us, paper use would be a good choice, as approximately "40% of the world's timber harvest ends up in paper ... [and] 130 million trees' worth of paper is discarded after use each year" in the United Kingdom alone! (Abramovitz, 1998, p. 8). Even little actions, if undertaken by many of us, could significantly reduce our plundering of the planet's forests. As an illustration, we will describe a self-control project based on reducing paper waste. As mentioned earlier, "reducing waste" is not really a specific behavior. We need to redefine the goal as more specific behaviors, such as the following:

- photocopy on two sides of page
- print drafts of manuscripts and informal memos on the backs of "junk paper"
- reuse envelopes for informal mail
- reuse gift wrapping received from others
- use scrap paper for lists, notes, and reminders
- use cloth towels and napkins instead of paper
- go to the public library to read magazines instead of purchasing your own
- bring a cloth bag to the grocery store rather than taking paper (or plastic) ones

Step 2

Make a public commitment to reduce paper waste by telling someone about the project.

Step 3

Graph the relevant behaviors over time in order to observe paper wasting behavior. To do that, assign points to each of the paper saving behaviors, which indicate the relative importance of those actions, as well as points for the wasting behaviors. Table 4.2 shows one example of how to set up the point system.

The next step is to count and graph these behaviors over a reasonable time period, say 2 to 3 weeks *prior to initiating any attempt at change*. This provides a **baseline** measure of behavior as it is occurring with naturally occurring contingencies. With this picture of unal-

TABLE 4.2
Paper Wasting Behaviors with Assigned Points

Paper Wasting Behaviors	Points
Photocopy on 1 side of page	1/page
Printing draft on new paper	1/page
Use new envelope for informal mail	1/env
Use new wrapping paper for gift wrap	1/gift
Use new paper for list, note	1/note
Use paper instead of cloth towel	1/towel
Buy magazine instead of using library	5/mag
Use paper bag at grocery instead of cloth	1/bag

tered behaviors, we can also monitor what situations are likely to accompany them. For example, you may be good at photocopying on two sides of the paper unless you are rushed. Because the photocopy machine is more likely to jam when making double-sided copies, you might avoid doing it when you have limited time. Similarly, it might be easy to use cloth napkins instead of paper when at home, but not when you go out to eat. Analysis of this kind might suggest that paper overuse occurs because of time pressure or convenience. Figure 4.2 shows

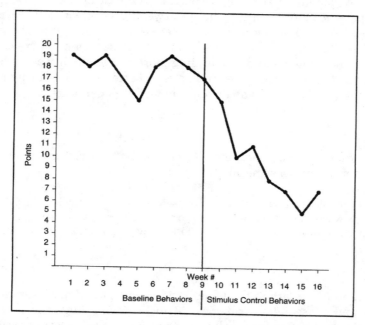

FIG. 4.2. Graph of paper wasting behavior before (baseline) and after implementing stimulus control procedures.

what a behavioral record would look like in graph form, both for the baseline period and the period involving changing the contingencies.

Step 4

Change S^Ds and S^Rs. With this analysis, behavioral contingencies can be designed that would be likely to reduce paper use. For example, you might decide that photocopying class readings must be done at least 48 hours before class, to ensure time to complete the reading. To reduce napkin use, you could keep a cloth napkin in your backpack so that you have it with you when you go to meals. You might notice that it is easier to reuse envelopes opened with a letter opener than ones that get torn when you open them by hand. Thus, placing a letter opener where mail gets opened will help with that part of your goal. By designing such antecedent conditions, we can more effectively manage our behavior.

Reward systems can also be very helpful. If you manage to change your behavior to specified levels, you could reward yourself with a special treat that is environmentally appropriate. Perhaps inviting a friend over for lunch, swimming for an hour, or watching a rented video would be reinforcing events. Similarly, you could institute punishers. By keeping a running account of the cost of paper waste, you can experience more directly the negative effects of waste: How much money is spent on gift wrapping, unnecessary photocopy paper, paper towels, and magazines? If these costs are not sufficient to create discomfort, then you could do something more active about waste: donating money for replanting tree projects, or better yet, replanting a certain number of trees for a certain amount of paper wasted.

Step 5

Behavioral change is more likely to be successful if you draw up a formal contract, such as the following:

> I, (Deborah Winter), will reward myself with a rented video if I bring my paper waste points down below 5 for any given week, or if I increase my paper conservation points above 20 for any given week.

Step 6

The last step is to graph the paper waste behaviors under altered antecedent and consequent strategies so that you can judge the extent to which the project is successfully changing paper use. Meeting predetermined goals indicates successful behavior change.

Self-control projects have an additional payoff besides changing the individual's behavior: They also provide the opportunity to model environmentally appropriate behavior for others. When we send a note on the second side of a piece of paper, reuse an envelope, or wrap a gift in the funnies, we demonstrate behavior to others that they may begin to enact as well. Modeling has been shown to be an effective form of antecedent control—remember the shower study.

Like all of the approaches described in this text, the behavioral approach does not guarantee instant success. In fact, the research on behavioral engineering has not been widely applied for several important reasons, delineated by Geller (2002). For one, the audience of the research is usually limited to psychologists, as it is published in professional journals and books. These individuals have "little interest or influence in large scale dissemination and application" or marketing the techniques (p. 526). Second, the target behaviors selected in the research studies may not be the most important. Overpopulation and overconsumption probably constitute the most important obstacles to achieving environmental sustainability (Howard, 2000; Oskamp, 2000), not litter control and recycling efforts, which have been the targets of most behavior change programs. Third, organizational and industrial practices are critical for sustainability efforts because of their polluting practices, the extent to which they can make "green" products available, and their contributions to an infrastructure that encourages or requires unsustainable behaviors (Stern, 2000). Fortunately, at least some businesses are starting to take sustainable practices to heart, and are discovering considerable financial benefits of doing so (e.g., Anderson, 1998; see also the discussion in chap. 8).

From a behavioral perspective, the most important obstacle to applying behavioral strategies may be that environmentally destructive behaviors are strongly habitual. Our past reinforcement histories have strengthened inappropriate behaviors to a point where they are difficult to change. Short-term reinforcers like convenience maintain inappropriate behaviors, and must be countered by stronger reinforcers like rewards. Switching behavior takes considerable practice. If you have ever tried to change your behavior, then you know that instant and permanent change does not happen. Any new behavior will be inconsistent and weak. However, weak behaviors can eventually become very consistent and durable, if reinforcement contingencies are appropriately maintained. Remember the cloth shopping bag example. Even though behavior change does not occur overnight, with conscientious and consistent practice, new habits can be firmly set.

Changing the consequences of the behavior of ourselves and others can be tricky, although waiting for natural forces to do it will be slow.

Eventually, our behavior will change to adapt to environmental contingencies, but the question is, how long will it take? Can humans effectively change the reinforcers controlling destructive behavior? And if so, why should we forego rewards and conveniences now in order to sustain a planet for future generations? What's in it for us?

Skinner directly posed this question in his book *Beyond Freedom and Dignity* when he asked "Why should I care whether my [culture or species] survives long after my death?" His answer was " 'There is no good reason why you should be concerned, but if your culture has not convinced you that there is, so much the worse for your culture' " (p. 137). In other words, Skinner himself had no real answer to this question. Instead he suggested that evolution selects cultures that *do* manage to get people to care about the next generation. This does not tell us *why* we should care, but only that we probably do. The question of "why" poses the perceptual problem of embracing future generations, so a worldview that emphasizes a responsibility toward future generations may be required. Although worldview is not a typical concern of behaviorists, Geller (1995), who did extensive work applying behavioral principles to environmental problems, has proposed that behavioral interventions should be designed to increase people's "active caring" about ecological issues.

APPLICATIONS OF THE BEHAVIORAL APPROACH

We can approach contingency management in several ways. Some approaches focus on the fact that contingencies are not yet powerful enough to change behavior, in part because they are still invisible. For example, we do not yet pay the true costs for most of our consumer purchases because current pricing does not reflect the resource depletion, pollution, and human poverty produced alongside the products. To make such costs more visible, we can urge lawmakers to institute real cost pricing mechanisms that represent the true contingencies that at present are invisible to us. We can provide cues and feedback for ourselves and others to facilitate behavior change, such as signs over light switches and photocopiers, information regarding energy use, or rewards for recycling.

All of these methods are useful, but can be expensive and difficult to accomplish on the individual level. Real cost pricing brings us into the domain of economic policy, international trade agreements, and political negotiations. We need to learn more about these processes, express our opinions to our elected leaders, and urge others to do so as well. Institutional changes can be addressed through task forces to examine energy use, conservation measures, recycling procedures, and so forth, and we can take initiatives to influence our schools, workplaces, communities, and municipal agencies.

From a behavioral perspective, climbing out of our environmental predicament will require that we change our behavior and facilitate the behavioral change of others by doing the following:

1. Observing, counting, and graphing environmentally relevant behaviors over time; noticing the stimulus conditions under which they occur.

2. Manipulating the antecedent conditions such as cues, instructions, reminders, and convenient tools.

3. Manipulating the consequent conditions such as feedback, reinforcement, and possibly punishment.

4. Focusing on our own behavior through self-control projects that will simultaneously model new behaviors to others.

5. Recognizing the individual contingency and social traps in which we are caught, and aligning long-term consequences with short-term contingencies.

6. Urging real cost pricing mechanisms so that economic and political structures maintaining inappropriate behaviors can be changed.

7. Focusing on reinforcing achievements rather than punishing inappropriate behaviors or using scare tactics. As Skinner (1991) noted, "The principle modus operandi of [environmental and other social] organizations is to frighten people rather than offer them a world to which they will turn because of the reinforcing consequences of doing so" (p. 28).

FORGOING FREEDOM

Before we leave behaviorism, we want to emphasize the important contributions this subdiscipline of psychology has made. First, behavioral principles help us examine particular features of our environment that control behavior. Because human behavior has caused many if not all of our environmental threats, human behavior must change if we are to extricate ourselves from them. Focusing on the particular elements of situations in which people behave gives us a strategy for changing behavior. In particular, examining both the S^Ds and S^Rs at work is a useful approach for planning change. The behaviorists have delivered a conceptual tool for designing a behavioral technology, even if changing the really powerful S^Rs gets us into the complicated social environments of interpersonal interaction and economic market analysis.

From this perspective, there is not only no need to focus our study on beliefs and attitudes, there is no need to worry about human freedom, because in reality, there is no such thing. To posit individual freedom is to draw a separation between the self and the environment, a separation that is arbitrary and false. It is true that we like to *experience* ourselves as free, and generally we do, *if* the reinforcers controlling our behavior are positive. Under those conditions, we usually experience ourselves choosing our behavior. For example, we believe that we choose to work on this book in order to communicate some ideas, an experience that has been reinforcing in the past. On the other hand, imagine if we were threatened with losing our jobs if we did not write this book. In that case, we would not feel free to write it; our behavior would be controlled by punishers, and we would feel controlled and manipulated. The behavior is controlled either way, but whether or not we *feel* free depends largely on the type of consequence. Our experience of freedom is also affected by knowing about the consequences controlling our behavior. When one is completely ignorant of the stimulus control, one may feel free. For example, selecting between several brands of toilet paper at the grocery store feels like a free choice. It is not always clear what controls the choice, so we misinterpret our ignorance as freedom. Noticing that one was made of recycled products and selecting it is experienced as a choice in order to help the environment (an S^R). If we were coerced or threatened with punishment to get the toilet paper for someone else, then we experience a punisher and would not experience the selection as a free choice. In either case, the choice is not really free, but we feel free if we do not know what the S^Rs are, or are controlled by positive reinforcers. Our behavior reflects the environmental contingencies at play, whether or not we develop verbal behaviors to describe them.

As you can imagine, Skinner had a tough time convincing U.S. citizens of his views about individual freedom. Our attachment to the concept of personal freedom is a central feature of democratic society. We experience personal freedom from our unusual degree of personal mobility (we drive cars, travel, and change residences far more than citizens of any other country); from our cultural heroes like Horatio Alger and Rocky, who teach us that anything is possible with personal effort; and from our political heritage, which emphasizes the pursuit of individual happiness. We not only think of ourselves as free, we feel belittled by the idea that we are not. Behavioral engineering elicits fears of Orwell's *1984* or Huxley's *Brave New World*. Sinister motives are attributed to those who would implement behavioral technology, and Skinner himself has been badly misrepresented and misunderstood as a cold, cruel scientist.

Reprinted with permission of Mark Stivers.

Although these reactions might be understandable, they are actually illogical and erroneous. All of us ask and pay for behavioral engineering when we send our children to school or hire consultants to help us solve problems. We revere teaching and learning, and expect others to derive methods for changing our behavior. To do so, we must temporarily acknowledge that we want others to "control" us. Because we are willing to see some behavior as controlled, is it not consistent to see all behavior as controlled, even if we experience personal choice? Such a view might cost us our traditional sense of "freedom"; it would also cost us our sense of "blame" and "accomplishment," because we merely reflect the play of contingencies in our behavior. But in return we may come to reconceptualize ourselves as more deeply integrated into our environmental context than we had ever before imagined.

CONCLUSIONS

Our behavior exists in a feedback loop where our actions change the environment and in turn the environment changes our actions. A clean delineation between self and environment is arbitrary and artificial.

Consider the example of a "shy" person who does not produce socially appropriate behaviors of smiling, making eye contact, or initiating conversation. Because these behaviors are not produced, they are not rewarded by others. In turn, others are not reinforced for their social behaviors toward this shy person, and their smiling, initiating communication, and eye contact behaviors are extinguished for lack of reinforcement. Now the social *environment* in which our shy person behaves is changed, making it even more difficult for the shy person to behave in socially appropriate ways. When we ask "who is shy?" we must answer that not only the individual is shy, but also *the individual in transaction with the social environment* is shy.

Similarly, as more people change to environmentally appropriate behaviors, industry and organizations will adjust accordingly. Demand for recycled products will increase their availability, and as they become more available, cost should come down, which in turn will increase their demand. Recycling is not only an individual action, it is a product of a social infrastructure (the recycling plant, the manufacturing and distribution of recycled products) that makes individual recycling possible. Thus, our actions depend on the environment and in turn change the environment in which we behave.

To see this point more clearly, imagine for a moment what a sustainable society might provide for transportation. All the cues encouraging driving alone would be gone. Nobody would be climbing into a car alone, cars would be expensive to operate, and roads would be less convenient. People would live within walking or biking distance to their workplace, commute in groups, or use public transportation. Electronic commuting would be far more frequent, with use of internet, fax, conference calls, and electronic mail to communicate with colleagues. Schools and shops would be arranged close by, allowing people to complete errands without the use of a car. A convenient system of vans or trams would supplement in cases of bad weather, heavy packages, or infirmed persons. Under such conditions, driving a car would be inconvenient, making more environmentally appropriate commuting behaviors easy to enact and maintain. We wouldn't try to change out of moral responsibility or pro-environment attitudes. We would emit environmentally appropriate behaviors because the environment had been designed to support them.

As Skinner (1991) wrote,

If human nature means the genetic endowment of the species, we cannot change it. But we have the science needed to design a world that would take that into account and correct many of the miscarriages of evolution.

It would be a world in which people treated each other well, not because of sanctions imposed by governments or religions but because of immediate, face-to-face consequences. . . . It would be a world in which the social and commercial practices that promote unnecessary consumption and pollution had been abolished. (pp. 26–27)

Behaviorists offer us the opportunity to experience the unity of our relationship with the environment, to see ourselves not as victims but as agents, consumers as well as restorers, reactors as well as designers. The behavioral approach illuminates the circular relationship between what we do and what is happening as we do it. Much of our present difficulty stems from our having considered ourselves separate from, or even above, our natural environment. Instead, our actions are both a product and a cause of the environment in which we behave.

KEY CONCEPTS

Behavioral engineering: antecedent and consequence strategies
Community-based social marketing
Conditioned stimulus, response; unconditioned stimulus, response
Conditioning: classical (Pavlovian), operant (Skinnerian)
Contingency management (consequence strategies)
Contingency trap, social trap (reinforcement dilemmas)
Discrimination, discriminative stimuli
Environmental contingencies
Extinguished behavior
Feedback
Freedom
Human nature
Information, modeling, prompts
Positive, negative punishment, punishers
Positive, negative reinforcement, reinforcers
Rational economic model
Real costs
Reward
Schedule of reinforcement: continuous, fixed, intermittent, interval, ratio, variable

S^D: Information, modeling, prompts
Self-control
Social reinforcers
Stimulus control (antecedent strategies)
Tragedy of the commons

5

Physiological and Health Psychology

I magine that you walk into a room. Immediately, your eyes start to water and you feel an irritation in your nose and throat. You notice that you are holding your breath, your heart is beating faster, and your face feels flushed. Then you see a sign indicating that the room was recently painted. Your heartbeat quickly returns to normal as you decide that "it's no big deal," and you calmly open a window to air out the room while you go for a cup of coffee. On the other hand, if you are a pregnant woman who has recently read that paint fumes may be toxic to the developing fetus, you will likely feel a much more intense stress response as your analysis increases the impact of the vapors.

This deceptively simple example illustrates the complex interactions between environmental conditions, physiological responses, and psychological processes such as cognition, emotion, and behavior. Several branches of psychology study these interactions, including:

- **Physiological psychology** (also known as **biological**, or **biopsychology**): a branch of the neurosciences (brain sciences) that

121

analyzes behavior as a function of physiological processes, often using nonhuman animal models.

- **Neuropsychology**: similar to biopsychology in its study of physiological effects on cognition and behavior, but focuses on the study of humans suffering from neurological (nervous system) disease or dysfunction.
- **Health psychology** (also known as **behavioral medicine**): psychology applied to the promotion of health and prevention/treatment of illness.
- **Environmental psychology**: the study of built and natural environments as they relate to behavior and experience.
- **Environmental psychophysiology**: the study of organism–place transactions and their physiological underpinnings.

In this chapter, we will look at the intersections of these subdisciplines as we argue that when our species damages "the environment," we damage ourselves. We have already seen how our behaviors, thoughts, and attitudes profoundly impact the natural world. Here we will show that environmentally destructive behaviors are just as toxic to our own health as they are to the planet's health.

Rachel Carson (1962) was the first to focus public attention on the link between environmental pollutants and compromised health. In Carson's words, "We have seen that [toxins] contaminate soil, water, and food, that they have the power to make our streams fishless and our gardens and woodlands silent and birdless. Man [sic], however much he may like to pretend the contrary, is part of nature" (p. 188). Forty years after *Silent Spring* was published, the use of toxic chemicals continues largely unabated in homes and industries. Yet, most people readily acknowledge their concern about "environmental" problems, such as air and water pollution, and their potential for causing adverse health effects.

Harm to humans from environmental toxins can occur in several ways:

1. Directly via the production, use, and disposal of toxic substances that stress physiological systems;
2. Indirectly through emotional responses such as anxiety that accompany exposure and environmentally harmful lifestyles; and
3. Indirectly by adverse effects on ecosystems critical for maintaining all life within a delicate balance.

We will begin our discussion by examining the most direct effect, the stress response, which is triggered by toxic environments and by contemporary lifestyles. Next, we will consider the physiological, neurological, and psychological effects of environmental toxins, as well as how stress itself impacts physiological systems and health. We conclude by offering ways to reduce damage to ecosystems as well as the self.

STRESS

Noxious odors, toxins, and physical or psychological demands stress our bodies and are referred to as **stressors**. Some researchers distinguish between the following types:

- **Environmental stressors**, including air pollution, traffic, noise, and catastrophic events like September 11, 2001, or nuclear accidents at Three Mile Island and Chernobyl;
- **Physical stressors**, for example, disease, aging, infection, surgery, malnutrition; and
- **Psychological stressors**, such as loss of a loved one, unemployment, disease diagnosis (Sarafino, 1998; Stein & Spiegel, 2000).

When you encounter an environmental stressor like paint fumes or any potentially threatening event, your **stress response** is activated. Regardless of the type of stressor, the stress response consists of physiological and psychological components (Evans & Cohen, 1987). The boundaries between the physiological and psychological are becoming blurred as neuroscience illuminates relationships between them. For example, the term **psychoneuroimmunology** was coined to reflect the interdependence of psychosocial processes, and nervous, endocrine, and immune systems. The **endocrine system** refers to glands that release **hormones**, which are chemicals that travel through your bloodstream and affect various physical processes (see Fig. 5.1). The **immune system** protects you from viruses, bacteria, and foreign substances via organs and cells distributed throughout your body.

Physiology of the Stress Response

Several pathways in your nervous system process environmental stimuli, although they function in an integrated manner. All stressors activate the **sympathetic division** of your **autonomic nervous system** (ANS). The ANS regulates respiration, cardiac function, and other life support mechanisms, and is a component of the **peripheral nervous system** (PNS). The PNS generally acts as an interface between the

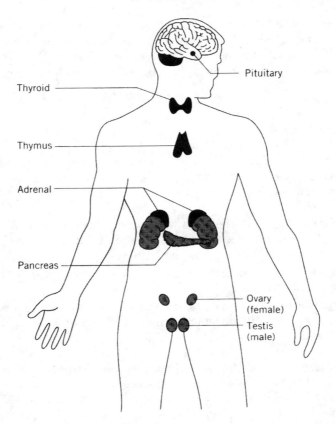

FIG. 5.1.   Some of the endocrine glands and their locations in the body. From
Sarafino, E. P. (1998). *Health Psychology: Biopsychosocial Interactions*, p. 42.
© John Wiley & Sons, Inc., New York. Reprinted with permission.

outside world and the **central nervous system** (CNS; brain and spinal cord; see Fig. 5.2).

Sympathetic nervous system activity, often referred to as the **fight
or flight response**, accounts for the increase in your heart rate and
facial flushing when you meet an acute (immediate) stressor such as
the fumes. Your body is mobilizing its energy stores to respond to the
threat. Part of the sympathetic response includes stimulation of glands
near your kidneys that release hormones. Thus, when you smell the
noxious odors, you feel a "rush of **adrenaline**" (also known as **epinephrine**), a hormone that is released by the adrenal glands (*ad renal*
means "toward kidney" in Latin; *epi nephron* means "upon the kidney" in Greek; Carlson, 1995, p. 65).

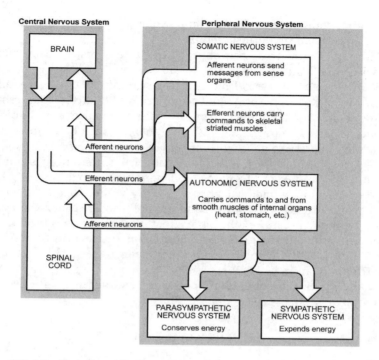

FIG. 5.2. Illustration of the flow and function of nerve impulses among the major parts of the nervous system. **Afferent** neurons carry sensory information to the central nervous system (CNS), **efferent** neurons carry motor signals to the periphery from the CNS. From Sarafino, E. P. (1998). *Health Psychology: Biopsychosocial Interactions*, p. 40. © John Wiley & Sons, Inc., New York. Reprinted with permission.

Your autonomic nervous system works in conjunction with your **endocrine system** via the **pituitary-adrenal axis**. This component of your stress response is triggered by long-term (chronic) stressors, and stimulates the release of several hormones, including **cortisol**. One effect of cortisol is suppression of your **immune system** (**immunosuppression**) (Parsons & Hartig, 2000), leaving you more vulnerable to infection during times of prolonged stress. The endocrine action mimics the direct sympathetic response, except that the additional hormones produce a much longer lasting outcome (Gevirtz, 2000). The overall result is an increase in your blood pressure, metabolism of **glucose** (which provides energy to cells throughout your body), and respiration. When a stressor terminates, the **parasympathetic division** of your ANS becomes active, enabling restoration and conservation of energy. Parasympathetic activity stimulates relaxation and digestion, a combination that accounts for the fatigue many of us feel after a large meal or intense activity.

Through the course of evolution, the stress response evolved to deal with a sudden and obvious threat like being chased by a saber-toothed tiger. According to Darwin's theory, animals that were able to respond in a way that protected them from the threat (successfully fighting it off or getting away from it) tended to survive and go on to reproduce, passing along the genes that enabled such behaviors. Other animals did not live to pass on their nonadaptive genes. As a whole, animal species became hard-wired to deal with threatening stimuli in sudden, intense bursts of energy and nervous system activity. However, because many modern stressors are ongoing (e.g., career and school responsibilities, crowding and air pollution), rather than acute as they were during our evolutionary history, the stress response is no longer well adapted to our environment. This distinction between our ancestral and current environments has been termed the **mismatch hypothesis** (Gaulin & McBurney, 2001), and may explain why chronic stress and other components of contemporary lifestyles produce such adverse health effects (e.g., Boaz, 2002).

Psychological Components of the Stress Response

Cognitive and behavioral factors are critically important in determining the duration and extent of the stress response. Your perception of stimuli in the environment, made possible by activity within the **cerebral cortex** of your brain, allows you to interpret and analyze your situation. Thus, **psychological stress** refers to your assessment of the meaning of environmental events, along with your evaluation of the resources you have to **cope** (deal effectively) with the events (Evans & Cohen, 1987; Lazarus, 1966; Lazarus & Folkman, 1984). These conscious, cognitive processes can either exacerbate or moderate your physiological response, and account for the more fearful reaction in a pregnant woman following her exposure to a potential toxin. The stress response can therefore be mediated by personal characteristics such as your cognitive appraisal of the situation, and your actual or perceived control over the stressor.

Coping efforts may help you escape, avoid, tolerate, or accept the threat (Sarafino, 1998), and can be "emotion-focused" or problem-focused" when resources are used to solve the problem (Spedden, 1998). Like Freud's defense mechanisms we discussed in chapter 2, emotion-focused coping can make a situation seem more manageable by creating distance or hope for future control, such as Scarlett O'Hara's approach in *Gone with the Wind* when she said "I'll think about that tomorrow." You could use emotion-based coping to ignore the fumes and stay in the room, telling yourself that you will get used to the smell and it probably will not hurt you (or the unborn baby). On the other hand, problem-focused strategies include problem solving, decision making, and direct action, like opening the window to air out the room, removing yourself from the situation by going for coffee, or putting on a gas mask. Both approaches can serve to reduce or increase distress, and either may be preferable depending on the specific situation, but problem-focused strategies are required for effective, long-term solutions.

ENVIRONMENTAL TOXINS AS STRESSORS

Toxic chemicals and their fumes are *physical stressors*, as they can directly cause symptoms such as hyperventilation, nausea and vomiting, and in severe poisoning cases, convulsions, unconsciousness, and death (Nadakavukaren, 2000; Weiss, 1997). Toxins are also considered *environmental stressors*, because they are present in environments where we live and work. Pollution, industrial chemicals, and consumer products are forms of environmental stressors. In fact, the medical profession adopted the term "environmental illness" to describe various allergies, chemical sensitivities, and "sick building syndromes" associated with air pollution (Arnetz, 1998).

Psychological factors, such as anxiety concerning potential poisoning, can produce the same physical symptoms as actual toxins, including hyperventilation, headache, and nausea (Wessely, 2002). Depression, a disorder that currently affects almost 10% of people in the United States (National Institute of Mental Health, 2002), is associated with environmental toxins. Depressive symptoms can result both directly from exposure to metals or pesticides (Weiss, 1998), and indirectly, when people feel pessimistic or stressed about the quality of the environment and their ability to effect change.

Environmental, physical, and psychological stressors interact in diseases like **asthma**. Every year, millions of people suffer asthma attacks, or breathing difficulties due to inflammation or mucus that obstructs their airways (Sarafino, 1998). Almost 300 children die each year from the disorder, making it the second leading childhood killer after accidents; 150,000 are hospitalized (EPA, 2002a). Although asthma is usually caused by irritation from allergens or air pollution (environmental stressors), it can also result from strenuous exercise (physical) or emotional (psychological) responses (Gevirtz, 2000; Sarafino, 1998).

Another example of the interaction between physical, environmental, and psychological stressors was observed following the terrorist attacks on September 11, 2001, and the subsequent anthrax incidents. Public fears about the attacks resulted in 2,300 false reports of anthrax exposure in early October 2001. Wessely (2002) observed that the social, psychological, and economic effects of "mass sociogenic illness" caused by psychological reactions and associated anxiety may be as significant as that which results from actual attacks.

As we write this chapter in summer 2002, the events of September 11, 2001, have faded from most people's everyday thoughts. Yet individuals who worked on rescue efforts at "Ground Zero" in New York or who live in the area are still experiencing serious respiratory illnesses, including asthma and bronchitis caused by exposure to massive amounts of particulate matter and dust (Prezant et al., 2002). Those exposed are at higher risk for **cancer** because of contact with **benzene**, **PCBs** (polychlorinated biphenyls, common industrial chemicals), and **asbestos** as the buildings collapsed and the debris settled (Ritter, 2002). Many experienced severe psychological trauma from witnessing the attack, or contending with its consequences. Such ongoing adverse impacts do not have the same dramatic appeal as hijacked planes flying into skyscrapers, and thus have not received much media attention. However, the number of casualties or illnesses resulting from environmental toxins far surpasses the few thousand deaths of that day. The World Health Organization (2000) estimates that 3 million deaths occur annually from respiratory and cardiac disease caused by various sources of air pollution. A recent analysis by the Environmental Protection Agency (EPA, 2002d) revealed that two thirds of people living in the United States (200 million people) are at an elevated risk for developing cancer due to exposure to toxic emissions released by automobiles and trucks, power plants, and other industrial sources. As we will see, environmental toxins can also cause neurological, cognitive, and emotional damage.

Many of the substances contained in vehicular and industrial emissions act as **persistent bio-accumulative and toxic pollutants** (PBTs; EPA, 2002c; also known as **persistent organic pollutants**; McGinn, 2002). They are *persistent*, meaning that they can remain in the environment for long periods of time (years or decades) without breaking down or losing their potency. *Bioaccumulation* means that such substances become more and more concentrated as they move through the food chain, becoming most toxic and potentially fatal later in the consumption cycle. In the 1950s, for example, phytoplankton in Clear Lake, California, absorbed low levels of a pesticide. The chemicals became more concentrated in the fish that ate the phytoplankton, and reached lethal levels in the birds that ate the fish (Nadakavu-karen, 2000). Because humans are at the end of many food chains, at least 40 states have issued advisories, especially to pregnant women, about eating fish that may contain high levels of PBTs.

Behavioral toxicology is the investigation of adverse cognitive and behavioral effects of PBTs (Weiss, 1998). All PBTs, including indus-trial emissions, heavy metals such as mercury and lead, and pesticides, are stored in fats and other tissues, and build up with repeated exposure (thus the term, bio-accumulative). These substances can be directly toxic by killing or damaging cells, or produce indirect effects by altering endocrine or immune system functioning. The developing nervous sys-tem is particularly vulnerable to the effects of toxins, and its study is re-flected in the subdiscipline of **developmental neurotoxicology**.

As many as 1 in 10 women are at risk of bearing children with learning disabilities and other neurological problems because of **mer-cury** exposure, putting 375,000 babies at risk annually (Motavalli, 2002b). Mercury, which impacts both pre- and postnatal brain develop-ment, acts directly as a **neurotoxin**. That is, mercury specifically damages or kills **neurons**, cells in the nervous system. Exposure to neurotoxins is associated with disordered cognitive development, in-cluding lowered IQ scores, impairments of memory and attention, and coordination deficits, or in more severe poisoning cases, mental retar-dation and cerebral palsy (G. J. Myers & Davidson, 2000). Other forms

of industrial chemicals such as PCBs also act as direct neurotoxins. J. L. Jacobson and S. W. Jacobson (1996) reported a difference of as much as 6.2% on IQ scores in children exposed to PCBs. The comparably harmful effects of **lead**, including retardation, attention deficits, and learning disabilities, are generally well known due to intensive public awareness campaigns. Lead damages neurological systems by interrupting the development of connections between nerve cells.

Even minimal amounts of toxins are cause for concern. As little as one seventieth of a teaspoon of mercury can disperse to contaminate a 25 acre lake for one year (McGinn, 2002). Although consumption of tainted fish is the most common source of exposure, airborne mercury is also quite common. Yet coal-fired power plants and municipal waste incinerators are still releasing mercury. Perhaps more disturbing is the fact that the medical and dental industries use and generate considerably more mercury-containing waste than other sources (Sattler, 2002), and mercury thermometers continue to be sold in most states. Because of consumer ignorance or carelessness in disposing of thermometers, mercury can be found in landfills where it can leach into water supplies.

Numerous PBTs in the form of industrial-use chemicals, manufacturing by-products, and emissions continually contaminate the air, wa-

"Just what goes in these hot dogs, anyway?"

ter, and soil. We consume tainted animals or their by-products (milk, cheese, and eggs), and PBTs "are found in everything from plastic wrap to computer terminals" (McGinn, 2002, p. 76). Many active ingredients of common agricultural, home, and garden pesticides also qualify as PBTs. All of these chemicals are a cause for concern because of their potential for causing psychological disabilities including retardation, attention deficit hyperactivity disorder, dyslexia, and autism; these disorders currently affect between 3% and 8% of children (Weiss & Landrigan, 2000). Thus, when Sue's next-door neighbor sprays pesticides on his lawn while carrying his young child in a snuggly on his back, she worries about the long-term implications for the child's development.

During the prenatal period, chemicals enter the placenta from the maternal bloodstream, affecting fetal growth and brain development (Weiss, 1997). PBTs are also present in the fat of breast milk. Breast milk contains levels of toxins that are even greater than that in the mother's blood, so breast-fed infants consume significant concentrations (Weiss, 1997). Young children also encounter higher levels of PBTs than adults, due to what Weiss (2000) called the **spatial ecology** of childhood. For example, because young children spend considerable time on floors, they stir up and breathe dust and residues, and their contact with dust may be 10 times greater than adults'. Children naturally explore their environments by putting contaminated items into their mouths. Perhaps most disturbingly, many children's toys contain **phthalates** (pronounced THAL-ates), which are additives that make plastics more pliable. In nonhuman animals, phthalates cause reproductive system abnormalities, birth defects, and cancer (McGinn, 2002). Finally, the fact that children ingest relatively more juice, fruit, and water than adults gives them increased exposure to residues and contaminants in those substances. Thus, "tolerance levels" set by the EPA for pesticide residues on food (EPA, 2002e) do not adequately protect children. The Food Quality Protection Act of 1996 requires regulators to consider these factors as well as possible cumulative effects in setting tolerance levels. However, tests conducted by the Environmental Working Group (2000) determined that dangerous levels of pesticides, including some that have been banned from production, continue to be found on popular foods such as apples. In their words, "two in 25 apples have pesticide levels so hazardous that a two year-old eating half an apple or less would exceed the government's daily safe exposure level."

Although most parents are aware of the risks of poisoning through accidental ingestion of household chemicals, an estimated 73,000 children suffered common household pesticide-related poisonings or exposures in the United States in 2000 alone (EPA, 2002b). Early signs of excessive exposure to some pesticides include nervousness, restlessness, and anxiety; not surprisingly, these symptoms are often improperly diagnosed (Weiss, 1998). More apparent indicators of acute poisoning are headache, weakness, and dizziness. Some pesticides cause severe abdominal pain, vomiting, diarrhea, difficult breathing, and potentially convulsions, coma, and death (Nadakavukaren, 2000; Weiss, 1997).

Moreover, long-term psychological impairment is common. One follow-up assessment demonstrated significantly lower IQ scores and greater deficits in visual-motor integration in children who had initially shown signs of central nervous system effects, such as lack of coordination, poor reflexes, "incoherence, loss of consciousness, [and] lethargy," following pesticide poisoning (Bellinger & Adams, 2001, p. 179). In rural populations where pesticides are regularly applied, frequent contact can produce deficits in balance, hand–eye coordination, and short-term memory in children. Prenatal exposure to a pesticide called **chlorpyrifos** interferes significantly with neurological development, resulting in brain atrophy and mental retardation.

However, conclusive evidence regarding the effects of environmental toxins, particularly for chronic low level exposure in humans, remains "disturbingly sparse" (Weiss, 1997, p. 246; see Table 5.1). Environmental toxins now bathe the entire planet, and even in the most remote places, people show measurable levels of PBTs in their tissues (Nadakavukaren, 2000); thus no unexposed "control" group exists to compare with exposed populations. Behavioral and cognitive effects from toxins are generally subtle and difficult to diagnose, so they may go unnoticed. In the words of a former director of the National Institute of Environmental Health Sciences, "Suppose that thalidomide, instead of causing the birth of children with missing limbs, had instead reduced their intellectual potential by 10%. Would we be aware, even today, of its toxic potency?" (Rall, as quoted by Weiss, 1998, p. 37).

Despite the lack of good control groups, it is highly likely that toxins combine with other factors to impact the developing brain (Bellinger & Adams, 2001; Weiss, 2000). A relatively small number of children experience clinical poisoning severe enough to require medical intervention (Weiss, 2000). A larger population is affected by subclinical poisoning, detectable by neuropsychological testing. Latent, or "silent," toxicity, "only emerges with additional challenges such as other pesticides, other environmental chemicals, or other health problems, and may not become apparent until additional challenges to function, such as the demands of the classroom, supervene" (p. 377; see Fig. 5.3). Early brain damage (i.e., fetal or neonatal) may not be observable until later in life when the brain is less adaptable (Weiss,

TABLE 5.1
Classification of Environmental Chemicals According to Availability
of Data Regarding Childhood Exposure and Developmental Effects

Amount of Information on Childhood Exposures	Amount of Information on Developmental Effects		
	Little or None	Some	Considerable
Little or none	hazardous waste sites municipal incinerators arsenic solvents manganese		
Some	pesticides cadmium inorganic mercury fluoride	PCBs (low dose)[1] methyl mercury (low dose)[2]	PCBs (high dose) methyl mercury (high dose)
Considerable			inorganic lead (high/low dose)[3]

Note: From Bellinger, D. C. & H. F. Adams (2001). Environmental pollutant exposures and children's cognitive abilities. In R. J. Sternberg & E. L. Grigorenko (Eds.), *Environmental Effects on Cognitive Abilities*, p. 159. © Lawrence Erlbaum Associates, Mahwah, New Jersey. Reprinted with permission.

[1]*PCBs (polychlorinated biphenyls):* PCBs are a diverse class of polycyclic hydrocarbon chemicals, now banned in the United States, but once used in a wide variety of industrial processes and products, including dielectric fluids in capacitors and transformers, hydraulic fluids, plasticizers, and adhesives. Current exposures are due primarily to residual contamination of soils and water. The consumption of sport fish taken from contaminated water bodies is a major pathway of exposure.

[2]*Methyl Mercury:* Mercury is a heavy metal that occurs naturally in the earth's crust and is released into the atmosphere by geologic processes such as volcanoes. The primary human activities that result in dispersal of mercury into the environment are emissions from power plants and waste incinerators, smelting processes, and industries such as paper mills and cement production. Dental amalgam, the material traditionally used to restore cavities, contains 50% elemental mercury and may produce chronic low-dose exposure. Inorganic mercury can be biotransformed to the organic form, methyl mercury, by bacteria in water body sediments. Methyl mercury undergoes "biomagnification," with tissue concentrations highest among organisms near the top of the food chain. Thus, fish consumption is the primary pathway of human exposure to methyl mercury.

[3]*Lead:* Lead is a heavy metal that has been mined and smelted for thousands of years. For decades, lead was added to residential paint to increase its durability and to gasoline to boost octane rating. The current primary sources and pathways include leaded paint still in place within homes, soil, and dust contamination resulting from these past uses, drinking water (primarily plumbing fixtures), industrial point sources such as smelters, and food processing procedures.

1998). Thus, diseases including schizophrenia, Alzheimer's, and Parkinson's may originate in prenatal toxic exposure.

As you are probably aware from personal experience, stressors do not affect the body independently, but interact with each other. If you are sick with the flu and stuck in traffic, things will feel worse than if you were dealing with either stressor alone. Similarly, the negative im-

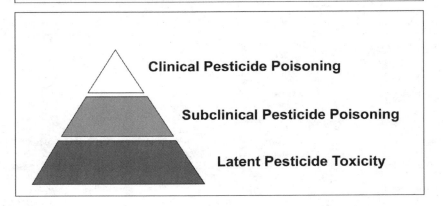

FIG. 5.3.   The toxicity pyramid for pesticides is designed to show that, although only a small proportion of children will manifest clear signs of excessive exposure, many more will show effects detectable by neurobehavioral testing, and even more will endure latent or silent toxicity that only emerges with additional challenges such as other pesticides, other environmental chemicals or other health problems. From Weiss, B. (2000). Vulnerability of children and the developing brain to neurotoxic hazards. © *Environmental Health Perspectives,* 108 (supplement 3), p. 377. Reprinted with permission.

pact of environmental stressors is often compounded by **social factors**. For example, **environmental racism** (also known as environmental injustice, as discussed in chap. 3) occurs because relative to higher status groups, minority and low income populations are exposed to more environmental pollution, and environmental and public health laws are often inadequately enforced in their communities (Bullard & Johnson, 2000). Economically disadvantaged and minority groups are more likely to live in regions containing toxic waste sites (Nadakavukaren, 2000), and lower income families often live in older houses where lead paint was used; roughly one third of urban African American children exhibit elevated levels of lead in their blood (e.g., McGinn, 2002).

Weiss (2000) advanced a conceptual model of how these factors interact. Intellectual development may be more compromised in someone born in a violent neighborhood following poor prenatal care and exposure to pesticides, than someone raised in a more privileged environment who is also exposed to toxins. Weiss' (2000) model illustrates how individual risk factors, none of which alone might exert obvious influence, can jointly produce damaging impacts on development (Weiss, 2000; see Fig. 5.4).

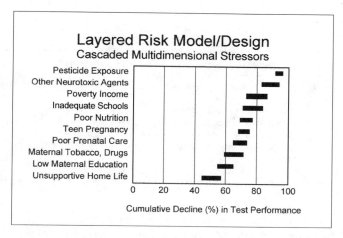

FIG. 5.4. Schematic model to show how individual components of a stressful environment might cumulate to reduce performance on IQ and other tests. The individual stressors are shown as overlapping to suggest a lack of independence, and their length is meant to indicate that no single component is overwhelming in isolation. From Weiss, B. (2000). Vulnerability of children and the developing brain to neurotoxic hazards. © *Environmental Health Perspectives*, 108 (supplement 3), p. 379. Reprinted with permission.

In addition to direct neurotoxic effects, PBTs that act as **endocrine**, or **hormone**, **disrupters** alter various aspects of nervous system activity. Specifically, PBTs can bind to naturally occurring receptors and block hormones from attaching, thus preventing the hormone from doing its job. Long-lasting effects can also be produced by alterations of the receptor cell's DNA when the substance attaches. The developing nervous system is particularly vulnerable to the effects of endocrine disruption. For example, PCBs and other industrial chemicals like **dioxins** impair thyroid function. Thyroid hormones are essential for normal brain development, so prenatal or neonatal exposure to thyroid-disrupting chemicals can cause significant neurological, including **neurotransmission** (chemical communication within the brain) abnormalities. Thus, deficits in overall IQ, learning, memory, attention, verbal skills, and reading comprehension have been associated with prenatal exposure to PCBs (Porterfield, 2000).

TOXIC EFFECTS IN ADULTS

Adults are not protected from the health risks of PBTs. The neurotoxic effects of PBTs such as pesticides may contribute to the development of **Parkinson's Disease** (LeCouteur, McLean, Taylor, Woodham, &

TABLE 5.2
A Summary of the Potential Effects of
Persistent Bioaccumulative Toxins (PBTs)

PBT Effects	Mechanism	Potential Outcome
Neurotoxic	Pre-, postnatal brain development	Cognitive impairment, developmental disabilities
	Adulthood—detoxification failure	Parkinson's Disease
Endocrine	PBTs bind to or block hormone receptors; alter receptor cell DNA	Reproductive abnormalities, birth defects, cancer
Immune	Greater susceptibility to bacteria, viruses	Infection, disease, cancer
Carcinogenic	Various tissues, organs	Cancer

Board, 1999), a degenerative neurological disorder that affects approximately 1 out of every 100 adults over age 65. Symptoms include difficulty initiating movement, tremors, and subtle cognitive deficits such as impaired processing of spatial information to guide movement, memory problems, or changes in mood (Strange, 1992). About 10% to 15% of Parkinson's patients experience **dementia**, a decline in intellect, memory, and abstract thinking, in the final stages of the disease. While Parkinson's Disease is also thought to have a genetic component (a family history increases one's risk for the disease), what may be inherited is a metabolic deficiency. In other words, the enzymes that normally break down and detoxify chemicals like pesticides fail to function properly in susceptible individuals (LeCouteur et al., 1999). (For a review of the effects of PBTs, see Table 5.2.)

Building the Perfect Beast: Our Use of Pesticides Compounds the Problem!

Health risks are not the only hazards of pesticides. What most homeowners probably do not realize is that attempts to eliminate or control "pests" will eventually backfire. You are probably familiar with the concept of **resistance**, when bacteria in the human body build up a tolerance to drugs like antibiotics. A similar process occurs with pesticide use: Any organisms that are not destroyed by the pesticides will multiply, and the characteristic that enabled the original survivors to escape the destructive effect is transmitted to their offspring. The pesticide is thus rendered ineffective for dealing with the new strain of organism. A compounding effect occurs via the **Volterra Principle**: Application of general pesticides can kill both pest and predator species. Thus, as consumers of pesticides or pesticide-treated products, we are contributing to the development of highly resistant strains of the very organisms we were hoping to destroy, and destroying the ones that would normally keep their populations in check. Eliminating "pests" will become increasingly more difficult for future generations.

Many people may not be aware of these principles or of the potential health hazards, and they may not realize that there are safe, effective alternatives to pesticide use, including pulling weeds by hand and buying organic products whenever possible. (For further information, see the Web site developed by the Northwest Coalition for Alternatives to Pesticides, www.pesticide.org.) Perhaps we can learn to be more tolerant of some pest damage or weeds, and lobby for increased use of **Agro-ecological** and **organic** (also called **integrated pest management** and **low impact sustainable agriculture**) techniques, which capitalize on natural controls and minimize environmental disruption (McGinn, 2002; Nadakavukaren, 2000). It is also important to evaluate **social norms** (see chap. 3) that compel us to have a weed-free lawn. Disregarding such pressure may be difficult, particularly when the proliferation of these chemicals support the social norm of chemical lawn care.

LEGISLATIVE ISSUES

As Weiss and Landrigan (2000) pointed out, more than 80,000 chemicals are registered with the EPA, and less than one quarter (23%) of the chemicals produced or imported annually at the highest volumes have been tested for effects on human development. Because of lack of testing, we are told that the evidence regarding toxicity is inconclusive, and the chemicals are deemed "innocent until proven guilty." This practice contrasts with the **Precautionary Principle,** where decision makers act conservatively to prevent harm to humans and the environment (Tickner, 1997), a principle that has guided legislation in European countries such as Sweden (Dinan & Bieron, 2001), and formed the basis of the Convention on Persistent Organic Pollutants. The resulting treaty outlines goals for dealing with the hazards of PBTs, including reducing their quantity and impact (McGinn, 2002). Some industry representatives and legislators might argue that it is too costly and impractical to increase regulation, especially by requiring evidence that the product is safe *before* allowing it on the consumer market. This position is ironic given the vast amounts of money spent on medical treatment of known toxin-induced illnesses, such as Parkinson's Disease and can-

"Where there's smoke, there's money."

cer. Slowing the progression of Parkinson's Disease by just 10% would result in savings of $327 million per year (Parkinson's Action Network, 2002), and the overall annual cost of cancer is currently estimated at $107 billion, including direct medical costs, mortality costs, and lost productivity (Cancer Research Treatment Foundation, 2002).

Apparently, we cannot count on industry or legislators to protect us from hazards associated with PBTs, perhaps because both factions benefit from the production and distribution of these substances. It is worth investigating political campaign contributions from industries that manufacture toxins or contribute to pollution. For example, energy companies (oil, coal, gas, and nuclear power) donated over $60 million to the 2000 U.S. presidential campaigns, more than 75% of which went to the Republican Party ("Who Gave," 2001). It should not surprise us then, that the George W. Bush administration promoted an energy policy that continues to rely on and subsidize those same industries, despite the overwhelming evidence regarding health, pollution, and other environmental impacts.

STRESS-ASSOCIATED HEALTH RISKS

Our review demonstrates that environmental toxins can significantly impact neuropsychological and physiological systems. The relationships between environmental factors, stress, and disease are complex.

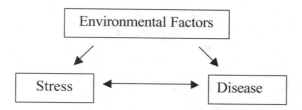

FIG. 5.5. The interaction between environmental factors, stress, and disease.

Environmental stressors can produce physical symptoms and directly cause disease; disease itself is a physical stressor; and a disease diagnosis for oneself or a loved one can create a great deal of emotional stress (see Fig. 5.5).

In addition, being *aware* that we live under potentially dangerous circumstances can cause stress. For example, did you feel stressed reading the foregoing sections? Unfortunately, such psychological stress is also toxic, in that it can directly produce adverse health effects. Emotional or psychological stress activates the same mechanisms that are recruited by physical and environmental stressors, and chronic activation of these systems can seriously compromise physical as well as mental health. We will review several of the most common health outcomes of stress, and conclude our discussion with some strategies for reducing it.

People often experience low grade infections and colds during prolonged periods of high stress because their immune systems are suppressed (**immunosuppression**). You may have experienced this yourself if you have ever gotten sick with a cold or the flu during final exams. Attending classes and living with lots of other people means that you are exposed to various bacteria and viruses capable of causing infection. Stress can interfere with normal immune functioning, decreasing or increasing immune system activity depending on many factors. The nature of the stress, whether it is acute or chronic, the person's interpretation and behavioral response, and access to resources such as social support, all influence the effect of stress on immunity (Goodkin & Visser, 2000; see Fig. 5.6). For example, feeling overwhelmed by exams and term papers, eating a poor diet, not getting enough sleep, and consuming caffeine or alcohol when you take breaks will compromise your immune system's ability to deal with the infectious agents you encounter in your residence hall and classes.

Symptoms of **depression** commonly result from stress, and recent studies suggest this effect may be mediated by the immune system. **Cytokines** (proteins that enable communication between cells) released during an immune response may contribute to depression

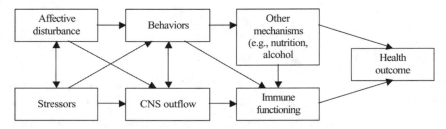

FIG. 5.6. Relationships among life stressors and affective disturbances. Both life stressors and affective disturbances determine central nervous system (CNS) outflow and behavioral responses. Behaviors may affect immune functioning directly or through effects on other mechanisms. CNS outflow also directly affects immune functioning. Behaviors, associated mechanisms, and CNS outflow all have an impact on health outcomes. From S. E. Keller, S. J. Schleifer, J. A. Bartlett, S. C. Shiflett, & P. Rameshwar (2000). Stress, depression, immunity and health. In K. Goodkin & A. P. Visser, *Psychoneuroimmunology: Stress, Mental Disorders, and Health*, p. 2. © American Psychiatric Press, Inc., Washington, DC. Reprinted with permission.

(Maddock & Pariante, 2001). The behavioral symptoms include "fatigue, loss of appetite, sleep disturbance, social withdrawal, decreased libido, depressed mood and general malaise" (p. 159), and are also observed to accompany infections. Maddock and Pariante (2001) suggested that these "sickness behaviors" actually produce depression (see Fig. 5.7).

Frequent mobilization of the stress response also increases one's risk for **stroke**, when blood vessels serving the brain are blocked or ruptured, or **heart attack**, a disruption of blood flow to the heart. Strokes usually impair cognitive processes such as speech production, comprehension, and memory, or motor functions such as voluntary movement. Many of the patients seen by neuropsychologists have suffered strokes, although tumors can compress or infiltrate brain tissue and produce similar symptoms.

Stress can exacerbate the risk of tumor development in several ways. First, immunosuppression leaves the body more susceptible to viruses and other organisms that can cause cancer (Boaz, 2002; Hardell et al., 1998). Second, immunosuppression resulting from stress can promote the growth of existing tumors (Stein & Spiegel, 2000). Third, cell proliferation repairs tissue damaged while "fighting or fleeing" a threat, and if the cells have genetic mutations, the result is a potentially cancerous tumor (Nadakavukaren, 2000). Finally, individuals who experience stress are more likely to engage in unhealthy behaviors such as smoking, eating a poor diet, or drinking alcohol excessively. Such behaviors directly increase the risk of several forms of cancer and other illnesses (Sarafino, 1998).

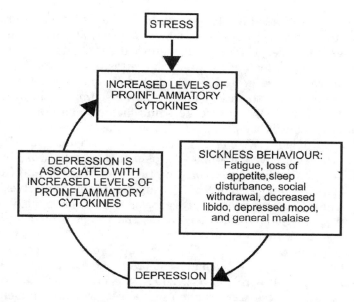

FIG. 5.7. The "stress, cytokine, depression" model. C. Maddock & C. M. Pariante (2001). How does stress affect you? An overview of stress, immunity, depression and disease. *Epidemiologia e Psichiatria Sociale, 10*(3), p. 160. Reprinted with permission of C. M. Pariante.

Stress-Associated Behavioral Disorders

Behavioral disorders such as overeating, smoking, and alcoholism are reaching epidemic proportions, and often are associated with feelings of stress. For example, stress can stimulate eating disorders (Arnow, Kenardy, & Agras, 1992), and many of us are aware that nutrition and healthy eating generally suffer when we are under stress. Such patterns are likely contributing to the epidemic of obesity in the United States and other developed countries. According to the U.S. Department of Health and Human Services (2002), 13% of children and adolescents and 61% of adults were overweight in 1999. Most overweight adolescents do not change their habits, and remain overweight in adulthood. Obesity is associated with an increased risk of cancer, heart disease, stroke, and diabetes, and almost as many deaths each year are associated with obesity as with smoking (300,000 vs. 400,000, respectively) (U.S. Department of Health and Human Services, 2001).

Eating and other addictive disorders have been analyzed as a metaphor for the psychopathology driving environmental problems (Riebel,

2001). For example, food is a limited resource that is taken for granted, as are water and fossil fuels. Awareness of internal states (e.g., feelings, hunger, or satiety) is numbed when we distract ourselves through addictions including food, coffee, and cigarettes or even television and music. Nature is disrespected as plants and animals are seen only in terms of their ability to satisfy food addictions. Impact on other humans such as exploited farm workers and factory laborers is ignored, and shared responsibility is denied, as eating disorders are seen as an individual's problem. "We consume the earth to ease our pain. But the success of this strategy is fleeting—the pain comes back, so we do more of the same, demanding more consumption-induced oblivion" (Riebel, 2001, p. 48). Riebel also noted that eating disorders themselves are a direct threat to the environment, because so much food is misused and wasted on them. This waste exacerbates the problem of overpopulation, necessitating further conversion of land for food production.

Regardless of whether we suffer from eating disorders per se, most Americans' choices of food are dangerous to their health. Again, evolution probably played a role (Boaz, 2002): We crave fats and salt because these substances were rare in our ancestors' environment and people needed to stock up when they encountered such substances. Similarly, sweetness indicated ripe fruit. With the current abundance of these flavors in grocery stores and fast food chains, we get more than our fill, and the consequences to our health are a testament. What is less widely known is that our appetite for meat, dairy products, and other fatty substances also increases our exposure to PBTs. Because PBTs accumulate in fatty tissue, eating animal-based products exposes us to even greater concentrations of these substances. Current agricultural practices compound this risk, as animals are routinely treated with growth hormones and antibiotics that can also adversely impact health (Motavalli, 2002a; Sherman, 2000).

Not surprisingly, the same food choices that negatively impact our health also adversely affect the rest of the natural world. Along with pollution from factory farms, massive environmental costs are incurred from using water, grain, energy, and land to produce meat. Hunger is pervasive throughout the world because of the eating behaviors of those in developed nations: "The feed cost of an 8 ounce steak will fill 45 to 50 bowls with cooked cereal grains" (Motavalli, 2002a, p. 29). In the United States, reducing meat production by just 10% would free enough grain to feed 60 million people. Animal rights and worker safety are also jeopardized by the meat industry because of the appalling conditions to which the animals and those who slaughter them are exposed (Schlosser, 2001).

Just as the experience of stress impacts our behavioral choices, many of our behaviors in turn create stress! Frequently people create more stress in their lives in order to maintain a certain standard of living that seems appealing or is socially valued. Most citizens in industrialized countries strive to earn a salary sufficient to pay a mortgage, make car payments, and buy "luxury" material goods. We purchase many more goods than are necessary for basic, comfortable survival, and consider it normal to do so. "What is 'normal'? Normal is getting dressed in clothes that you buy for work, driving through traffic in a car that you are still paying for in order to get to the job that you need so you can pay for the clothes, car, and the house that you leave empty all day in order to afford to live in it" (Goodman, 2001, p. 1).

STRESS-ASSOCIATED PSYCHOLOGICAL DISORDERS

In addition to adverse health and behavioral effects, stress is *psychological*, and can include serious outcomes such as acute and posttraumatic stress disorders (PTSD). Both conditions are forms of anxiety disorder, and include re-experiencing traumatic events through thoughts or dreams, flashbacks, increased arousal, and attempts to avoid reminders of the triggering experience (American Psychiatric Association, 2000). Other signs of stress disorders include social withdrawal, emotional numbing, depression, anger, sleep disruption, nightmares, and somatic symptoms such as gastrointestinal distress and aches and pains. Symptoms are frequently observed as long as a year or more after the traumatic event (Bell, Greene, Fisher, & A. Baum, 2001). A personal trauma or witnessing of environmental and social disasters such as the attacks on September 11, 2001 (Center for Disease Control, 2002) and nuclear accidents (Davidson & A. Baum, 1996; Lundberg & Santiago-Rivera, 1998) can produce stress disorders. Acute stress disorders and PTSD are differentiated by the timing of onset and the duration of symptoms: Acute stress disorder develops within one month of exposure to an extreme trauma; the onset of PTSD can be delayed up to several months or even years (American Psychiatric Association, 2000).

Acute stress and PTSD can overlap with dissociative disorders, which are characterized by a disconnection between consciousness, memory, identity, or perception, functions that are usually integrated (American Psychological Association, 2000). For example, during a flashback, the person behaves as if the traumatic event is being experienced at that moment. This dissociation from the present time can last from a few moments to several hours or even days.

In addition to personal trauma and natural or human-made disasters, many chronic stressors can cause stress disorders. For example, living in a community near a hazardous waste site, nuclear plant, or lake where fish are inedible, can produce considerable mistrust, anxiety, depression, or anger concerning obvious or invisible health effects (Bell et al., 2001; Lundberg, 1998). Yet one does not need to reside near a toxic waste dump in order to feel the effects of environmental stressors. Simply living in an urban environment and enduring the noise, pollution, and crowding produces stress and physiological arousal, adverse effects on mood, and deficient cognitive performance (Bell et al., 2001). Urbanized settings can even increase the propensity for aggression and violence (Kuo & Sullivan, 2001). Mood disorders such as depression (Lundberg, 1998) and panic attacks, which include heart palpitations, accelerated heart rate, sweating, shortness of breath, dizziness, and a fear of losing control (American Psychological Association, 2000), are also associated with stress. These disorders can overlap in symptomology with acute stress disorder and PTSD (Lundberg, 1998).

Less severe psychological effects include self-reports of stress and related symptoms (e.g., nervousness, tension), negative affect and interpersonal behaviors, and deficits in task performance and concentration (Evans & Cohen, 1987). These impacts are likely familiar to most readers of this text. For example, when you envision the typical middle-class family in the industrialized world (perhaps even your own family), do you picture harried people who often work more than 40 hours per week and have little leisure time to relax with their families and friends? Perhaps members of your family suffer from the symptoms of stress: headaches, tension in their shoulders and backs, stomach ulcers, high blood pressure. Perhaps they have been diagnosed at risk for a heart attack or stroke. They might engage in behaviors that further compromise their health, yet may help them to *feel* more relaxed: smoking, consuming alcohol, or using illegal drugs. Maybe they simply zone out in front of the television because they are too tired to spend quality time in more meaningful or productive activities. Unfortunately, that picture has become increasingly common and our collective health, along with the health of the planet, is suffering for it.

Social Considerations

The infamous Ted Kaczinski (the Unabomber) was quoted as "attribut[ing] the social and psychological problems of modern society to the fact that *society requires* people to live under conditions radically different from those under which the human race evolved" (quoted by Wright, 1995, p. 50; italics added). Kaczinski's statement is consistent with the mismatch hypothesis, but it also illustrates a common misconception—that our society or culture produces stress. The problem with that explanation is that the terms "society and culture" simply refer to how a group of people tends to behave. We behave in materialistic and consumptive ways; therefore, we live in a materialistic, consumptive society. The reverse is not true: Some abstract "society" is not causing us to be materialistic or consumptive. Thus, the idea that society causes stress is circular: Stress is caused by behaving in ways that produce stress! The implication, however, is profound: If we are behaving in ways that produce stress, presumably we could do otherwise. If that is true, then why don't we?

Most of us engage in activities that stress our bodies and brains because there is some gain from doing so. We have become dependent on various technologies and chemicals that are hard to give up despite their potential for hazard. We have developed behavioral habits and patterns of consumption that are very difficult to change. In addition, there are certain incentives for many stress-inducing behaviors. For example, Sue has been working for the last 12 hours on revisions to this chapter. When she lets herself think about it, she feels physically stressed, with tension in her shoulders, back, and legs. She also feels emotionally stressed from working under a deadline. On a broader level, she is stressed about the myriad environmental problems we are addressing in this book. Yet she is also aware of the benefits to this work. She believes that the book is a useful contribution to our discipline, and hopes that students and other faculty will benefit from using it. Because knowledge is power, she also thinks that books like this can help change destructive patterns. On a personal level, Willamette University has expectations for faculty scholarship, and so contributing to this book will help her professional record. Finally, if we meet our upcoming deadlines, Sue will reward herself with a vacation to Mexico over the January break (although the psychological benefits of her vacation will be mitigated by the guilt associated with the tremendous use of fossil fuel for air travel).

As this example illustrates, we are drawn to living a stressful lifestyle because of the personal, professional, or social reinforcers we receive (see chap. 4). Does that mean that we are doomed to suffer the adverse health effects associated with stress and the toxins to which our technology subjects us? We don't think so. There are many ways in which we can reduce our stress, and positively affect the state of the environment, as well.

SOLUTIONS: DECREASING OUR TOXIC LOAD, INCLUDING STRESS

"The well being of the ecosystem of the planet is a prior condition for the well being of humans. We cannot have well being on a sick planet, not even with our medical science. So long as we continue to generate more toxins than the planet can absorb and transform, the members of the earth community will become ill" (Swimme & Berry, 1992, as quoted by Clinebell, 1996, p. 3).

Because it can negatively impact task performance and concentration as well as health, one's ability to engage in problem-focused coping is compromised by stress. Not surprisingly, full recovery and restoration from stress requires removal of environmental stressors (e.g., PBTs) and involves positive changes in all aspects of the stress response, including cognitive appraisal and behavioral strategies (effective coping and reduced avoidance of problems) (Ulrich et al., 1991).

Behavioral Solutions

Sue and her partner recently bought a new bed. They wanted to make the most environmentally friendly choices possible, and found futon mattresses made with cotton that had not been treated with pesticides. However, as a matter of course and in compliance with federal regulations, the company usually treats the mattresses with a flame retardant. Because of environmental and health concerns, they both felt uncomfortable with the application of such a chemical, so they asked the company to provide an untreated mattress. The company was only able to do so if a physician provided documentation of a chemical sensitivity. Fortunately, their family doctor was willing to make that statement. This example illustrates our frequently unconscious acceptance of chemical risk and is, as Sherman (2000) put it, "inherently the antithesis of a democracy. . . . How did [the flame retardant] legislation get written in the first place? Who benefits, and who doesn't?" (p. 205). Somebody decided for all of us that the risk from fire is more important than the risk of long-term chemical poisoning. The public is not typically given the opportunity to provide input regarding such risk decisions (more is said on this topic of risk assessment in the next chapter).

Rather, the norm is for citizens to be exposed to potentially toxic materials, putting the consumer in the position to request alternatives where available. The ability to seek out nontoxic or less toxic options requires knowledge of the risk in the first place, as well as having resources to purchase what are often more expensive items. The average consumer is usually disadvantaged by lack of access to information, or resources, or both, and the public has little control over the majority of toxins to which we are exposed: in the air we breathe, the water we drink, and much of the food we eat. Knowing that we lack control can produce considerable anxiety, and many people avoid thinking about it in order to reduce those unpleasant feelings—remember Freud's defense mechanisms? However, ignoring problems will not help us solve them. Taking even small steps toward improving a situation can create a feeling of empowerment and even greater motivation to work for change.

Although there is a strong tendency for both legislators and citizens to react to crises rather than attempt to prevent them, there are alternatives. We do not need to continue supporting industries that are willing to put the health of people and the planet's ecosystems at risk until the chemicals it sells are *proven* dangerous. Nadakavukaren (2000) recommended the following behaviors to reduce your own exposure to PBTs and the resulting stress to your physiological systems:

1. Avoid use of chemical pesticides to the greatest extent possible; don't permit children or pets to play on pesticide-treated lawns;
2. Heed state-issued fish advisories; don't fish downstream from golf courses due to pesticide runoff from these heavily-treated grasses;
3. Limit consumption of fatty meats and dairy products;
4. Wash fruits and vegetables thoroughly to remove pesticide residues; better yet, grow your own chemical-free produce or buy organic products whenever available;
5. When using a microwave oven, don't allow plastic wrap to touch food. (p. 238)

You have probably heard about the health benefits of **exercise**, including its role in reducing stress. Again, the mechanism probably relates to the evolution of the stress response. Human anatomy and physiology is specifically adapted to an active life, and the *fight or flight response* by definition prepares us for physical exertion (Boaz, 2002). By channeling that energy into a physical activity like exercise, we use the mechanism in the way in which it evolved, and enable the parasympathetic system to provide more complete recovery. Yet, urban environments typically discourage physical activity by emphasizing road building for vehicular travel, rather than providing significant access to walking and bicycle paths. Thus, land use planning and public policy decisions guiding the design of built environments have important implications for environmental impacts on health (Frank & Engelke, 2001; Lawrence, 2002), including:

- reducing environmentally harmful behaviors (e.g., burning fossil fuels from automobiles), and subsequent exposure to the associated pollutants;
- decreasing stress such as that associated with traffic congestion and vehicular noise (Bronzaft, 2002); and
- enhancing public health through encouraging exercise, which is beneficial both directly and via reducing the impact of stress.

Interestingly, exercise can also aid in detoxification from hazardous chemicals by mobilizing fatty tissues that store toxins, to speed their excretion (Sherman, 2000). Despite these benefits, however, fewer than one third of Americans meet the federal recommendations to engage in at least 30 minutes of moderate physical activity, 5 days a week. Forty percent of adults engage in no leisure-time physical activity at all (U.S. Department of Health & Human Services, 2001). Eating a nutritious and balanced diet, and taking the time to notice and enjoy what one is eating, can also aid in reducing the experience of stress (Peurifoy, 1995). As a further benefit, we can make food choices that are better for our individual health, as well as for the rest of the planet.

The interpretation or analysis of a threat can either increase or decrease the intensity of the stress response. *It is not what happens to a person that is important, it is what one thinks happened* (author unknown). Fortunately, that means that we have a certain amount of control over the extent to which we are adversely affected by stressors. For example, **cognitive behavior modification** techniques emphasize calming self-talk (e.g., Peurifoy, 1995): "This isn't a crisis; I don't need to over-react. What do I need to do to solve this problem? Relax, take a deep breath. . . ." Exerting any form of control during a stressful situation also minimizes adverse health effects. If you are anxious about air pollution, modify your behavior to reduce consumption of fossil fuels (e.g., buy a more fuel-efficient vehicle, walk whenever possible, reduce your home energy use). These behaviors can help you feel more in control and empowered, and enhance activity of your immune system. Participating in community efforts to restore native plants, or dealing with polluting industries, can be both environmentally and personally beneficial, as these behaviors positively impact one's immediate environment, enhance a feeling of community and social connectedness, and increase control over stressors (S. Kaplan, 2000). Clinebell (1996) urged all of us to "green and clean" our cities and the buildings in which we live, work, play, and worship, in order to heal ourselves as well as our environment.

Psychological well-being, cellular immune measures, and physical health are inextricably connected, and all benefit from the following (Feaster et al., 2000):

1. adequate social support;
2. use of active coping strategies (including planning strategies, problem solving); and
3. positive attitudes including optimism, and feelings of social connection. Humor can also have many positive effects (Stein & Spiegel, 2000).

These social and personality factors enable stress modulation and improved health outcomes.

Restorative Environments

Have you ever felt mentally and emotionally refreshed by walking in a park, or gazing at a lake? Just as behaviors that are destructive to the environment are damaging to our health, contact with **natural** or undisturbed settings can have many beneficial psychological results (Frumkin, 2001; Ulrich, 1981). R. Kaplan and S. Kaplan (1989) defined "natural" environments as those containing vegetation or water, and lacking buildings and cars. Such settings evoke strong preferences and provide restoration from stress, including that associated with prolonged directed attention (S. Kaplan, 1995). For example, Sue has been struggling to stay on top of her class preparations as well as continue working on this manuscript. She started to experience **attentional**, or **mental**, **fatigue** (R. Kaplan & S. Kaplan, 1989), approaching exhaustion. We suspect many of you can relate to that worn-out feeling that accompanies long-term cognitive effort (e.g., during mid-term and final exams). The Kaplans noted that one can suffer from such fatigue even when the work is enjoyable, and subsequently, one's productivity can suffer as well. Although not synonymous with stress, attentional fatigue often co-occurs with feelings of stress, and natural, **restorative environments**, can mitigate the effects of both (S. Kaplan, 1995). The Kaplans (1989) identified four criteria for maximal effect of such environments:

- "being away" from the demands of regular life;
- "soft fascination" with sensory dimensions of the setting that are inherently appealing;

- "extent," or "scope," that gives a sense of vastness or connection between the experience and one's knowledge of the world; and finally,
- "compatibility" with the person's activity preferences.

Although literature on restorative environments focuses on positive psychological impacts rather than negative ones (wilderness settings can also be terrifying, although no one since Freud mentions this point very often), we think that most readers can relate to the point that natural settings frequently offer healing experiences. As an example, Sue went to the Oregon coast one weekend to recover from her mental fatigue. She got away from her work, and was captivated by watching the waves crash, noticing patterns of light in the water droplets as they were blown from the waves' crests (i.e., soft fascination). She chatted with her partner, laughed as their dog chased the waves and seagulls, and took long walks. The beach, like other natural settings, offers extensive physical scale, and is compatible with her enjoyment of walking and watching wildlife. Little by little, she felt more relaxed, and when she returned to work on Monday, she approached her work with rejuvenated zeal. In other words, the coast served well as a restorative environment. Wilderness experiences like backpacking are also purported to have various healing properties (Greenway, 1995; Harper, 1995; S. Kaplan & Talbot, 1983; White & Heerwagen, 1998).

Recognizing the value of restorative environments is important; although doing so could also lead to exploitation. Saving natural resources only for the ways in which they can benefit humankind is a limited and anthropocentric view. As Greenway (1995) put it, "Perhaps the clearest evidence of our recovery will be that we do not demand that wilderness heal us. We will have learned to let it be. For a wilderness that must heal us is surely a commodity, just as when we can only look at wilderness as a source of endless wealth" (pp. 134–135).

Fortunately, you do not always have to leave town in order to experience the restorative effects of nature. Ulrich (1984) showed that hospitalized patients with a window overlooking a natural environment (deciduous trees) recovered more quickly and required less medication than patients who could only see a brick wall out their windows. People with views of nature from their workspace reported fewer headaches, greater job satisfaction, and less job stress (R. Kaplan & S. Kaplan, 1989). "Natural" landscapes are preferred in a variety of settings, and provide the opportunity for "micro-restoration" (R. Kaplan, 2001). Activities such as gardening, caring for indoor plants, and interacting with animals such as pet dogs, all can reduce stress (Frumkin, 2001). Interestingly, restorative experiences in nature can also help to motivate environmentally responsible behavior such as recycling (Hartig, Kaiser, & Bowler, 2001).

Evolutionary processes may help explain the power of natural environments (Ulrich, 1983). It is likely that natural settings, particularly those containing water or resembling savannahs, are preferred and provide restoration because such environments have signified opportunities for obtaining food and avoiding certain risks throughout our evolutionary history (S. Kaplan, 1992; Ulrich et al., 1991; White & Heerwagen, 1998). For example, Prospect Refuge Theory predicts that we prefer environments where we can see without being seen, and where we are protected from the elements; these features were also critical to our ancestors' survival (Appleton, 1975).

CONCLUSIONS

The uniquely human ability to significantly alter the world around us has led to the production and use of synthetic compounds, chemicals, and fossil fuels, with some unfortunate, if not devastating, consequences. Our species is also unique in its ability to recognize some of those consequences, experience concern and other feelings, and (hopefully) change our behavior accordingly.

> Yet, how can we motivate people to make the difficult lifestyle changes that will be needed to save the biosphere [and ourselves]? One key is to awaken widespread awareness of the heavy price our lifestyles are costing us in terms of personal health as well as the environment. These costs will continue to soar until increasing numbers of us change our lifestyles drastically in ways that are simultaneously self-caring and planet-caring. . . . We humans display blatantly contradictory attitudes and behaviors in our individual health practices and in the ways we treat the environment. . . . For example, [every day] Americans jog 27 million miles for their health, but eat 3 billion gallons of ice cream (mainly fat and sugar), and produce one and a half million tons of toxic waste. (Clinebell, 1996, p. 3)

Environmental health hazards are, for the most part, preventable. The use of many toxins proliferated because of their beneficial uses (pesticides and fertilizers gave us the Green Revolution and the subsequent increase in the global availability of food). However, the myriad detrimental effects on ecosystems and species should lead us to question whether the benefits are worth the costs. We must choose whether to continue purchasing and supporting the use of such products. To do this, we must become informed: informed consumers, voters, and citizens. We can exercise more and eat in more healthful and planet-friendly ways. We can observe economic benefits to such choices, either directly (spending less money on gas while we walk or bike) or indirectly (reduced health care costs). We can choose to buy organic products, and make choices based on environmental implications rather than cost.

However, as Sherman (2000) argued, "This is not enough, for what [will] save the less-well-off, the poorly educated, or the family, unaware of hazards? Unless the common good is provided, none will be safe. . . . **Every** family should be able to obtain water, food, and air, free from . . . contamination. In the long run, what is more humane and cost-effective than to prevent [health risks]?" (p. 233). As citizens in a democracy, we have the right to contact our representatives in government and urge them to make environmentally responsible policies a reality. We also have the responsibility to help shape policies that provide healthy environments for all people. We can vote for individuals whose expressed concern for environmental issues is consistent with their legislative decisions, and hold accountable those who weaken air and water quality controls. In fact, democracy does not exist where citizens are uninformed and uninvolved. As Woody Allen put it, "80% of success is showing up."

KEY CONCEPTS

Addictive behaviors

Adrenaline, epinephrine

Asthma

Behavioral toxicology

Cognitive behavior modification

Coping: emotion-focused, problem-focused

Depression

Developmental disabilities (attention, autism, dyslexia, learning, memory, mental retardation)

Endocrine system, hormones

Environmental illness, "sick building syndrome"

Environmental racism

Fight or flight response

Immune system, immunosuppression

Integrated pest management

Mismatch hypothesis

Nervous system: central (brain, spinal cord), peripheral

Neurological

Neurotoxin

Parkinson's disease

Peripheral nervous system: autonomic (sympathetic, parasympathetic), somatic

Persistent bioaccumulative toxin (PBT): industrial chemicals, lead, mercury, pesticides

Pituitary-adrenal axis

Precautionary Principle

Prenatal development

Psychoneuroimmunology

Resistance

Restorative environments

Social support

Sociogenic illness

Spatial ecology of childhood

Stress (acute, chronic) behavioral, cognitive, emotional factors

Stressors: environmental, physical, psychological

Stress response

Subfields: Biopsychology, physiological psychology, environmental psychology, environmental psychophysiology, health psychology (behavioral medicine)

Toxicity

Toxicology: behavioral, developmental neurotoxicology

Volterra Principle

6

Cognitive Psychology

Do you recycle paper? Why or why not? Please take a moment to record your response before continuing.

If you answered "yes" to this question, your reasons probably included thoughts about the importance of saving natural resources. You may have mentioned that it takes a lot of energy to convert trees to wood pulp and subsequently to paper products, and much chemical processing is required. Even if you did not consider these technical facts, you probably contemplated the importance of conserving scarce resources. If you answered "no," perhaps you reasoned that it does not really make that much difference, or that recycling bins are never available when you need them, or that recycling is just a fad. These responses illustrate a basic tenet held by cognitive psychologists: In order to understand behavior, we must understand people's thought processes.

Cognitive psychology is defined broadly as the study of mental processes, and from this perspective, understanding the way people process information about environmental problems is crucial for understanding their responses to them. However, cognitive (along with social) psychologists have shown us that the relationship between our beliefs and behavior is much more complicated than we might suspect; that we like to think we are more rational and logical than we actually are; and that we are easily tricked by the limitations of our own perceptual and reasoning processes. Cognitive and perceptual biases, errors, and shortcuts cause us to overreact to some hazards and underreact to others. Yet, our cognitive and perceptual processes are crucial organizing features of our behavior. These mechanisms were shaped by eons of evolution, are modified by our personal experiences, and generally function pretty effectively. If they didn't, none of us would have survived very long.

In this chapter, we will explore environmental issues from the perspective of cognitive psychology, and consider why it is so difficult to respond to our current challenges. We will base our discussion on an information-processing model that assumes that behavior is a function of the quality of available information, and how adequately we process it.

INFORMATION-PROCESSING MODELS

Cognitive psychologists use models to describe how we mentally represent, manipulate, and store information. Information-processing models emphasize the adaptive nature of the brain, enabling us to be "cognitive misers;" we only take in as much information as is required to navigate in a particular situation. We create cognitive, or mental, "maps" of various situations or experiences, each map consisting of an organized collection of considerably more information than can be processed at one time. Maps allow us to anticipate, react, and consider possible upcoming events (S. Kaplan & R. Kaplan, 1981). Public reactions to environmental issues are impacted by such maps. For example, in the mid-1990s, Mitsubishi planned to build a desalination plant in a pristine area of Mexican coastal waters that serves as a birthing and nursery area for grey whales. After international environmental groups and celebrities publicized the development plans, more than one million letters of protests, coupled with public boycotts of Mitsubishi products, were successful in terminating the project in 2000. People's mental maps of the area consist of whale habitat, not industry. Mental maps thus impact our experiences and judgments, and whereas they speed processing time and efficiency, they sometimes result in biases or inaccuracies.

One of the most influential information-processing models built on Hebb's (1949) idea that when events occur close together in time, associations are formed between the elements in the brain (neurons) that represent those events (S. Kaplan & R. Kaplan, 1981). **Neural networks** are built from interconnected units of conceptual information (Collins & Loftus, 1975), and **learning** occurs via this associative mechanism: Connections between nerve cells (neurons) are changed by experience in ways that subsequently alter behavior. For example, we can learn to associate paper with recycling bins rather than trash bins. Neural network theory predicts that when one concept in a network is activated during cognitive processing or memory retrieval, activation spreads to all related concepts. Individuals create different **associative networks** based on their specific experiences, memories, and beliefs, and thus can have very different responses to the same concept. For example, when an environmentalist thinks of the concept "logging," the related concepts of "habitat loss," "species extinction," and "watershed degradation" become activated. A logger would think of "jobs," "provide for family," "wood products" (see Fig. 6.1).

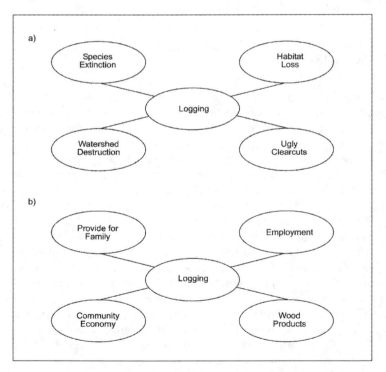

FIG. 6.1.   Different associative networks, representing an environmentalist's (a) and a logger's (b) cognitive concepts associated with logging.

Such differences in associative networks can account for many environmental conflicts. Negotiations often fail because each side assumes the other's goals directly oppose theirs, an assumption that Bazerman (1983) termed the "mythical fixed pie." Instead, by examining associative networks, areas of overlapping values and agreement can be addressed, and focusing on that overlap is the route to conflict resolution (Mayer, 2000; C. Moore, 1996). For example, forest practices (including cutting old growth and natural fire cycle suppression) that do not maintain the health of the forest ecosystem will adversely impact all interested parties: the timber industry; the community that depends on the associated employment and economic opportunities; and the various species that require healthy forests for oxygen, habitat, and watershed protection, among other services. For these reasons, finding common ground between the associative networks of competing groups is the road to sustainability (Kitzhaber, 2002; see Fig. 6.2). Thus, all factions would benefit from restructuring their neural networks so that their associations to the common goal of sustainable forests is activated first, before more divisive concepts and goals. Changing our thinking about our environmental challenges means changing our neural networks.

Artificial intelligence (AI), a branch of computer science, utilizes Hebb's concept of neural networks by creating artificial, neuronlike units and linking them together based on the strength of their associations. The linkages can be modified by the computer program's "experience;" thus, AI systems can learn in a way that presum-

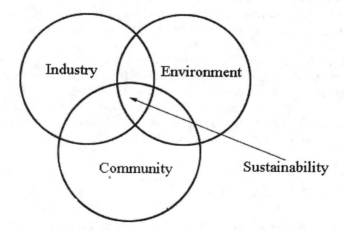

FIG. 6.2. Venn diagram, illustrating overlapping interests of industry (economic), community and environmental interests. The area of intersection represents sustainability.

ably resembles human learning. Since the 1950s, computers have been used to simulate human cognition, including problem solving, reasoning, and learning (Matlin, 2002).

THE COMPUTER REVOLUTION

It is probably not overstating things to say that the creation of the computer revolutionized the field of cognitive psychology. Originating in military research and development, computers quickly emerged as a principal tool for processing information. By 1948, computers were compared to human brains in terms of their apparently similar operations (Hunt, 1993), and the metaphor of the brain as a computer had instant appeal. Both seem to depend on digital events: the firing of a neuron and the firing of a bit are on–off occurrences. More importantly, both the brain and the computer "process information": Data are fed in, transformed according to some rules or decisions, and output is generated. Complicated but orderly decision sequences enable both the machine and the brain to behave intelligently.

Despite considerable advances in computer science, the capacity and ability of the human brain continues to amaze and challenge researchers in various disciplines. Computer modeling, cognitive psychological approaches, and neuroscientific techniques like brain imaging, together with theoretical insights from linguistics and philosophy, have converged to launch the interdisciplinary field of **cognitive science**. This collaborative approach to the study of human information processing is now one of the most dynamic areas of international research and curricular development. Yet even a sophisticated, efficient, and intelligent system like the brain does not always work perfectly. Thus, one way to understand environmentally destructive behaviors is to see them as outcomes of faulty information processing. Faulty processing can result from inadequate information, or inadequate processing of available information. As we shall see, both problems can contribute to current environmental problems.

THE CONSTRAINTS OF GIGO

There is a familiar saying in computer science: garbage in, garbage out (GIGO). No computer can do a good job if the incoming information is flawed. If our minds are like computer programs, then our behavior is dependent on the accuracy of the information on which we operate. If the information is limited or distorted, then the resulting behavior will likely be inappropriate. Among other problems, information can be inadequate because it is inaccurate, because it is limited, or because it is irrelevant. We will look at these three types of information problems in turn.

Wrong Information

Obviously, GIGO can result from wrong information. Good decision making requires accurate knowledge, but information that appears accurate in the present can later be discovered to be inaccurate. For example, since World War II, the Atomic Energy Commission has continually lowered the maximum permissible radiation doses for both nuclear plant workers and the general public (Gerber, 1992). Early nuclear tests were conducted without adequate protection to workers in part because officials mistakenly believed that small and moderate doses were not harmful. No information is perfect, but a commitment to improving information and revising decisions accordingly is an important principle of all good policy.

Limited Information

Information can also be inadequate because it is limited. First of all, we are limited by the hard wiring of our sensory apparatus. For example, our visual systems respond to only a tiny range of the entire spectrum of electromagnetic radiation—namely, wavelengths between approximately 400 and 700 nanometers, which we call light. Yet the continuum of electromagnetic energy extends from short cosmic rays of 4 trillionths of a centimeter, to long radio waves, traveling up to several miles. We are blind to the vast majority of this information: "Instead of experiencing the world as it is, people experience only about one trillionth of outside events: a small world indeed!" (Ornstein & P. Ehrlich, 2000, p. 73).

Furthermore, the vast majority of us who are not visually impaired are **visually dependent**. Sight uses a greater part of the cortex of the human brain than do the other senses, hearing, smell, touch, or taste, leading us to rely more heavily on visual information than any other kind. As Ornstein and P. Ehrlich (2000) noted, "Tree-dwelling . . . made it inevitable that human beings would become predominantly 'sight animals' rather than 'smell' or 'taste' animals. This sensory emphasis on sight has many consequences in today's world. We notice the 'visual pollution' of litter much more readily than we do carcinogens in automobile exhausts, potentially deadly chemicals in drinking water, or toxic contaminants in cooking oil" (p. 21). If we cannot see some-thing we are not likely to find it important. This visual dependency makes it difficult to respond to ozone depletion or global warming. Be-cause we cannot directly see chlorofluorocarbons (CFCs) or greenhouse gases, it is less likely that we will notice their significance, or keep their importance paramount in our thinking. Because of visual depend-ence, it is difficult for the public to make accurate distinctions between the environmental risks of greenhouse gases and CFCs (Bostrom & Fischhoff, 2001).

Most institutions concerned about public opinion try to apply the principle of visual dependence to their advantage. For example, using the notion of "out of sight, out of mind," the U.S. Forest Service (USFS) has officially sanctioned sets of cosmetic strips, that is, intact forests directly bordering public highways. The USFS calls these strips "viewsheds" and they are maintained in order that the public not be overly concerned or reactive about logging practices. In published plan-ning documents for each National Forest, the size and placement of viewsheds are explicitly specified. "Special rules apply to timber har-vesting within 'visually sensitive corridors' along designated high-ways" (Oregon Department of Forestry, 2000, p. 17). Furthermore, "Areas (viewsheds) with high visual sensitivity (as seen from selected travel routes, developed use areas, or water bodies), are managed to at-tain and perpetuate an attractive, natural-appearing landscape. Tim-ber is managed on a scheduled basis and used to develop a large tree appearance and vertical diversity" (U.S. Department of Agriculture Forest Service, 1990, p. S-29).

Visual dependence is a powerful principle of our information-processing system, a principle that has been exploited by all sides of environmental debates. Sometimes, however, our reliance on vision can backfire. Consider the "owl vs. jobs" controversy, which the press claimed signified the debate about the forests of the Pacific Northwest during the early 1990s. Spotted owls depend on old growth forests, that is, forests that have not been previously cut and replanted. Old growth forests are more complex ecosystems than are replanted for-ests, so spotted owls serve as an **indicator species**: Their presence signifies the health of a complex system of interdependent species and habitat, and the ability of other species to survive. The only available legal means for saving the dwindling amounts of old growth forest was for environmentalists to argue that the 1972 Endangered Species Act protects the owl from extinction. Any number of other species could have been selected, from the red-backed vole to the mycorhizal fungi (Maser, 1988), but environmentalists were smart to choose the owl: Owls have a strong visual image and are a lot cuter than a vole or a

Time Magazine © Time Inc./TIMEPIX. Reprinted by permission.

fungus. An owl has large eyes and a small nose, comprising what physiologists call a **neotenic face**, which is a face that approaches the proportions of a baby's face. We have a built-in, genetically hard-wired response to neotenic faces (Ornstein & P. Ehrlich, 2000): We find them "cute." We like them, and we feel protective of them.

But the owl's visual appeal has also backfired. When the debate is framed as "owls vs. jobs," families whose livelihoods depend on the timber industry quite rightly ask how environmentalists could possibly think that saving some owls would be more important than feeding their children. Because of the owls' visual appeal, it is difficult for the public to remember that the owl signifies an entire forest ecosystem, comprising hundreds, perhaps thousands of species, on whose healthy functioning humans are also dependent. An *endangered ecosystem* is really the issue. Analogously, some environmental philosophers (Callicott, 1994; Leopold, 1949, 1993) have argued that we must develop a "land aesthetic" that goes beyond our naïve visual dominance. Our uneducated reliance on vision leads us to value wilderness only when it is pretty. Instead we must learn to perceive much more complex ecosystems, even if such perception requires seeing beyond prettiness.

In addition to the limitations imposed by visual dominance, three additional principles of our perceptual systems are likely to result in GIGO. The first is the principle of **selective attention**. Even though we perceive an extremely small range of electromagnetic information, if we were to notice everything in that range, our experience of the world would be chaotic—a "buzzing, blooming confusion" to use William James' well-known phrase. Instead, our perception is quite selective. In order to make sense of the world, we must relegate large portions of it to "ground" as we focus on some "figure." We unconsciously make these decisions all the time. We do not notice the left foot stretching in front of the right as we walk; instead we concentrate on where we are going. Similarly, we do not notice the fossil fuel burning in the gas tank as we drive, the electric power feeding the computer as we write, or the trees used to build the rooms in which we sit. As cognitive misers, we delegate attention only to those items that need it, and tune out the rest.

In chapter 2, we discussed the role of defense mechanisms, devices that produce motivated selective attention and enable us to avoid potentially anxiety-provoking stimuli. Even without the role of anxiety reduction, however, we do not notice many features of our environment because of a second principle of the hardwiring of our nervous system: **Sensory adaptation** occurs if stimuli do not change. Our nervous systems are built to signal changes in our environment, rather than constancies. Stimuli that do not change quickly lose their ability to activate neural transmission; consequently, situational features that remain the same fade from our awareness and those that change too slowly never reach our awareness at all. Like the frog who will jump out of a pot of very hot water if suddenly thrown in, but will allow itself to be boiled to death if placed in a very slowly heating pot, we humans will endure quite noxious environmental events if they are introduced gradually enough.

The smog level of Los Angeles is a good example of the role of sensory adaptation. As Ornstein and P. Ehrlich (2000) put it,

7.31.02

a visitor to the LA. basin, arriving on a smoggy day, is often immediately appalled by the quality of air he or she is expected to breathe. But, as with many other constant phenomena, the locals hardly notice. A few years ago one of us arrived at John Wayne Airport in Orange County in the early evening to give a lecture. Every streetlight was surrounded by a halo of smog, and his eyes immediately began watering profusely. As a visitor from the (relatively) smog-free San Francisco area, he felt obliged to kid his host: "Well, at least we have a nice clear night for the lecture." His host's serious response: "Yeah—you should have been here a couple of weeks ago. We had a lot of smog then." (p. 76)

Sensory adaptation is exacerbated by another limitation of our perceptual capacity: **proximal cognition**, the tendency to be more motivated by short-term, concentrated benefits rather than long-term widespread costs (Bjorkman, 1984). You might recognize this concept as the "contingency trap" described in chapter 4. A related concept is illustrated by economic models of **subjective discount rates** (Howard, 2000, 2002). In this context, future benefits are less compelling than short-term costs. For example, it is difficult to expend money now to purchase a new refrigerator or upgrade the insulation in your home, even though these actions would save significant amounts of money in the long run in reduced electricity costs. Perhaps subjective discount rates can explain why Deborah has not yet replaced her inefficient, double-paned windows (chap. 1). Behaviors undertaken to increase energy efficiency can result in a return on investment of from 30% to 50% per year, compared to the much lower performance of most stocks, bonds, and money market funds (Bazerman & Hoffman, 1999). Yet, we tend to be focused on ourselves and what is affecting us in the present, preventing us from engaging in behaviors that have future impacts. The impacts of these traps are historically unprecedented, because our knowledge about, and ability to conduct, large-scale environmental destruction has not occurred until recently in human evolution (Vlek, 2000).

The mechanisms for visual dependence, selective attention, sensory adaptation, and proximal cognition all make sense from an evolutionary point of view. The current environment is quite different from that in which the human species evolved. Our ancestors were probably well adapted to their environment *precisely because* of these ways of processing. Yet now these mechanisms are "limitations" because they contribute to GIGO. The media reinforce this problem when they use brief headlines that oversimplify issues ("owls vs. jobs" is a classic example), and cater to a public with a limited attention span. We get only fleeting stories quickly taken up and then dropped by the press, television, and radio. Because of these cognitive mechanisms, the same old bad news about population growth, global warming, and resource depletion will not sell papers or retain viewers. Thus, most of us need far more information than we currently receive or actively seek out, so our ability to make sophisticated decisions about complicated issues is jeopardized. In addition, corporations do not advertise the environmental consequences of consumer choices.

For example, governmental agencies require food labeling to inform the consumer of the nutritional dimensions: fat content, calories, and chemical additives are listed. No information is yet made available, however, about relevant environmental concerns: number of gallons of gasoline used to grow and distribute a food product, number of people injured by the use of pesticides, whether or not the food was produced in the United States or on foreign soil where environmental regulations are more lax, and whether genetic engineering was used to produce the foods or protect them from pest damage or disease. Thus, making informed consumer choices on food and other products is not easy, although reframing food choices in these terms would lead to the obvious conclusion that buying strawberries in January in North America is a less environmentally appropriate action than buying them at the local farmer's market in June.

Encouragingly, more and more companies are responding to an emerging market for organically produced foods, and products that bear fewer negative environmental and social impacts. For example, some companies are becoming sensitive to social issues like farm worker health and safety, and environmental issues like biodiversity. In this case, more information about corporate practices can lead to better environmental choices.

Irrelevant Information

Too much information can also produce GIGO if the information confuses us; many reasoning difficulties come from being distracted by or using **irrelevant information**. We encounter irrelevant information in advertising, and at times we actively pursue it through using confirmation biases and misinterpreting events as being meaningfully related to our behavior. In this section, we will elaborate on each of these points and argue that humans are not as rational as they think.

Advertisers often employ irrelevant information to increase the desirability of their products (see Fig. 6.3). Ink regulation and incineration are irrelevant information, as plastic bags are rarely burned at high enough temperatures to be nontoxic. Claiming the product is "recyclable" borders on the fraudulent, because fewer than 1% of plastic bags are recycled at all, and this company neither recycles nor uses re-

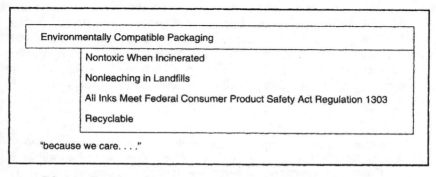

FIG. 6.3. The information printed on a grocer's plastic bag demonstrates the use of irrelevant information to make a product appear environmentally friendly.

cycled bags. "Reusable" would have been a more appropriate term. Inaccurate and irrelevant information is displayed in an attempt to make this company appear environmentally conscious, a practice termed "greenwashing" by some environmental groups.

However, we do not need the efforts of advertising to become confused by irrelevant information. There are two ways in which we actively **pursue** irrelevant information. One is called the **confirmation bias**. When testing our hunches against incoming data, we make the mistake of looking for confirming information rather than disconfirming information (Wason, 1960). This tendency is consistent with associative network theory, as it is more difficult to process and store material that conflicts with the attitudes and concepts comprising our cognitive networks. For example, when Sue was doing research for the physiological and health chapter of this book, her bias was to look for evidence showing adverse health effects of pesticides. She tended to discount studies that found no effects, concluding that they were methodologically flawed or politically motivated (i.e., funded by a pharmaceutical company). She had to work hard to present a more balanced perspective, that is, to create associations contrary to her preexisting ones between chemicals and disease.

Seeking lots of confirmatory information feels good, but is not very useful. People generally do not like to experience disconfirmations, so they do not seek them. Consequently, environmentalists tend to read material that confirms their views, such as publications of the *Sierra Club* and *Natural Resources Defense Council*, rather than *The National Review* and *Our Land* (a Wise Use movement publication).

In addition to using confirmation biases, we may interpret random events as meaningfully related to some human action out of our need to believe that we have some control over our world. The principle of **regression toward the mean** illustrates this tendency. In brief, chance events fall on a normal curve, with extreme occurrences far less likely than more typical ones. Because extreme events are rare, the next event is likely to be less extreme, simply due to chance alone. For example, extremely hot days are more likely to be followed by cooler ones than by hot ones, simply by chance. But human beings, looking for meaning, are prone to explain occurrences in terms of human actions. In the words of environmental educator Lee (1993):

The significance of regression artifacts in environmental science may seem less important than in the allegedly "softer" social sciences, until we recall that environmental remedies are applied precisely because some aspect of the environment is in an extreme state. Regression to the mean predicts, for example, that after a species has been declared endangered it will tend to become more abundant. This is not an effect [of the 'endangered' declaration] at all, but a reflection of the fact that the human decision to declare a population in bad trouble is based upon its being *in extremis*. To the extent that that condition is caused by a variety of factors—as is virtually always the case in the natural setting—some of them will fluctuate in the next year, and the fluctuations will on average tend to bring the population up. In the early years of the Columbia Basin program, before any of the rehabilitation measures could be carried out, there was a resurgence of salmon populations from the historic lows of the late 1970s, when the Northwest Power Act was passed. It took a special effort of political will not to take credit for this change, even though there was as yet no cause to which such an effect could be attributed. (pp. 71–72)

In other words, because human beings are prone to make up explanations for random events, we can easily misinterpret our actions as causing something that is happening purely by chance.

If problems are presented simply enough, we can usually come up with an appropriate answer, but unfortunately, life is usually not very simple. Even when we are not being manipulated by advertisers or actively looking for it, irrelevant information can get in the way. For example, consider the following set of statements (based on a problem Zukier, 1982, presented to his laboratory participants):

1. Assuming you have access to sunlight, heating a house with passive solar heat costs from 30% to 40% less over the lifetime of the house than heating with conventional systems, such as electricity, gas, coal, or oil. If you want to save money on heating, which system should you choose?

2. You are planning your dream home, which you plan to live in for the rest of your life. Assuming you have access to sunlight, heating a house with passive solar heat costs from 30% to 40% less over the lifetime of the house than heating with conventional systems, such as electricity, gas, coal, or oil. Passive solar systems add from 5% to 10% more to the construction costs. Some people believe that rooftop solar collectors are ugly and detract from the architectural design of a structure. In order to get the maximum efficiency from your passive system, you have to open and shut windows and shades to regulate heat distribution, although this could be accomplished by an inexpensive computer. Your access to solar energy could be disrupted if someone decided to build an interfering structure, because right now there are no laws to guarantee owner access to sunlight (such legislation has been opposed by builders of high-density developments). If you want to save money on heating, which system should you choose?

The irrelevant information (irrelevant to the question of saving money) contained in the second problem is likely to distract readers from the crucial sentence "heating a house with passive solar heat costs from 30% to 40% less over the lifetime of the house than heating with conventional systems" and confuse the issue. Because most environmental questions are complex and involve many different considerations, it is difficult not to get waylaid.

The public's tendency to be distracted by irrelevant information is a concern among policymakers whose job it is to convince the public to reduce energy use. Most energy conservation programs are designed under the assumption that the public is primarily interested in saving money and will act rationally to do so. This view is called the *rational-economic model*, which we encountered in chapter 4. According to Stern (1992), the rational-economic model rests on the assumption that if a technology will save its owners and operators money over the life of the equipment, it "will be adopted once the owners become aware of the benefits" (p. 1224).

However, research shows that instead of using a purely "rational economic model" for decisions about conservation issues, most people rely on a "folk model," which looks irrational to energy experts. In the words of social psychologists Costanzo, Archer, Aronson, and Pettigrew (1986):

> The "folk model" typically used by individual consumers calculates current dollar savings as compared to pre-adoption expenditures and fails to reveal that the initial cost of the investment is paid back faster because of rising fuel prices. Thus, folk calculations based on naive and "irrational" assumptions cause consumers to make fewer energy-saving investments than an expert analysis would recommend. In addition, a variety of noneconomic factors (e.g. style, status, performance, safety, comfort, and convenience) influence decision making and contribute to the apparent irrationality of conservation behavior. (p. 525)

These additional dimensions are important to consumers, often more important than price. Thus, the concept of **bounded rationality** is useful, as it acknowledges that humans do not function in order to fully maximize potentially beneficial outcomes (Gardner & Stern, 2002; Gigerenzer, 2000; S. Kaplan & R. Kaplan, 1981). Rather, "bounded rationality . . . necessarily takes shortcuts, simplifies complex problems, uses certain tricks, and shows certain biases . . . which work reasonably well" most of the time (Gardner & Stern, 2002, p. 228).

The concept of irrelevant information brings us to the question "irrelevant to whom?" When experts (either policy analysts or cognitive psychologists) define a problem, they typically do it in narrower terms than laypersons do. We will say more about this problem of definition later in the chapter when we talk about risk analysis.

ADDITIONAL CONSTRAINTS ON INFORMATION PROCESSING

Our cognitive systems evolved to process information quickly and efficiently, using previous experiences to guide subsequent decision making. Yet sometimes our biases and shortcuts get in the way of making good decisions. Thus, GIGO is not our only information-processing problem. Even when we have accurate, comprehensive, and relevant information, we sometimes overuse preconceptions and expectations. Reasoning shortcuts (**heuristics**) that help us make judgments based on limited information may lead us to "snap" decisions. We have difficulty with quantitative processing, particularly with large numbers, presumably because such information was only very recently encountered in our evolutionary history. Finally, we are influenced by the way information is framed, or the context in which it is presented. In this section, we will discuss each of these cognitive mechanisms and their relationship to environmental issues.

Learning and experience, and subsequent associative networks or mental maps, give us a framework for how to interpret information and situations. The world would be totally chaotic without some **preexisting biases** based on our previous experiences. To paraphrase Bloom (1987), too much open-mindedness would make our brains spill out! Preexisting beliefs are necessary, but they can also get in our way, or potently affect our perception and interpretation of an event. Consider how two different people interpreted the same traffic accident on I-95 in Springfield, Massachusetts, involving a tractor trailer carrying 11,000 pounds of radioactive uranium that overturned and burned:

> A representative of the antinuclear group Nuclear Information and Resource Service [said] that "People should be plenty concerned," since the accident signaled more trouble in the future: "Accidents happen at the same rate to nuclear shipments as for all other shipments—one per every 150,000 miles the truck travels." In contrast, a representative for the U.S. Council for Energy Awareness, which is supported by the nuclear industry, took the accident as a signal of assurance: "The system works," he said. "We had an accident including fire and there was no release of radioactivity." (Cvetkovich & Earle, 1992, p. 8)

Because people use their preexisting biases to interpret events, discourse about specific environmental problems can be divided, if not derisive. As we previously suggested, it is critical for interested parties (industry, community representatives, and environmentalists) to find common goals and learn to work together to achieve them. This process can be facilitated by encouraging all parties to see the other's side of the issue (C. G. Lord, Lepper, & Preston, 1984). Although acknowledging the opposite viewpoint is not easy, its effects are valuable. To illustrate this point, pick an environmental issue about which you have a strong opinion and consider the other side. For example, we think the United States should sign on to the Kyoto Protocol to address global warming, but the George W. Bush administration disagrees. Although acknowledging the reality of global warming and its relation to human activities, President Bush refused to sign on in 2002. He argued that the "Kyoto Protocol would have required the U.S. to make deep and immediate cuts in our economy to meet an arbitrary target" (Bush, 2002). When we make the effort to seriously consider that argument, we realize that workers in industries such as coal, oil, and automobiles would be significantly affected. One study showed that the Protocol would eliminate 2.4 million United States jobs, reduce United States total annual output by $300 billion (in 1992 dollars), and reduce the average national household income by nearly $2700 (WEFA, 1998). Whereas Sue and Deborah still believe that the economic and social costs of *not* responding to the threats of global warming are greater (Goodstein, 1999; Gelbspan, 1998), arguing the other side forces us to appreciate the complexity of the issue, and understand the President's concerns about the well-being of some U.S. citizens.

Reasoning Strategies: Heuristics

In order to comprehend a complex world, people not only depend on biases, but also heuristics. A heuristic is any reasoning device that helps us think quickly and efficiently. For example, on our campuses, male administrators can usually be distinguished from faculty at a distance because the former wear coats and ties, but the latter do not. However, heuristics do not always work, and can lead us into wrong snap judgments. For example, consider the following problem based on cognitive psychologists Tversky and Kahneman's (1983) now classic experiment.

John is a 31 year old white male, single, outspoken, and very committed to environmental issues. He and his friends have demonstrated in many confrontational protests over logging, mining, and land use operations. Which statement is more likely:

1. John is a bank-teller
2. John is a bank-teller and a member of EarthFirst!

Most people think Statement 2 is more likely because it fits the stereotype of an EarthFirst!er, or what cognitive psychologists call a **representativeness heuristic**. This heuristic refers to the tendency to judge an event as likely if it represents the typical features of its category (Medin, Ross, & Markman, 2001). Objectively, however, Statement 1 is more likely based on probability: The conjunction of two events can never be more likely than either event alone. That is, any one event occurs more frequently alone than it occurs with another event. In this case, using a representativeness heuristic leads to poor reasoning. Such errors often appear in our choice of language, for example, the frequency with which conservatives refer to environmentalists as "radical environmentalists." Exclusive use of this phrase suggests that their mental representation of an environmentalist does not include room for moderates or conservatives.

Similarly, the **availability heuristic** refers to a tendency to form a judgment on the basis of what is readily brought to mind, often due to one vivid experience that produces a memory so strong that only it is available when we encounter that category. For example, Deborah met the parents of a particular Whitman College student a few years ago, and got to talking about a recent lecture given by Dennis Hayes, founder of Earth Day. Deborah mentioned she had just written about much of the same material (e.g., overpopulation, overconsumption) in this book. The student's father expressed an enthusiastic interest, asked Deborah to let him know when the book came out, and handed her his card. When she looked at it, she had to swallow her shock: He was a high-ranking officer of the Weyerhaeuser Company, the largest timber company in the country. Deborah found it surprising that he would be so pleasant and genuinely interested in reading a book about environmental problems.

Why? She felt this way because of her reliance on heuristics. When confronted with new information, we compare it to a mental image already formulated about that category. Deborah's mental representation of Weyerhaeuser officials was based on one presentation by a forest management executive several years earlier, who seemed to her at the time to be defensive and rigidly technocratic. He argued that Weyerhaeuser engages in sustainable forestry, but Deborah was unconvinced by his numbers and by the way he handled questions from the audience. Consequently, she believed that all Weyerhaeuser officials would have the same manner. She formed an entire mental category from one vivid example, and used it to interpret new information. Deborah was amazed by the warmth and interest of this new person with whom she was lucky enough to chat before applying her faulty availability heuristic. As D. Myers (1993) said, "People are remarkably quick to infer general truths from a vivid instance" (p. 55).

The availability heuristic can be used to encourage environmentally responsible behavior, which was done by researcher Marti Gonzales and her colleagues when they persuaded people to sign up for energy conservation home improvements:

> They trained California home energy auditors to communicate their findings to homeowners in vivid, memorable images. Rather than simply point out small spaces around doors where heat is lost, the auditor would say "if you were to add up all the cracks around and under the doors of your home, you'd have the equivalent of a hole the size of a football in your living room wall." With such remarks, and by eliciting the homeowners' active commitment in helping measure cracks and state their intentions to remedy them, the trained auditors triggered a 50 percent increase in the number of customers applying for energy financing programs. (p. 56)

By drawing a vivid image of a "hole the size of a football in your wall" these researchers were much more convincing than when speaking in more abstract, conceptual terms. In both cases, the information is the same, but the vivid example is more persuasive because it creates a memorable image that is more available to memory.

Quantitative Illiteracy

Unless we have some technical training in a quantitative field, most of us have difficulty conceptualizing very large and very small numbers, a limitation termed **quantitative illiteracy**. A billion may as well be a trillion or a gazillion—we do not deal in these types of numbers often enough to have a well-developed understanding of their differences. Consequently, when environmental problems are described in quantitative terms, many of us lose track of the numbers and reason poorly. In Washington state, for example, cleaning up the Hanford Nuclear Reservation's plutonium, toxic chemicals, heavy metals, leaking radioactive waste tanks, ground water and soil contamination, and seepage into the Columbia River has already cost $35 billion and is expected to cost at least another $50 billion to complete (Stiffler, 2002). How does this number compare to the United States national debt? To the annual cost of social security? To federal expenditures on education?[1] For most of us, these numbers are too big to comprehend or relate to each other. Consequently, it is difficult for us to make good decisions about environmental clean-up relative to other societal projects.

Similarly, our pro-environment behaviors are often undertaken with less than optimal results because we do not understand their quantitative dimensions. For example, electric lights use about 5% of home electricity. In the 1970s, the energy crisis induced many people to conserve energy by being conscientious about turning off lights. When their behaviors failed to show impact on their electricity bills, people gave up trying to save energy altogether. Unfortunately, they did not realize that home heating and cooling uses from 50% to 70% of domestic energy, so that turning down one's thermostat in the winter and turning it up in the summer by just a couple of degrees would save far more energy than conscientiously turning off lights. Here's a key point: Choosing major appliances that are energy efficient is the single most important class of behaviors for reducing energy use; refrigerators alone use about 19% of household energy. Likewise, many people are quite conscientious about recycling but less aware that **reducing use** is a far more effective way to save natural resources. For example, buying products in refillable plastic containers (e.g., shampoo from local health foods stores) is much more important than recycling plastic bottles, yet far fewer people use refillable bottles than recycle.

Framing Effects

Finally, we are also susceptible to **framing effects**, which are induced when the same information is structured in different ways. For example, people like to think of themselves in positive terms, so are more likely to deny harming the environment than to claim that they help it (Bazerman & Hoffman, 1999). Moreover, people were more likely to invest in a water-heater wrap if it was presented as a way to avoid losing money, rather than as a way to save it (Yates, 1982)!

---

[1]The figures are as follows: The national debt (2002) was $6.02 trillion (6,019 billion) (U.S. Treasury Department, retrieved online at http://www.publicdebt.treas.gov/opd/ opdpdodt.htm); Social Security expenditures in 2001 totaled $463.3 billion (Social Security Administration, retrieved online at http://www.ssa.gov/finance/2001/fy01acctrep.pdf, p. 6); the amount spent on education in 2000 was 90.6 billion for total education expenses (representing 5.1% of the federal budget), about half of which went toward elementary and secondary education (Census Bureau, 2002), retrieved online at http://www.census. gov/prod/2002pubs/01statab/educ.pdf.

Using Cognitive Psychology to Solve Environmental Problems

The picture that cognitive (and social) psychology paints of human beings is not an especially attractive one. We can be duped by our biases, reasoning errors, the need to justify our actions, and inexperience in quantitative matters. We like to think of ourselves as rational and open-minded, but research shows that our rationality is bounded. Add these limitations to the emotional influences of anxieties and defenses (discussed in chap. 2) that also affect our decision making, and it is easy to conclude that only experts should be making environmental decisions. Unfortunately, experts are just as likely to make errors, as we shall soon see.

Because all this seems to undermine the point of this book, which is to understand the psychological dimensions of environmental problems so that we might start doing things differently, let us add a very important point here. Although we all are easily deceived by these processes, we do not have to be. Instead we can learn to avoid errors by understanding how they function. As psychology professors, we demonstrate how cognitive biases and shortcuts work by giving students problems to work on. We find that if the students have already read the chapter in which the reasoning problems are described, they will avoid making them. What this means is that we can learn to reason more effectively if we learn to avoid our naïve errors, and if we put forth the necessary effort to overcome these powerful predispositions.

From a cognitive perspective, we can start changing environmentally inappropriate choices by getting better information about the effects of our actions. All institutions have some vested interest in their own point of view, and may distort information in order to maintain it. This is no less true of environmental groups than it is for businesses, governments, military organizations, or local landowners. Thus, we can become better environmental citizens by doing the following three things:

1. *Getting better information and acting on it*. For example, asking difficult questions about environmental issues; pursuing answers, even when they are not forthcoming; learning more about the environmental consequences of our actions, especially our consumer choices; and expressing our preferences to store managers and legislators. (A number of good guides are available that give information about the environmental impact of consumer goods; we have described some of them in the appendix.)

2. *Noticing and correcting our reasoning errors.* Specifically, forcing ourselves to make a counterargument in order to appreciate other sides of complex issues; being willing to admit that our information and/or reasoning is flawed, and being open to learning more about our limitations.

3. *Taking personal responsibility,* by being confident enough about our intelligence to learn more about complicated issues, and refusing to leave environmental solution efforts entirely to experts who may have different priorities.

This last point is so important to effectively addressing environmental problems that we will spend the remainder of the chapter looking at it in more detail.

RISK ASSESSMENT: WHOSE QUANTIFICATION PROBLEM IS IT?

We learned in the previous chapter that many environmental conditions threaten human health and well-being. How do we objectively evaluate the risks of such conditions? Who is responsible for determining risk to the general public? An important area where cognitive psychology has been applied to environmental problems is called **risk assessment**. In risk assessment, human health hazards associated with various substances and activities are evaluated and quantified. This section will summarize the process of risk assessment. We will discuss the discrepancies between how experts and the public evaluate risk, and the implications of these discrepancies.

To get a feel for how risk assessment works, please rank order the following hazards according to your perception of how much of a health risk each poses. After you have completed your rankings, look at the footnote to see how your answers compare with those of others in the U.S.[2]

| Medical x-rays | Stress | Pesticides in food |
| Cigarette smoking | Nuclear waste | Motor vehicle accidents |

---

[2] A study by Slovic, Flynn, Mertz, Poumadere, and Mays (2000) found that U.S. respondents rated smoking and nuclear waste in the highest risk category, followed closely by stress. Motor vehicle accidents and pesticides in food were perceived as posing moderate risk, and medical x-rays were seen to pose the lowest risk.

Since Rachel Carson's (1962) publication of *Silent Spring*, public concerns about environmental risks has continuously grown, becoming an important issue in government and industry circles. The United States Environmental Protection Agency (EPA), founded in 1970, is charged with enforcing over 9,000 environmental regulations. Risk assessment forms the basis of the EPA's regulatory decisions, and involves four factors: Identifying hazards, estimating probabilities of damage, reducing risks, and communicating risk to the public. All of these tasks are important arenas for the application of cognitive psychology.

Professionals who assess risk usually define it as the number of deaths caused by a hazard in one year (or some other time unit): for example, 400,000 deaths from smoking (U.S. Department of Health and Human Services, 2001), 32,000 from handguns (Center for Disease Control, 1999), and about 50 direct deaths from nuclear radiation since World War II, with most of those occurring during the accident at Chernobyl in 1986 (J. A. L. Robertson, 2000). Government reports estimated that the worst case scenario for a nuclear accident would result in 3,400 deaths. Thus, according to the experts' index, smoking is 8,000 times more risky on an annual basis than nuclear power has been to date, and about 117.5 times riskier than the maximum fatalities of a nuclear accident.

Number of fatalities per year is easy to count, and thus easy to conceptualize. However, counting fatalities gives the impression that death is the only relevant outcome of a risk, and that everything important can be quantified. These illusions are furthered by the use of complicated formulas that estimate exposure rates, event probabilities, and financial costs. For example, computer programs can estimate the number of deaths caused every year by a hazard, compared to the price of regulation controls and the cost of one death. Thus, risk assessment programs require that a number be given for the value of a human life. Social costs are then calculated to be a sum of the regulation and mortality costs. These approaches rest on the rational-economic model described earlier (Stern, 1992).

Because of this kind of quantitative effort, some people, including former EPA policy analyst Ken Bogen, call risk assessment a form of "probabilistic cannibalism" (G. T. Miller, 1993), which trades lives for dollars. Abstract numbers can hide the effects of environmental hazards; as risks become quantified, their social dimensions get lost. Consider the issue of pesticides, for example. Legal levels of residues from pesticides licensed for use in the United States cause between 2,000 and 10,000 cancer deaths in real, but nameless United States citizens each year, who were not given the opportunity to give informed consent (G. T. Miller, 2002).

When cigarettes, alcohol, and drug abuse presently cost hundreds of thousands of lives, billions of dollars, and tremendous human suffering, trying to eliminate environmental risks might appear wasteful and unjustified (Finucane, in press). Yet relative to drugs and alcohol, people who are harmed from environmental toxins and contaminated food are not informed, or presented with a choice. They are also unequally distributed among the population: Environmental risks are incurred more often by lower income groups, minorities, and children (Bullard & Johnson, 2000; Laituri & Kirby, 1994; Opotow & Clayton, 1994).

However, these considerations disappear when risks are quantified and are therefore irrelevant to risk analysts. But they are not irrelevant to the public. The public cares more about personal health and safety than about quantifiable data or the environment (T. A. Miller & Keller, 1991), and rarely agrees with experts about specific risks. For example, one study showed that nonexpert groups rated nuclear power as the highest risk among 30 hazards, whereas experts rated it quite low (20th out of 30; Slovic, Fischhoff, & Lichtenstein, 1979). The public thus feared nuclear power much more than the experts, a trend that remains 20 years later (Slovic et al., 2000).

Such rating discrepancies occur because the public and experts use different definitions of risk (Slovic, 2000). To illustrate public perception of risk, Slovic, Fischhoff, and Lichtenstein (1985) proposed a model based on two dimensions: degree of controllability (including fatality, equitability, risk to future generations, voluntariness) and the degree of observability (including knowledge of those exposed, delay of effects, amount of scientific knowledge available; see Fig. 6.4).

Yet, matters of observability, voluntariness, equitability, and knowledge are much more difficult to quantify than are number of deaths per year. Some critics of risk assessment suggest that we will never be able to quantify them adequately, and so should not use risk assessment to make major policy decisions. For example, it may be impossible to compare risk hazards. "How does one compare a case of lung cancer in a retired petrochemical worker to the loss of cognitive function experienced by an urban child with lead poisoning?" (Durenberger, Mott, & Sagoff, 1991, p. 50). Others argue that risk assessment is an inadequate, even a dangerous way to make policy decisions because it fools us into thinking that we can make rational, objective decisions based on numerical formulas derived from epidemiological and nonhuman data, which may be flawed or inappropriate. In Morgan's words, "Risk management is, fundamentally, a question of values. In a

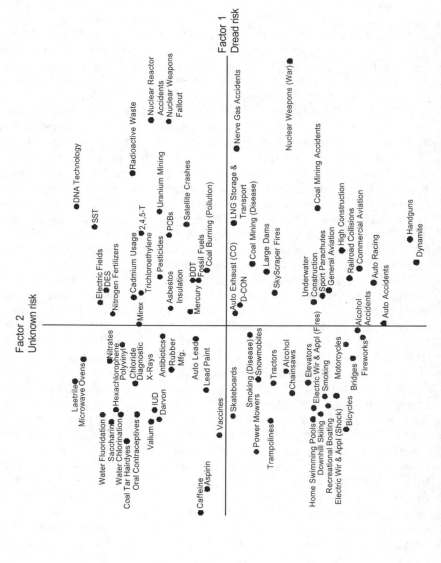

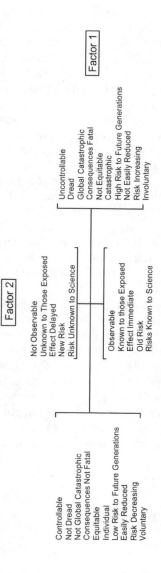

FIG. 6.4.   Location of 81 hazards on Factors 1 (controllability) and 2 (observability), derived from the interrelationships among 15 risk characteristics. Each factor is made up of a combination of characteristics, as indicated by the lower diagram. From Slovic, P., Fischhoff, B., & Lichtenstein, S. (1985). Characterizing perceived risk. In R. W. Kates, C. Hohenemser, & J. X. Kasperson (Eds.), *Perilous Progress: Technology as Hazard*, pp. 91–123. Boulder CO: Westview. Reprinted by permission of P. Slovic.

democratic society, there is no acceptable way to make these choices without involving the citizens who will be affected by them" (Morgan, 1993, p. 32).

Thus, effective risk assessment requires the experts to work with the public. There are at least three ways in which public participation is critical to risk management (Finucane, in press). Public support increases the success of implementing risk decisions; members of the public possess wisdom to offer to the process; and the individuals directly affected by regulations have the right to participate in decision making.

It is well worth monitoring the way in which experts think about and document risk assessment because without public input, their judgments (like everyone's) are likely to be distorted by the institutions that train them, hire them, and pay them. Cognitive processes, including perception of risk, are not entirely rational, whether they are made by experts or by lay people. For example, framing effects influence both physicians and patients (McNeil, Pauker, Cox, & Tversky, 1982). Specifically, treatment preferences (e.g., surgery or radiation for cancer) change depending on whether the prognosis is framed as probability of living versus the probability of dying. Thus, risk evaluation by both the experts and nonexperts is impacted by the way the risk is framed.

Heuristics also impact perceptions of both the public and experts, especially when the experts are out of their area of expertise (Finucane, in press). For example, fear of hazards are affected by the availability heuristic, as we tend to overestimate the incidence of infrequent events (e.g., nuclear accidents, botulism, or the incidence of anthrax exposure) and underestimate the incidence of frequent ones (e.g., automobile accidents). This error is understandable in light of the amount of press coverage devoted to different events. Unusual situations get a lot of media attention, and more commonplace occurrences are much less publicized. Consequently, we may fear less likely hazards more than likely ones (Fischhoff, 1990).

THE ROLE OF EMOTIONS IN OUR JUDGMENT OF RISK

Emotion, also known as **affect**, can contribute to the judgment of risk, primarily as it influences the availability of certain memories. We are more likely to recall emotionally charged events than more mundane ones. When a hazard evokes feelings of dread (e.g., cancer), it will be perceived as posing a greater risk than less dreaded events, such as traffic accidents (Slovic, Finucane, Peters, & MacGregor, 2002). Slovic and colleagues referred to this process as the **affect heuristic**, where judgment and decision making are guided by images that accompany positive and negative feelings. The effect can occur without conscious awareness, accounting for **subliminal** influences. Advertising capitalizes on such effects by showing smiling people using potentially hazardous substances (pesticides, cigarettes).

The affect heuristic influences our assessment of the relative risks and benefits of potential hazards. If people enjoy an activity, they judge the risks low and the benefits high; but if they dislike the activity, they do the opposite, and judge the risk high and the benefits low (Slovic et. al., 2002; see Fig. 6.5). For example, someone who enjoys eating meat (positive affect) will tend to downplay the health and environmental risks more than someone who doesn't like the taste of meat. These effects may be due to associative networks. Thus, certain feelings or moods will enable recollection of any concepts previously connected to that emotion, and can influence our judgment and decision-making processes (Forgas, 1999).

Clearly, affect does not always correlate with the objective risks or costs. People may respond with very little fear to guns, automobiles, and unsafe sex even though these can pose very dangerous risks. On the other hand, stimuli such as spiders, snakes, and heights can evoke profound fear reactions, despite awareness that one really has little to fear from these stimuli. This pattern can be explained from an evolu-

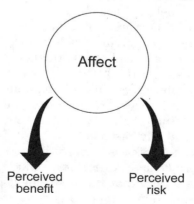

FIG. 6.5.   A model of the affect heuristic explaining the risk/benefit confounding observed by Alhakami and Slovic (1994). Judgments of risk and benefit are assumed to be derived by reference to an overall affective evaluation of the stimulus item. From Finucane, M. L., Alhakami, A., Slovic, P., & Johnson, S. M. (2000). The affect heuristic in judgments of risks and benefits. Journal of Behavioral Decision Making, 13, p. 4. © John Wiley and Sons, Limited. Reprinted with permission.

tionary perspective, and fits with the **mismatch hypothesis** (described in chap. 5). Evolution has not yet prepared us to respond seriously to modern hazards (e.g., Slovic et al., 2002). Thus, the discrepancy between our ancestral and current environments can account for a variety of cognitive limitations that contribute to ecological problems.

RETAINING A VOICE

The danger of current risk assessment practices is that public participation is not typically sought or respected by the experts. This situation threatens our health and security because the experts' oversimplified model fails to take into account outcomes other than death. Many of us assume the experts know what they are doing, even though public trust in industry and government officials is not high (Covello, 1993; Slovic et al., 2000). Leaving important risk decisions to experts while not entirely trusting them is paradoxical, but results when we assume the questions are too complicated, too enormous, and too overwhelming.

In many arenas, leaving decisions to experts makes sense. For example, automobiles and buildings should be designed by engineers and architects with far more knowledge than the public could ever be expected to possess. Because we live in a representative democracy, we entrust elected and nonelected leaders alike to be good stewards of society, to be educated in their areas of influence, and to make responsible decisions. However, engineering problems and risk assessments are fundamentally different arenas because the latter involve human values. There is no reason to think that experts can make the crucial judgments about the monetary value of human life any better than the layperson. What authority would an industry official have over a full-time parent in determining how many lives are worth risking for any particular technological advancement?

Despite the fact that risk assessments are not perfect, and tend to differ between lay people and experts, it is unlikely that we can afford to dispense with the service that risk assessment performs: forcing us to explicate our assumptions, empirically measure what we can, and consider the diversity of concerns that different people will bring to the problem. For these reasons we believe that risk assessment should not be abandoned but rather improved, by including more effective public participation in decisions that impact our lives and well-being. We appreciate Freudenburg and Pastor's (1992) three stage analysis of the history of risk assessment. First, the public was called irrational, ignored, and blamed. In the second phase (where we are now), scientists are attempting to understand and include the public. Now, a third phase is needed: to understand the larger systems that create victims and risks in the first place.

CONCLUSIONS

The main contribution of cognitive psychology to approaching environmental problems is the view that inappropriate environmental behaviors can result from inadequate, mistaken, distorted, or missing information about the consequences of our actions, or processing biases and heuristics. Our perceptual and cognitive systems can lead us to both overestimate or underestimate risks, depending on the available information and how we process it. Unless trained to do otherwise, experts are just as likely to make these errors. If we recognize that much of human behavior relies more on nonconscious preferences rather than rational calculation, we can become more conscious in our decision making. For example, making environmentally appropriate consumer choices requires conscious consideration of what constitutes a sustainable lifestyle and making decisions accordingly. The biases discussed in this chapter can be overcome, *if* we are alerted to them and intentionally and consistently practice methods of subverting them. We all must address problems of sustainability with a rigorously attuned intelligence, an intelligence that is strengthened, rather than undermined, by learning about our cognitive limitations.

KEY CONCEPTS

Artificial intelligence

Associative networks

Bounded rationality

Confirmation bias

Framing effects

"Garbage in, garbage out" (GIGO; wrong, limited, irrelevant information)

Heuristics (affect, availability, representativeness)

Indicator species

Information processing models
Neural networks
Mental maps
Mismatch hypothesis
Pre-existing biases
Proximal cognition
Quantitative illiteracy
Rational economic model
Regression toward the mean
Risk assessment
Selective attention
Sensory adaptation
Subjective discount rates
Visual dependence

7

Holistic Approaches: Gestalt and Ecopsychology

What would you call the following?:

If you answered "T," then you are responding to the relationship between these dots, rather than to the dots themselves. Instead of answering "10 dots" you perceived a meaningful configuration of them, based on the way they are organized.

Your response illustrates the central theme of this chapter: The relationship between parts can often be more important than the parts themselves. If we presented the same configuration of small x's, you would still respond with "T," even though all of the separate elements have changed. Both of the psychological perspectives we will talk about in this chapter emphasize this principle of **holism: The whole is more than the sum of its parts**. From this perspective, environmental problems are best approached by considering the system in which they are created. Just as you cannot understand how a person would answer "T" if you insisted on reducing the study of this configuration to the study of 10 separate dots, our environmental problems cannot be adequately addressed if we focus exclusively on individuals as isolated actors. A system cannot be reduced to its elements.

Because of this emphasis on nonreductionism, both Gestalt and ecopsychology look at aspects of human experience that are sometimes difficult to measure. Consequently, some psychologists would argue that they are not *real* psychology, because they are not *real* science. Science is a method of knowing which tests hypotheses under controlled conditions with empirical observations, observations that are typically quantified (Banaji & Crowder, 1989). Because it is more arduous, perhaps impossible, to measure some of the topics we will be discussing in this chapter, mainstream psychologists tend to pay less attention to them. But from the perspective of these holistic approaches, the fact of their marginalization is part and parcel of our environmental difficulties. From the holistic approach, environmental problems are caused by our failure to see the whole. Both our modern worldview, which emphasizes individualism, and contemporary psychology that is conducted as a science, assume that things can be separated from each other. Both assume that experience can be reduced into smaller elements, that individuals are separate from each other, and that people are separate from their culture or from the natural world. Instead, holistic approaches stress our interconnected existence within a complex system. Consequently, it should be no surprise that these approaches are marginalized, but we should not dismiss them simply because they are. Rather, their marginalization expresses their potential contribution: something important to say about a more holistic way of seeing ourselves. In this chapter, we will lay out a few fundamental principles of holistic psychology and then see how they can be applied to environmental problems.

GESTALT PSYCHOLOGY

Gestalt is a German word that does not have an easy equivalent in English, but we can roughly define it as form, whole, structure, or meaning. The "T" you saw in the dot formation above is a gestalt—a form or whole. The term *gestalt* was first used in this context by von Ehrenfels (1890, cited by Boring, 1950) who illustrated the idea with melodies. If you transpose a tune from the key of C to the key of D, every note would change, but the melody would still be recognizable. Thus, the melody is defined by the relationship between the notes, rather than the notes themselves. The melody forms a gestalt, independent of its notes. From this perspective then, environmental problems result from our inability to accurately perceive our relationship with larger ecosystems, and solving environmental problems will require that we learn how to perceive them differently.

The work of Gestalt psychologist Wolfang Kohler (1974–1975), who described learning as perceptual reorganization, can help us here. In his famous studies with apes and chimpanzees, he put bananas out of range of the hungry animals. In order to reach the fruit, they had to stand on boxes or ladders, and use sticks as tools to knock the bananas down. Kohler noticed that his monkeys learned how to solve these problems quite suddenly. Instead of a gradual change, the monkeys roamed around for a while and then suddenly placed the objects in the correct position to reach the bananas. Moreover, once the monkeys had solved the problem, they could quickly solve it again. Kohler argued that his animals showed **insight learning**: a sudden perceptual reorganization of the field so that a box was no longer seen as a box but as a stepping stool. With these demonstrations, Kohler asserted that learning is not a consequence of associated responses built up over time, as the behaviorists argued. Instead, learning depends on perception; it is a consequence of perceptual reorganization. Such insight learning could be crucial for solving our environmental problems.

For example, when Deborah's niece, Danielle, was 9 years old, she visited one summer. While they were hanging up towels on the clothesline outside, Danielle asked why they didn't just put them in the electric dryer. Deborah explained that we should always let the sun do whatever work it can, because when we use electricity instead, we create problems. In the Pacific Northwest, electricity comes from hydroelectric dams and those dams are killing salmon. So whenever we use a dryer without needing to, we also help kill fish without needing to. Danielle's response was "Oh no, we don't want to kill those fish," and she enthusiastically helped hang up the towels. Kohler would say that she experienced a sudden perceptual reorganization that allowed her to see her behavior related to the well-being of another species. Her response was an enthusiastic embrace of more environmentally responsible behavior.

LABORATORY CONFIRMATION: GROUP EFFECTS
IN SOCIAL DILEMMA GAMES

If Gestalt principles apply to environmental issues, we ought to see people behave in more environmentally appropriate ways when they are reminded of their group membership. Individuals who act from pure self-interest would be more likely to deplete a resource base than those who realize their behavior affects the well-being of the group. In general, research with social dilemma games supports this principle.

Remember from chapter 4 that laboratory research has validated Hardin's notion of "the tragedy of the commons." When laboratory psychologists ask participants to simulate management of common resources, people usually behave quite individualistically, grabbing as much as they can quickly, and exhausting the commons so that its resources are quickly depleted. Thus players will overharvest their trees (Bell et al., 1989), forfeit other long-range payoffs (Dawes, 1980), or overspend their credit cards in order to procure smaller but more immediate individual rewards. Apparently, resource depletion can be driven by the fear that others will use it first (Lynn, 1992).

Deborah experienced this kind of hoarding when she served as a camp cook for her husband's geology field camp one summer. Although she did her best to estimate group uses of various foods, within a week in the wilderness area, she realized that they were running low on hot chocolate. She hoped that as scarcity became apparent to other camp members, its value would go up and they would be more careful about using it, rationing it until the end. Instead, as soon as scarcity became apparent, the remainder of the hot chocolate disappeared very quickly, much faster than it was used before scarcity was obvious. Apparently, camp members wanted to be sure they got their share before it completely ran out. Being somewhat of a hoarder herself, Deborah wanted to put the chocolate away and use it only on special occasions, so that it would last. Simply perceiving a commodity as scarce will increase the demand for it. Restaurant servers use this principle when they strategically hint to their customers that they should pre-order the chocolate truffle cake because there aren't many left, and then sell a record breaking number of the dessert. Shopkeepers that emphasize a sale "while supplies last" capitalize on this phenomenon and encourage unnecessary consumption.

Although scarcity and individualism can drive self-defeating competitive behavior, a huge number of studies show that cooperation can replace competition if group membership is highlighted. There are at least three ways to make group membership more obvious: First, limit the size of the group so that individuals feel more responsible to it; second, allow group members to communicate with each other; and third, appeal to altruistic norms. We will briefly examine the evidence for each of these.

Limit Group Size

At least in the laboratory dilemma game, the smaller the group, the more cooperatively players behave. Two-person groups are more cooperative than those with three persons, and those with three persons are more cooperative than those with six persons (Dawes, 1981). Researchers have concluded that in the smaller group, people feel more identified with each other, and with the group's success. Smaller groups give people an "illusion of efficacy" (Kerr, 1989). When Kerr manipulated group size, it proved to have a bigger impact on cooperation than the number of investors, even though investor size was actually the more crucial variable for payoffs.

Promote Communication Between Players

To quote one of the most extensive reviews of the social dilemma literature, "the salutary effects of communication on cooperation are ubiquitous" (Dawes, 1980, p. 185). Whenever experimenters allow their players to talk to each other about their choices and strategies, cooperative behavior is increased. Even partial communication is helpful. When players' choices are made public to other players, their behavior is more cooperative than when they are allowed to behave competitively in private (J. Fox & Guyer, 1978; Jerdee & Rosen, 1974). Communication appears to increase cooperation through several processes: Players humanize other players, they understand the social dilemma better, and they commit to cooperative policies. Attempts to separate these explanations have focused on the importance of interpersonal commitments. One study, for example, showed that cooperative behavior was enhanced by discussion only when all members promised to cooperate (Orbell, van de Kraght, & Dawes, 1988).

Appeal to Altruistic Norms

Although Hardin argued that we cannot solve our commons problems by appealing to altruistic norms, research on laboratory gaming has suggested he's wrong. Although it is true that players often get trapped into what they know is self-defeating and group-defeating behavior, when moral appeals are given prior to group play, cooperative behavior can be dramatically increased (Dawes, 1981). We can certainly think of many examples of self-sacrificing behavior by people who are committed to others: Parents sacrifice for their children, soldiers for their country, and donors for their charity.

Thus, from a Gestalt perspective, we can reason that ecological problems have been exacerbated by mistakenly thinking of ourselves as separate individuals whose behavior has little effect on other humans, much less on the biological and physical dimensions of our planet. For many centuries, people assumed that what human beings do would have no impact on the ecosphere. The thought that humans could actually change the atmosphere or climate would have seemed absurd two decades ago; now the human-induced depletion of ozone and build-up of carbon emissions are troubling realities. The perceptual shift of seeing behavior embedded in a larger system will be required before we will be able to change to environmentally appropriate behavior.

APPLYING GESTALT PSYCHOLOGY

Why don't we see our embedded relationship with fellow human beings and the ecosystem more consistently? One answer comes from **Gestalt therapy**, a form of group and individual psychotherapy that became popular in the 1970s and is still widely practiced in the United States and Britain today. Gestalt therapy was founded by Frederick (Fritz) Perls (1893–1970) (Perls, 1969, 1971, 1978), who was trained as a psychiatrist, and worked as a clinician.

We can understand Perls' work as a synthesis of Gestalt and Freudian theory. As a neo-Freudian, Perls' first concern was the unconscious. Perls agreed with Freud that much of what we do is based in unconscious motives. According to Perls, unconsciousness results from a fragmentation of various parts of the psyche. Awareness brings about an integration of these dissociated parts. Perls used Freud's concept of projection to describe how we see our fragmented parts in others when we judge them harshly. Hostility arises from our inability to recognize the same shortcomings in ourselves, and compassion results when we accept our limitations. For example, when we notice the same greed in ourselves that we deride somebody else for, we are less likely to be so judgmental.

So far, such recognition and transcendence of the defenses is not so different from Freud's approach. But Perls' use of Gestalt brought him into sharp disagreement with Freud, and he spent a great deal of energy criticizing classic psychoanalysis. According to Perls, in order to become conscious, one must more effectively examine the **present**, rather than erecting entertaining but irrelevant explanations from the **past**. Our full integrity actually exists in the present, but we are unaware of it because we block out so much of what is actually happening right now. We stay unaware by refusing what Perls called *contact*. Contact is the sensual registering—seeing, hearing, smelling, touching, and moving—in the present. By shutting down our contact, we become numb to our unified being. We also become victims of intellectual abstractions that cannot communicate the unity of being. Instead, overintellectualizing and underexperiencing our present moment leads us into neurosis.

For Perls (and the ecopsychologists we will consider soon) the way out of our plight is through direct sensory experience of the here and now. Stopping the endless chatter that goes on in our heads (thoughts, hopes, worries, judgments, attributions, excuses, explanations) and opening up to the more direct, nonverbal ways of knowing leads us to the experience of ourselves as whole persons. Holistic experience enables us to know our ecological selves, and frees energy that was previously used to maintain the defenses so that we can better know and love the world we live in.

Several thinkers have used Gestalt principles to approach our ecological problems (Abram, 1987; Calahan, 1995; Cohen, 1993; Scull, n.d.; Swanson, 1995). One good example is the work of Sewell (1995, 1999), who argued that sensory experiences of taste, smell, sight, touch, and hearing are the primary access to the world. Because our senses have been deadened by modern life, we do not fully experience our deeply embedded existence in physical ecosystems. We must learn how to attend to present experience more fully, quietly, and deeply, to see, hear, taste, and feel more clearly. Sewell argued that practicing mindful attention will bring us a more accurate and richer picture of who we are in the ecological world, and will help us discover the beauty of it. In Sewell's (1995) words,

> the earth calls continually. She [sic] calls us with beauty, sometimes truly breathtaking, sometimes heart wrenching, and always provocative and visceral. We are embedded in a multidimensional web of beauty. It is where we are, now. . . . The moment calls for the reperceiving of our Earth, for perceiving the myriad and magical relations that may inform an ecological ethic. If we are receptive to the ways in which the landscape speaks to us, or the ways in which perception serves as a channel for communication, we may reawaken and preserve a sense of human integrity within the family of all relations. (p. 215)

Thus, Sewell claimed that environmental problems rest in the periphery of our perception because we are so accustomed to partial seeing. We

MUTTS   By Patrick McDonnell

Reprinted with special permission of King Features Syndicate.

"sort of" see the effects of excessive fossil fuel use, and we "sense" its relationship to environmental destruction, but we allow the connection to remain "blurry." We are so habituated to dulled senses and numbed experience that we continue our destructive behavior. Changing our behavior will require first that we clearly see its connection with the beautiful natural world of which we are always a part. This argument reminds Deborah of one of her favorite poems by Mary Oliver:

> You do not have to be good.
> You do not have to walk on your knees
> for a hundred miles through the desert, repenting.
> You only have to let the soft animal of your body love what it loves.
> Tell me about despair, yours, and I will tell you mine.
> Meanwhile the world goes on.
> Meanwhile the sun and the clear pebbles of the rain
> are moving across the landscapes,
> over the prairies and deep trees,
> the mountains and the rivers.
> Meanwhile the wild geese, high in the clean blue air
> are heading home again.
> Whoever you are, no matter how lonely,
> the world offers itself to your imagination,
> calls to you like the wild geese, harsh and exciting—
> over and over announcing your place
> in the family of things.
> —Mary Oliver (http://www.frii.com/~parrot/joy/poem2.html)

From the Gestalt view, the world calls itself to you, over and over. We do not need to be perfect. We simply need to see and hear and taste and feel the presence of the world, sensing the soft animal of our body, the physicality of ourselves in the world, and we will discover interdependence with it.

THE ECOLOGICAL SELF: THE SELF BEYOND THE SELF

To experience our place in the world gives us an expanded sense of who we are. The holistic approach to environmental problems suggests that ordinary perception of ourselves as isolated beings encapsulated in separate skins is misleading and dangerous. To successfully address environmental problems requires that we also recognize our "ecological selves," a term first coined by Arne Naess (1985). Naess argued, as have many after him (Cohen, 1993; Conn, 1991; Hillman & Ventura, 1992; Keepin, 1992; Roszak, 1992; Shepard, 1982) that changing environmentally relevant behavior will require that we experience a larger, more connected sense of self (Bragg, 1996).

We experience our ecological self when we feel the connection between our self and other people, other life forms, ecosystems, or the planet. We experience it when we sense a deep resonance with other species and a quality of belonging and connection to the larger ecological whole. As you might imagine, people frequently experience their ecological self in wilderness settings, especially forests (K. Williams & Harvey, 2001). But we might sense it any time. For example, one evening, Deborah walked out of a seminar she was attending and suddenly saw the stars above her. They seemed to be twinkling at her, reminding her of how huge and close the cosmos is. Suddenly, the people in the seminar, in the city, and in the world seemed to be together under the twinkling benevolence of the shining stars. Deborah felt the clear connection between the planet and the rest of the universe, each twinkling at each other in their shared space. She felt herself a part of the Earth and the stars, and was moved by a deep sense of belonging.

The ecological self has several dimensions. Bragg (1996) suggested that there are at least three psychological elements to the ecological self:

1. *Cognitive*: a heightened sensitivity toward information about the well-being of other people, species, and ecosystems.
2. *Emotional*: feelings of sympathy, caring, empathy, and belonging toward other people, species, and ecosystems.
3. *Motivational*: a concern about and intention to ensure the well-being of other people, species, and ecosystems.

From this perspective, the ecological self leads to environmentally appropriate behaviors, not out of a sense of self-sacrifice or self-denial, but out of a sense of love and common identity. In Naess' (1988) words:

We need environmental ethics, but when people feel they unselflessly give up, even sacrifice, their interest in order to show love for nature, this is probably in the long run a treacherous basis for conservation. Through identification they may come to see their own interest served by conservation, through genuine self-love, love of a widened and deepened self. (p. 43)

How could we possibly become so identified with nature that we protect it as we would protect ourselves? W. Fox (1990a), an ecophilosopher, argued that we develop identification by experiencing the joys and pains of others. Small children learn to identify with others as they observe others' happiness, disappointment, anger, or joy. Similarly, we identify with the natural world when we experience commonality with it. We usually find it easy to identify with our pets—Deborah has no trouble believing her dog Sophie has emotional reactions of happiness or shame. But it is more difficult to identify with a slug that crawls into Sophie's food dish.

Difficult but not impossible. A few years ago, Deborah attended several meditation weekends over the course of a summer. The days and evenings were filled with sessions of sitting meditation, silent walking, silent meals, or silent gardening of the lawn and flower gardens. Sitting in the meditation hall one of those afternoons, she grew very quiet and heard many sounds that she would not normally hear: the creek babbling nearby, a bird's wings flapping, a dog snoring across the yard. Someone walked by on the lawn and Deborah was filled with tenderness as she felt the blades of grass being crushed. It wasn't that she felt those boots crushing her, but she could feel them crushing the grass. She felt the vulnerability and the fragility of the natural world—a feeling she is ordinarily not in touch with. In Fox's words, she identified with the grass. She knew that she was Deborah, sitting in the meditation hall, and that the grass was outside being crushed. But she felt an enormous commonality with that grass, as if she could feel what happened to it, as if she could feel it happening to someone whom she deeply loved.

In this sense, the ecological self is an integration of two selves: the separate physical self, what we normally experience as people in the Western world, as well as the larger self that identifies with the ecosphere. We cannot trade a small separate self for a larger spiritual self. Instead, the larger self is integrated with the normal smaller self. Ecopsychology builds on the insights originally outlined by object relations theorists (discussed in chap. 2). We construct our sense of self out of our relationships with others. But the holistic framework would go further, and argue that our ecological self is a natural part of the developmental process, and that realizing our eco-selves is necessary for us to address environmental problems.

Thus, from this perspective, our standard sense of self as a separate, autonomous being seriously jeopardizes our ability to live harmoniously within the ecosphere. Environmental problems are not so much a crisis of technology as they are a crisis of insight: Mistaking social or bureaucratic identity for our core sense of self, we quite naturally abuse the environment with which we feel no identification. However, through a deeper inquiry into our true dependence on other people and other species, we may come to a more intelligent, deeper sense of relationship to the ecosphere, which gives us a sense of common identification. When we act from our ecological self, we do not have to *try* to make environmentally responsible choices. Instead, our choices are naturally less intrusive, more sensitive, less toxic because we appreciate the larger context and care about those whose well-being our behavior affects.

ECOPSYCHOLOGY

The importance of the ecological self is a key focus of a newly emerging field called **ecopsychology**, the study of human experience in its ecological context. In *The Voice of the Earth* (1992), Roszak formulated the term to "bridge our culture's long-standing, historical gulf between the psychological and the ecological" (p. 14). Roszak sharply criticized traditional psychology, especially its Freudian elements, as part and parcel of urban madness and argued that overconsumption of resources is a form of madness, promoted by urban industrial settings. The environmental destruction this madness causes destroys us along with it.

In cities, alienation from nature and from others is allowed to flourish, so that modern psychiatry has ignored the most primal part of our psyche: our **ecological unconscious**. In Roszak's (1992) words, "The contents of the ecological unconscious represent . . . the living records of cosmic evolution, tracing back to distant initial conditions in the history of time" (p. 320). This emphasis on the early, pre-human memories in our unconscious gives us an "inherent sense of environmental reciprocity" so that "when the Earth hurts, we hurt with it" (p. 308). A central element of ecopsychology is that we must recover the child's "enchanted sense of the world," our deeply rooted sense of ethical responsibility to the planet and to other people.

Roszak (1992) posited that "the whole of the cosmos is a single great organism" (p. 140), an organism with feeling, intelligence, soul. We are all born with knowledge of this principle. Children instinctually know it, which is why the great developmental psychologist Jean Piaget called their thinking "animistic." To Piaget, and the other traditional psychologists who followed, animism represents an immature and confused stage of cognitive development. To Roszak and other ecopsychologists (Mack, 1992), animism represents an earlier and wiser stage of cognitive development.

Thus for ecopsychologists, animism is more, rather than less, sophisticated. To support this point, Roszak drew on the thinking of astrophysicists Lovelock and Margulis (Lovelock, 1979). Their Gaia (pronounced Guy-ya) hypothesis proposes that the Earth is a living system. In Lovelock's (1990) words,

> the atmosphere, the oceans, the climate, and the crust of the Earth are regulated at a state comfortable for life because of the behavior of living organisms. Specifically, the Gaia hypothesis says that the temperature, oxidation state, acidity, and certain aspects of the rocks and waters are at any time kept constant, and that this homeostasis is maintained by active feedback processes operated automatically and unconsciously by the biota. Solar energy sustains comfortable conditions for life. The conditions are only constant in the short term and evolve in synchrony with the changing needs of the biota as it evolves. Life and its environment are so closely coupled that evolution concerns Gaia, not the organisms or the environment taken separately. (p. 19)

In other words, the system of living organisms (the biota) is so intricately tied to inorganic systems through feedback loops and homeostasis that the Earth's entire organic–inorganic system can be considered a living being. Lovelock and Margulis named this living system "Gaia" after the Greek goddess of the Earth. Their subsequent discussions with scientists led them to emphasize the changing features of Gaia, noting that the evolution of life forms has undergone large periods of homeostasis, sprinkled by quantum leaps of change, so that homeostasis is a relative, not an absolute principle. The central feature of Gaia, however, still holds: "There is no clear distinction anywhere on the Earth's surface between living and non-living matter" (Lovelock, 1990, p. 40). Lovelock thus called for a discipline called geophysiology, which would study the Earth's systems as a single living organism. From this perspective, environmental problems are symptoms of Gaia's "disease": the "carbon dioxide fever" of global warming, "the acid indigestion" of pollution, "the dermatologists' dilemma" of ozone depletion.

Seeing the Earth as a living being helps us identify with its (in this case, her) well-being. However, Lovelock (1990) also stated that it is the health of the planet that matters, not that of some individual species of organisms. This is where Gaia and the environmental movements, which are concerned first with the health of people, part company. [Environmental problems] are real and potentially serious hazards but mainly to the people and eco-systems of the First World—from a Gaian perspective, a region that is clearly expendable. It was buried beneath glaciers, or was icy tundra, only 10,000 years ago. (p. xvi)

Thus, Gaia will go on. If "her" systems take a sudden turn for the worse (worse to humans, that is), other species will evolve to fill the available niches, whether or not humans survive. Human existence is thoroughly dependent on the current balance of Gaia's regulatory systems; human survival is certainly not assured.

Ecopsychology's claim that humans are born with a sense of unity with the ecological world is paralleled by E. O. Wilson's (1984) biophilia hypothesis, "the innate tendency to focus on life and lifelike processes" (p. 1). Wilson and other scientists (Kellert & E. O. Wilson, 1993) argued that our survival on the planet will require that we recognize this affinity for life that is so deeply a part of us.

Ecopsychologists would urge us to experience Gaia and biophilia, and thereby realize our eco-self. More recently, Reser (1996) laid out several fundamental tenets of ecopsychology which summarize many of these points:

1. The core of the human mind is the ecological unconscious, repression of which causes a collusive madness; to heal ourselves and the planet we must become aware of our fundamental, primal connection to the system of our ecological home by recovering the repressed ecological unconscious.

2. The ecological unconscious contains a record of cosmic evolution, connecting us to all other life forms.

3. There is a synergistic relationship between planetary and personal well-being, such that as one is healed, so is the other. In this healing we will find ways to design small-scale social institutions and personal empowerment that nurture our ecological selves, and withdraw us from the "gargantuan urban-industrial culture" that destroys the ecosystem along with our psyches.

We would add the following points from other writings:

4. Overconsumption is a form of narcissism brought on by disconnection from our ecological self (Kanner & Gomes, 1995).

5. Through ecologically based transcendent experience, people can learn to reclaim their ecological selves. Transcendent experiences of ecological connections are induced through a variety of techniques, including shamanic rituals (Gray, 1995), perceptual practice (Sewell, 1995), horticultural therapy (Clinebell, 1996), community restoration (Shapiro, 1995), and wilderness trips (Harper, 1995).

EVALUATING ECOPSYCHOLOGY

Despite understandably skeptical receptions from environmental psychologists (Reser, 1996), ecopsychology is a flourishing field with a solid literature (Scull, http://www.island.net/~jscull/ECOINTRO.pdf), graduate programs (Naropa University, Project NatureConnect), techniques for developing awareness of the eco-self (Cohen, 1993, 1997; Kahn, 1999; Swanson, 2001; Thomashow, 1995), and a growing number of practitioners. Some of its claims seem quite reasonable and have been endorsed by mainstream psychologists. For example, consider the point that human beings are distressed when ecosystems are distressed. Writing for mental health professionals, White (1998) agreed that anxiety in clients about environmental problems should not be treated as displaced anxiety, but should be taken seriously in clinical settings and treated accordingly. Evidence is accumulating about the therapeutic effects of mindful contact with nature (Frumkin, 2001; Irvine & Warber, 2002). We believe ecopsychology will continue to grow because it speaks to deeply felt concerns and experiences that people have about their relationship to the natural world.

More recently, Fisher (2002), a psychotherapist, laid out four projects for ecopsychology:

1. *Psychological*: to acknowledge and better understand the human–nature relationship. This work emphasizes human relationship with nonhuman species, and would use, for example, Shepard's (1982) focus on childhood immersion in wilderness, and subsequent learning about a "mature, reciprocal, harmonious relationship with the larger natural world" (p. 8).

2. *Philosophical*: to bring the psyche (or soul) back into our understanding and experience of the natural world.

3. *Practical*: to develop experiential methods for restoring connection to the natural world, including vision quests, ecotherapy, and experiential workshops.

4. *Critical*: to seriously question the tenants of both ecopsychology and the larger intellectual climate from which it emerged. Here for example, ecopsychologists deal with the real problem that it is sometimes easier to empathize with nonhuman species than with people. Referring to ecopsychologists' work on helping people "think like mountains" (Seed, Macy, Fleming, & Naess, 1988), Anthony (1995) argued that "There is a blind spot in ecopsychology because the field is limited by its Eurocentric perspective, in the same way that the environmental movement as a whole has been blind to environmental racism. . . . Why is it so easy for . . . people to think like mountains and not be able to think like people of color?" (pp. 264, 273).

We believe these four tasks are important for the field of ecopsychology, but we want to add a fifth project: to examine empirical research that might support or contradict the basic claims of ecopsychology. Here we depart from some ecopsychologists such as Fisher (2002), who claimed that scientific data are irrelevant because the scientific method is a form of dualistic thinking that separates people from their environment (pp. 31–33). In contrast, as trained experimental psychologists, we believe that looking at empirical evidence is one useful way of evaluating a set of ideas, although not the only way.

Before we tell you about some of this research, you can get a good feel for it by taking the following scale that Schultz (2000) asked his participants to complete, with the following instructions:

People around the world are generally concerned about environmental problems because of the consequences that result from harming nature. However, people differ in the consequences that concern them the most. Please rate the following items from 1 (not important) to 7 (supreme importance) in response to the question: I am concerned about environmental problems because of the consequences for _____

1. _____Animals
2. _____Plants
3. _____Marine Life
4. _____Birds
5. _____Me
6. _____My future
7. _____My lifestyle
8. _____My health
9. _____All people
10. _____Children
11. _____People in my community
12. _____My children

Finally,

Please circle the picture that best describes your relationship with the natural environment. How interconnected are you with nature?

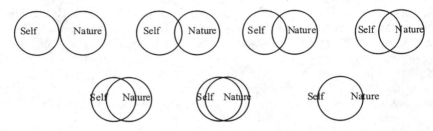

FIG. 7.1.   Nature and Self: pick the pair which best describes your relationship with nature. From Schultz, P. W. (2002). Inclusion with nature: Understanding the psychology of human–nature interactions. In P. Schmuck & P. W. Schultz (Eds.), *The Psychology of Sustainable Development*. New York: Kluwer Academic/Plenum Publishers. Reprinted with permission. Adapted from Aron, A., Aron, E. N., & Smollan, D. (1992). Inclusion of other in the self scale and the structure of interpersonal closeness. Journal of Personality and Social Psychology, 63, 596–612.

You can score your responses by comparing the sum of your scores for Items 1–4 (Biospheric) versus Items 5–8 (Egoistic) versus Items 9–12 (Social/Altruistic). Then give yourself a score on the circle question as Schultz did: 1, if you chose the first set on the left, where the circles touch but do not overlap, through 7, if you chose the last set where the circles are entirely overlapping.

Using these measures, Schultz examined the environmental concern of thousands of college students and United States citizens and found, as Stern and Dietz (1994) had previously proposed, that people's concerns about environmental problems can be separated into three related types:

1. *Egoistic*: concern about environmental protection because it will affect one's own well-being.
2. *Social-altruistic*: concern about environmental problems because they pose a threat to other humans.
3. *Biospheric*: concern about the impact of environmental problems on other species, or all living things.

Schultz also found that women scored higher on all three measures than men (Schultz, 2001). This finding relates to our earlier discussion (in chap. 3) of gender differences in environmental concern.

More importantly, when Schultz showed his participants photos and asked them to try to take the perspective of animals being harmed by environmental conditions, he found higher Biospheric Concern scores (Schultz, 2000). This result suggests that we can increase Biospheric Concern and enlarge our scope of justice (recall this discussion from chap. 3) by intentionally taking on the point of view or perspective of those normally outside it.

Most importantly for the question of changing behavior, Schultz found that environmentally responsible behavior (recycling, avoiding driving, purchasing environmentally friendly products) was correlated with Biospheric Concern. That is, people who have more Biospheric Concern report more environmentally helpful behaviors. Environmentally responsible behaviors were also correlated with NEP scores (chap. 3), empathic concern, and a measure of eco-self, which was scored with the last item using circles. Those who chose the circles with greatest overlap between self and nature showed more responsible behaviors. From the perspective of ecopsychology, they can be said to have a stronger ecological self.

More recently, Schultz, Shriver, Tabanico, and Khazian (in press) developed a measure of the ecological self that uses an implicit measure. Because ecological identity is often not articulated nor experienced directly, it must be measured in indirect ways. As you might have noted with the circle question, a sense of connection with nature is not necessarily very conscious. It may even be called a "primitive belief" (Dunlap et al., 2000) because we are not often asked to articulate it, so we find it difficult to explicitly respond to questions about it. To measure the implicit quality of this concept, Schultz presented his participants with a word such as "car" or "animals," and asked them to decide whether it is more like "nature" or "built," more like "me" or "not me." Reaction times to each question were recorded. By comparing response rates on a long series of these types of questions, he measured participants' implicit connection with nature. The degree to which "me" and "nature" produced similar responses was positively correlated with biospheric concerns, and negatively correlated with egoistic concerns.

We believe this research offers good support for the ecopsychologists' claim that environmentally responsible behavior comes from (or with) a sense of connection and concern for the well-being of the natural world. It also demonstrates that our sense of ecological self is not necessarily very conscious, a point that the ecopsychologists have been making with the term "ecological unconscious," but that until recently stood in the way of ecopsychology being taken seriously because unconscious processes are so difficult to measure. For some of us, ecological identity is more conscious than for others. Schultz' research also shows that we can teach ourselves and others to have a larger ecological self by empathizing and taking the perspective of non-human beings.

Teaching people to take the perspective of non-human beings is exactly what Seed and Macy have been doing with their Council of All Beings Workshop (Seed et al., 1988). In this workshop, participants role-play different creatures or elements in the ecosphere by expressing their unspoken reactions to human impact. Through fantasy, role-play, and dialogue, participants develop a deeper identification with their animal, plant, or element, whose reactions are ordinarily not heard or recognized. Most people who complete this workshop experience it as deeply powerful in shifting them from an identification with the smaller separate self to a larger, ecological self. Empirical research shows that people answer the question "Who am I?" with more ecological statements (I am water, I am hawk) after the workshop than before it (Bragg, 1996).

BIODIVERSITY FROM AN ECOPSYCHOLOGICAL PERSPECTIVE

From an ecopsychological perspective, the planet's diverse species are precious, and saving them from extinction is crucial. As we discussed in chapter 1, however, we are losing species at a rate which experts call "mind-boggling" (Ryan, 1992). Current estimates range from 3 to 200 per day (G. T. Miller, 2002, pp. 175–180), faster than any since the decline of the dinosaurs, some 65 million years ago. Humans are watching the greatest episode of extinction ever to occur since we have been on the planet (Rodgers, 1994). Scientists have catalogued about 1.4 million species; estimates of how many species exist vary from 10 million to 80 million. Because we do not know how many species we are destroying before we destroy them, our losses are literally incalculable.

Why should anybody care about the end of a species that we don't even know about? With 80 million (or even 10 million), one would think there are plenty to spare. Variations in answers to this question reveal the particular vantage point of the ecopsychological perspective. Most frequently, lawmakers and scientists involved give answers in economic terms. A clear example was articulated in chapter 4, where the dollar amounts of tropical deforestation were listed:

> Forests provide the following economic services: gene pools (including wild plants exported for $24 billion in 1991); water regulation and flood control (estimated in India alone to be worth $72 billion); watersheds which reduce soil erosion (worth $6 billion a year in lost hydropower due to siltation of reservoirs); fish (the Pacific Northwest salmon industry alone is worth $1 billion); climate control, through mitigation of greenhouse gases

and carbon storage (worth $3.7 trillion a year) and recreation (estimated in the United States to be worth more than timber, grazing, mining and other commodities). Wood, then, which is extracted with unsustainable procedures, is astronomically expensive. A mature forest tree in India, for example, is estimated to be worth $50,000. The real cost of a hamburger from cattle raised on cleared rainforest is $200. And a wild Chinook salmon from the Columbia River is estimated to be worth $2150 to future sports and commercial fishers. (Durning, 1993, p. 21)

Even if biodiversity is not translated into such specific monetary terms, most tropical forest advocates argue that species should be saved because of their as-yet-unknown utility to humans, and for their potential contributions to meeting future human needs. For example, N. Myers (1984) argued that tropical forests are essential as sources of new foods, pharmaceutical medicines, and energy products such as green gasoline, as well as important regulators of climate and producers of the global oxygen supply.

Ecopsychologists would give a different answer. They would join deep ecologists in arguing that "all things in the biosphere have an equal right to live and blossom and to reach their own individual forms of unfolding and self-realization within the larger Self-realization. This basic intuition is that all organisms and entities in the ecosphere, as parts of the interrelated whole, are equal in intrinsic worth" (Devall & Sessions, 1985, p. 67). Species are important to save, not by virtue of what they can do for us humans, but because they are part of an intricate ecosystem to which we belong, one that we do not own. And that ecosystem is our larger ecological self. No matter how oversimplified the dilemma of "owls vs. jobs" may be, the debate over the ESA brings us to the heart of the ecopsychological approach. Should species be protected for their economic and utilitarian features, or simply because they exist and have a "right to unfold"?

EMOTIONAL DIMENSIONS

The passion that human beings feel toward wildlife has been noted even in an environmental law textbook. Introducing a discussion of the Endangered Species Act, Rodgers (1994) noted that our relationship to

> wildlife taps the deepest wellsprings of human emotion and behavior.... It is a source of inspiration and art, recorded from the Paleolithic cave works to the contemporary cartoons of Gary Larson. It is the font and fodder of religion, as no one would doubt who has seen images of the spotted

owl nailed to the cross in the heart of logging country in Forks, Washington. It is the crucible that forges the best thinking about human ethics and morality. It is the subject of a worldwide network in trade that is staggering in its scope, avariciousness, and destructiveness. And it is the arena in which some of the most passionate performances of contemporary environmental conflict are played out, in the dangerous and violent confrontations to protect marine mammals at sea, in the no-holds-barred sabotage and other "monkeywrenching" activities on land, and in the courageous and lonely undercover work necessary to beat the poachers at their own game. (pp. 993–995)

In other words, connection with wildlife taps into our deepest core. The religious and spiritual dimensions of protecting biodiversity are not only recognized by ecopsychologists, but by experts in law and forestry. Those spiritual dimensions lead us to safeguard the Grand Canyon, the Acropolis in Athens, even Central Park in New York City, which would otherwise be seen as "economic wastes of top-value real estate" (N. Myers, 1984, p. 352).

But, as Rodgers also noted, the religious dimension fuels "passionate performances" by people on both sides of the issue. Members of EarthFirst!, who chain themselves to trees and risk bodily harm to themselves and others, express their deepest conviction about the importance of saving wilderness, just as those who nail a spotted owl to a cross communicate their similarly intense, although opposite, convictions. Rigid, unbending zealousness about wilderness has been criticized by Arnold in his anti-environmental manifesto *Ecology Wars* (1993). Arnold blamed environmentalists for what he called the religion of "wildernism":

Wildernism provides most if not all the characteristics of a standard religion as recognized by scholars of the subject: a sense of distinctiveness and community, of awe and cosmic unity, standards of morality and irreproachable beliefs, rituals, tests of faith and grounds for expulsion, a central dogma that must be protected and so on. The adherents of wildernism are convinced of their moral and ethical superiority, are blind to reason on the questions of dogma, and feel that they have an exclusive hold on the truth. It all adds up to religious behavior, and one does not expect objective rationality from religious behavior, one expects devotion, and at the extreme, zealotry. (p. 44)

Because of the depth to which people experience their ecological selves, we can expect that controversy over the Endangered Species Act (ESA), which we talked about in chapter 3 to be passionate. The ESA is one of the world's toughest environmental laws, making it illegal for United States citizens to engage in any practices that endanger

a species, such as buying, selling, hunting, killing, collecting, or injur-
ing. Species listed as threatened or endangered by the Fish and Wildlife Service or the National Marine Fisheries Service are thereby le-
gally protected. The law also makes it illegal to engage in habitat
destruction, which is why the listing of the Northern Spotted Owl in
1990 and wild salmon in 1992 by the Fish and Wildlife Service produced such fury. Consequently, many extractive industries lobby Congress to amend the ESA to take economic considerations into account
in the classification of endangered species.

Although ecopsychologists tend to emphasize the experiential,
rather than empirical, basis of caring about other species and the
health of the environment, a few research scientists have examined the
importance of feelings on our concern about the environment (Vining
& Ebreo, 2002). For example, Kals et al. (1999) demonstrated that
emotional affinity is a powerful predictor of behavior that protects the
environment, as is indignation about insufficient protection. Emotional affinity results from positive experiences in wilderness settings,
especially in the company of friends and close relations. Fear, anger,
and guilt about the environment are also positively related to pro-
environmental attitudes (Kals & Maes, 2002). Other researchers have
examined the relationship between sacred space and place attachment
and concluded that "sacred spaces evoke strong emotional ties of commitment and connectedness, a sense of history, belonging, and rooted-
ness" (S. Mazumdar & S. Mazumdar, 1993, p. 237).

Direct experience in nature is usually required for these deeper
kinds of emotional responses and spiritual understandings. We usually
cannot feel the full depth of our ecological being, nor the accompany-
ing feelings, from information on paper. For example, poet Terry Tem-
pest Williams claimed that wilderness experience is required for us to
make appropriate environmental decisions because such experience
opens us to feelings, to a deeper sense of caring, and to matters of the
heart. In a testimony to the United States Congress regarding the logging of the Pacific yew tree, valuable because of its potential in treating breast cancer, she urged her listeners to make their decisions from
more direct experience, and from their hearts:

> I am asking you as members of this subcommittee, as my lawmakers, my
> guardians of justice, for one favor. Will you please go visit the trees? See
> them for yourself—these beautiful healing trees growing wildly, mysteri-
> ously, in the draws of our ancient forests, and then go visit the adjacent
> forests, and then go visit the adjacent clear-cuts, walk among the wreck-
> age, the slash piles, forage through the debris, and look again for the Pa-
> cific yew. Think about health. Think about the women you love—our bod-
> ies, the land,—and think about what was once rich and dense and green

with standing. Think about how our sacred texts may be found in the forest as well as in the Psalms, and then, my dear lawmakers, we ask you to make your decision with your heart, what you felt in the forest in the presence of a forgotten language. And if you cannot make a decision from this place of heart, from this place of compassionate intelligence, we may have to face as a people the horror of this nation, that our government and its leaders are heartless. (T. T. Williams, 1994, pp. 130–131)

From this perspective, our difficulty stems from limited experiences of the complexity, beauty, magic, and awesome power of the natural world. Our hearts and spirits are closed down because our culture emphasizes separation and autonomy, convenience and efficiency. Housed in separate homes, often not even knowing our neighbors, much less the natural physical world that supports and surrounds us, we maintain psychological separation from each other and from the ecosystem of which we are an integral part. Decisions about how much timber should be harvested out of ancient forests in the Pacific Northwest are made by officials thousands of miles away, using abstract logic and knowledge, in concrete cities, staring at information on video screens. But we will need more than severed intellects, no matter how information rich they are, to make wise decisions about the sustainability of the planet. Decisions must also be based on a deeper identification with the natural world, a sense of the interconnectedness of all people and species, and a sense of awe for the exquisite beauty of creation. These sensitivities just cannot be produced in an office, with symbolic information as our only experience.

To assume that logic and rationality are the only bases for intelligent decisions is to continue what neurologist Damasio (1994a) called, in the title of his book, *Descartes' Error*. Without essential anatomical knowledge, Descartes believed that the body and mind could be separated into two dichotomous realms, the body housing the emotions and the mind housing rational intellect. Yet modern research shows the complex interconnections between emotional and cognitive centers in the brain, making intelligent decision making dependent on emotion and passion. As Damasio (1994a) claimed, "Absence of emotion appears to be at least as pernicious for rationality as excessive emotion" (p. 144).

This is not to say that everyone must experience wilderness directly in order to reap the spiritual wisdom it can teach us. Artists and writers also deliver this awareness through evoking connection with the natural world. There is a large literature from the lyric poets such as Whitman, Tennyson, Keats, as well as more modern poets and writers such as Gary Snyder, Annie Dillard, Wendell Berry, and Barry Lopez, which powerfully communicates the awareness of ecological selfhood. Whether we find this consciousness through literature or in wilderness, the key is a sense of reverence and respect for the natural world, "a profound courtesy, an unalloyed honesty" to use Lopez's (1990, p. 49) words. This respect will mean seeing nature less as a commodity and more as a teacher, less as property and more as a shrine.

A similar point has been made by Roszak, in his discussion of urban madness: Ecopsychology

> deeply questions the essential sanity of our gargantuan urban/industrial culture. . . . Now thoroughly rationalized and accepted as "normal", the city dates back to the fantasies of megalomaniac pharaohs and conquering god-kings. It was born of delusions of grandeur. . . . The walls and towers, pyramids and ziggurats of ancient cities were declarations of a wishful biological independence from the natural environment. For many centuries that isolation was only partial; the wild environs were never far away. With the passage of time and the growth of technology, we have gained the power to reify the wish. Soon there will be no great beasts that are not in zoos or on reservations; there will be no tribal peoples who remember a different relationship to the planet than that of the urbanites. (pp. 219–220, 321)

For these reasons, an essential dimension of human experience that must be restored is the aesthetic appreciation of the natural world.

CONCLUSIONS

The basic principle to be drawn from both Gestalt and ecopsychology is that ordinary experience of ourselves as separate autonomous beings is incomplete and inaccurate. Recognizing our embedded role in the larger ecosphere will require a perceptual shift (emphasized by Gestalt psychology) and experience (emphasized by ecopsychology) of ourselves as wider and deeper ecological selves. This shift is more than a cognitive event—it is also a profoundly emotional and/or spiritual event. One feels identified with the planet and with other species and peoples on an experiential, rather than simply an informational, level. (Lifton, 1993, made a similar point when saying that we need to develop a species mentality to solve our global problems.) This shift is more powerful, and also more ineffable than simply taking in new knowledge. It is less about information and more about identification. Less of a decision and more of a dropping into a fuller experience of oneself. Less about behaving, and more about being. Less about knowing and more about appreciating. Thus the ecological self is an expanded, more gracious, and more spacious sense of self realized through direct experience.

An important quality of direct experience is silence, either through solitude or shared silence. Silence is often scarce in our modern world, which is filled with entertainment, convenience, and comfort. Fritz Perls would have endorsed this point, as he frequently noted the ways in which head "chatter" blocks fuller experience of wholeness. Because this experience rarely occurs while people are chatting, we are more likely to "fall into it" when we allow ourselves to become very quiet, as in Deborah's experience in the meditation hall described earlier. When we are quiet, senses open, perceptions grow richer, acuity sharpens, and we become aware of the subtleties and richness of the natural world, subtleties missed when we are thinking or talking. Rituals can enhance our experience of nature, for example, singing or chanting to celebrate the rising of the full moon, gatherings to mark the changing of the seasons (e.g., equinox and solstice); or simply taking time to go outside to appreciate a summer rain, a snowfall, a sunset, or a sunrise.

It is not difficult to imagine that most of us enjoy and even crave these kinds of experiences, yet find them difficult to schedule in increasingly busy lives. As the field of horticultural therapy (Clinebell, 1996) now demonstrates, growing geraniums is a healing activity. Going for a walk, relating to a landscape or a non-human being is inherently restorative. Ecopsychologists would simply remind us to expand these activities, promoting experiences in which we learn about and appreciate the biotic world (without trying to manipulate or change it) and other animals (without owning them).

As the larger ecological self claims more of our existence, the environmentally depleting, smaller self claims less. We will want to commit ourselves to more environmentally appropriate actions and activism, not from a sense of guilt or moral ideology, but out of a sense of love and devotion. As we identify ourselves as part of the larger unity, environmental activism becomes a natural extension of our sense of self.

From the holistic vantage point, the consumer culture is a sign of spiritual affliction; it arises from and feeds on small, segmented selves that make us feel impoverished and hungry for something to fill the void. Our driven, materialist society runs on a core experience of emptiness, and we use consumer products to try to satiate that inner vacuum. Thus, overconsumption is caused by greed, craving, and lack of understanding of our truer selves. When we experience our ecological selves, however, we are filled with a sense of perfection and completion. We stop craving, wanting, scheming, worrying. We rejoice in the incredible beauty of the ecosystem and our role in it. We don't have to *train* ourselves to stop overconsuming because experiencing our ecological selves replaces that inner craving with a deeply satisfying sense of wholeness and abundance. From this perspective, the way out of the shopping mall is back into an earlier connection with the natural world, through silence, ritual, art, or simply spending more time outside in biotically rich settings. As all spiritual traditions of the world teach, fulfillment comes with simplicity and quiet awareness, not with material wealth.

This kind of spiritual awakening will also lead to dissatisfaction with the status quo, however, because seeing the larger picture illuminates social injustice and environmental deterioration. Freed from the compulsion of satisfying cravings, we will naturally focus more energy on solving bigger problems, and we will be naturally drawn to environmental projects that heal both the planet and ourselves. Ecopsychologists like Conn (1995) would encourage us to become active in local, regional, national, or global environmental issues, working with them from a sense of devotion and caring, as well as playfulness and lightness. Because we are connected to the whole, we are also part of that which appears to us as "the enemy"—the unconscious guzzling consumer, the advertising executive, the "wise use" advocate, the antienvironmentalist, the slash and burn farmer, or the weapons manufacturer. Social action not only helps solve a pressing environmental problem, but it helps us heal ourselves. As we come into contact with others who do not share our views, we are forced to remember our underlying connection, the human bond with each other and with the ecosystem on which we depend. Social action is a way to practice these basic spiritual values. Hence, healing the planet and healing ourselves are both possible if we undertake environmental activism as spiritual learning. Our ecological goals can heal our psyches, and the psychological work required can reverse environmental damage.

KEY CONCEPTS

Animism

Biophilia hypothesis

Cooperation: group size, communication, altruistic norms

Ecological self

Ecological unconscious

Ecopsychology

Ecotherapy
Environmental concern: emotional dimensions;
    egoistic, social-altruistic, biospheric concern
Gaia hypothesis
Gestalt psychology and Gestalt therapy
Holism
Insight learning
Sensory contact

8

Putting It Together: Using Psychology to Build a Sustainable World

One day fairly soon we will all go belly up like guppies in a neglected fishbowl. I suggest an epitaph for the whole planet: . . . "We could have saved it, but we were too darn cheap and lazy."
—Kurt Vonnegut (1990, as quoted by Mack, 1992, p. 246)

*I*n this book we have described the seriousness of our environmental problems and tried to show how psychology can help us solve them. That assumes, of course, that our human civilization is worth saving, and that we could save it if we really want to. As the coauthors of this book, we do believe that we can save it, and yet, we are not convinced that humans will survive. Vonnegut may be right. In order to endure, we will have to confront the dangerous direction we are going. And we will need a robust psychology to help us make crucial changes in our behaviors, thoughts, feelings, and values. How to sustain human existence on the planet could become psychology's core question, offering an intellectual coherence to a discipline increasingly fragmented by diverse concerns.

COMPARING THE SIX APPROACHES

We hope your reading of the previous chapters has convinced you that each of the six different psychological approaches has something important to contribute to the project of building a sustainable world. Each provides insights about changing individual behavior, thoughts, feelings, physiological reactions, or beliefs. Let's review some of these points, comparing and contrasting the contributions from each approach.

Chapter 2: Freudian Psychology

Freud contributed a great deal toward helping us understand the uniqueness, as well as the irrationality, of individual human behavior. Without Freud's notion of defense mechanisms and their various manifestations, we would be less likely to notice our own and others' environmentally destructive behaviors and excuses, less able to correct them, and less willing to experience the uncomfortable feelings that the defenses occlude. Knowing more about our own personal patterns of defenses allows us to be less habitual in our use of them. Also, without the Freudian perspective, we might be too impatient with our attempts to solve environmental problems because we wouldn't understand the deeply rooted instinctual needs the problems represent. Object relations theorists have contributed an updated version of Freud's theory by focusing on how we build a sense of self out of our relationship with others. Their insights relate directly to the way we experience a connection with nature, and why people experience that connection differently.

On the other hand, Freudian (and perhaps objects relations) theory is culturally limited. Nor do these theories give much direction for what to do about our environmental difficulties once we have noticed the instinctual or deeply unconscious basis for them. If we focus on explaining our mess rather than developing solutions to it, we will have a lot of insight, but not much change in our behavior. Because the psychoanalytic approaches focus so much on our early experience, they do not have as much to offer about how to change behavior in the present.

Chapter 3: Social Psychology

Social psychology underscores the importance of immediate social situations on environmentally relevant behaviors. Norms, roles, and reference groups continually exert their potent influence on what we mistakenly assume to be private, personal views. By demonstrating the degree to which we like to maintain a consistent, coherent view of the world, social psychology offers insights into how to change people's attitudes by subtly changing their behavior first. Social psychology highlights the importance of how we create meaning for our actions. Our attribution process can help or hinder changes toward environmentally responsible behavior. Personal values, scopes of justice, as well as gender, all affect the way we think about and behave regarding environmental issues. On the other hand, by emphasizing the meaning that is created in social and cultural contexts, social psychology has less to say about how to change behavior when people are not aware of their choices. Social psychology assumes we are conscious, although not particularly rational.

Chapter 4: Behavioral Psychology

Behaviorism's focus on actual behavior rather than meaning and underlying motivations is therefore also valuable. Behavioral psychologists insist that we examine and change environmentally destructive behaviors without worrying about their deeper causes. Skinner advanced the insight developed by social psychology about the importance of the immediate situation on our behavior, and he extended this principle by arguing that what we do is a function of the consequences of our behavior. The behaviorists' emphasis on specification, measurement, and stimulus control helps us to recognize and thus modify the environmental contingencies that signal and maintain environmentally irresponsible behavior. Yet, because much of our behavior is rooted in institutional structures with their global, political, and economic dimensions, we must also work toward changing larger organizations that reinforce destructive behaviors. The behavioral approach may also be limited because ignoring unconscious motivations could lead to "symptom substitution." For example, stress is a particularly potent cause of environmentally destructive behaviors. Until we reduce underlying stress, getting rid of one damaging behavior (e.g., overeating) will likely result in adopting another (e.g., compulsive shopping).

Chapter 5: Physiological and Health Psychology

Environmental pollution and toxic chemicals directly activate human stress responses. Current practices soil the air and water with wastes, and push agricultural production to the extreme by applying fertilizers and pesticides. As a result, we stress our own physiological systems to the point of malfunction, disease, and psychological damage. In the mad rush to consume, we suffer emotionally and therefore physically. Physiological and health psychology helps us see that taking better care of the Earth translates into taking better care of ourselves and the children of future generations.

Chapter 6: Cognitive Psychology

On the other hand, a lot of environmentally destructive behavior is an outcome of inadequate or bad information, leading us to value the contributions of cognitive psychology. Cognitive psychology helps illuminate inadequate information, erroneous beliefs, and imperfect processing patterns. Although we are prone to make cognitive errors in the interest of efficient and rapid processing, becoming alert to potential errors aids us in making better judgments about complex situations. Thus, the cognitive approach can help us become better decision makers by improving the quality and use of information. But because cognitive psychology underscores the tendency of humans to take cognitive and perceptual shortcuts, cognitive psychology may also disempower the public in the face of "experts," who conceptualize environmental risks in different terms. It also assumes that the key to our difficulties rests in better information. Yet, because we know much more than we are willing to act on, information cannot be our only problem.

Chapter 7: Holistic Approaches: Gestalt and Ecopsychology

Holistic approaches suggest that part of our problem is the mistaken experience that we are separate from each other and from ecological systems. Gestalt and transpersonal approaches emphasize our embeddedness in the larger world. By highlighting relationship and wholeness, psychologists working with these models offer a rich set of methods for enhancing our identification and connection with the natural world, methods that are increasingly being used by ecotherapists. The basic insight they deliver—that we are part of nature, rather than outside it—is a fundamental theme of our closing remarks later. On the other hand, because holistic psychology has devoted less attention to empirical tests of its claims, many mainstream psychologists dismiss or ignore it.

Each of the approaches we have talked about in this book can help us understand our current predicament and suggest ways out of it. You may at this point be wondering, which is most useful? Which is the best?

We believe the question of "which psychology is best?" is problematic for a number of reasons. First, human behavior is so complex no one approach can capture everything. It may be easier to focus on information or emotions, social settings, or hormones for the short run, but we think that all of these explanatory devices are useful at different times. Environmental behavior is multiply determined, as Hallin (1995) showed with research on household related behaviors in Minnesota: People cite a wide variety of reasons for changing their environmentally relevant behavior, including past experience, role models, altruism, convenience, and rewards.

Second, the debate about which approach is better can distract us from solving our problems. Because we value each of the perspectives we examined, we attempted to demonstrate their value without disparaging others. The century-long history of psychology is filled with intriguing as well as bitter debates and intellectual struggles, and you can easily find proponents of one view who will use vitriolic attacks on others. The differences that propel these arguments are not resolved; indeed, we do not believe they ever will be. You probably have some sense of what they are by now:

1. Is environmentally relevant behavior innate (nature) or learned (nurture)? Does it come from our genes and evolutionary history or from our environment? Is it primarily a physiological reflex, or are cognitive and emotional dimensions more important?

2. Are we more conscious or unconscious? Rational or irrational? Selfish or altruistic?

3. Should we study human beings by focusing on the smaller, more elemental parts (reductionism) or look at behavior in its complexity and context (holism)?

4. Do we need to understand what goes on in people's heads? Or can we just focus on behavior as the most direct route to fostering less destructive behavior?

5. Can we effectively concentrate our attention on the individual, or must we also pay equal attention to the larger sociological, political, and economic structures within which individuals behave?

Different approaches have different answers to these questions, and we could spend a lot of time discussing and debating them. Instead, we chose to emphasize their relevance to environmental problems by concentrating on their utility. However, **common vision is also possible because common fate is assured**. Ecosystems will not care if we spend our time debating the relative merits of behavioral or cognitive theory, nor which theory wins the most followers. Ecosystems will collapse whether or not we win our intellectual debates. Only changing our behavior will make any difference to the outcome of our crisis. We suggest getting on with using psychology rather than deliberating about it.

The third reason picking a winning theory is not very interesting to us is that although it is intellectually strategic to focus on emotions or physiology, thinking or behavior, information or consciousness, as a theoretical starting point, each of us is already whole. Thus, choosing to change one element of our functioning will in turn change others. From this perspective, it does not matter which theory you choose to act on; the more important point is that you **choose to act**.

We would like to go on and suggest six operating principles for how to proceed. Each principle comes from our reflections about how to effect change. As you will see, each of these principles has psychological rationale and connects to psychological theory and research. The six principles are:

- Visualize healthy ecosystems
- Work with small steps and big ideas
- Think circle instead of line
- Consider ways in which less is more
- Practice conscious consumption
- Act on personal and political levels, especially community participation

VISUALIZE AN ECOLOGICALLY HEALTHY WORLD

Any serious look at environmental problems presents a troubling future. No matter how it is accomplished, sustaining human life on the planet will require huge changes in the way societies are organized and conducted, changes that may or may not be pleasurable. For example, whether or not we design sustainable technologies, we will end our dependence on fossil fuels soon because the global supply is quickly running out. There simply is not enough oil on the planet to forever run the number of automobiles currently produced, much less a car for every Chinese household, a goal recently adopted by China. A car in every Chinese garage would require 80 million barrels of oil a day, much more than what the world now produces (Brown, 2001) or will ever produce, because world oil production will peak in the next 10 to 20 years (MacKenzie, 2000). We will reduce our dependence on fossil fuel one way or another, whether by intelligently designing alternative technologies, or fighting over the last reserves in armed conflict. As we write this chapter, another United States attack on Iraq is in progress. The United States' massive militarization of the Middle East is just one of the huge and ugly costs of oil dependency. Modern warfare parallels ecological collapse for its destructive capacity, and both bring tremendous human suffering.

Do you ever wonder why more people are not concerned about these issues? Does it seem odd to you that most people you know seem curiously oblivious about the dangerous path that civilization is on? That they buy their SUVs with little thought about how doing so supports both international war and global warming? We have come to agree with Roszak (1994) that a big part of the public's problem in seriously confronting these issues is "Green guilt and ecological overload." Roszak blamed environmentalists for disregarding the fear, anxiety, and denial caused by their messages and suggests that they should do a "Psychological Impact Statement" (p. 537) whenever they discuss disturbing information. Instead of trading on fear, guilt, and despair, Roszak urged environmentalists to find ways of tapping into hope, joy, and nobility, as we confront our environmental problems.

We agree with Roszak that it is important to build motivation from a positive, rather than a negative source. Positive images of a possible future are desperately needed to spur both our own and others' commitment to solving environmental problems. Consequently, when Deborah found the following passage a few months ago, she was deeply grateful:

> Imagine for a moment a world where cities have become peaceful and serene because cars and buses are whisper quiet, vehicles exhaust only water vapor, and parks and greenways have replaced unneeded urban freeways. OPEC has ceased to function because the price of oil has fallen to five dollars a barrel, but there are few buyers for it because cheaper and better ways now exist to get the services people once turned to oil to provide. Living standards for all people have dramatically improved, particularly for the poor and those in developing countries. Involuntary unemployment no longer exists, and income taxes have largely been eliminated. Houses, even low-income housing units, can pay part of their mortgage costs by the energy they *produce*; there are few if any active landfills;

worldwide forest cover is increasing; dams are being dismantled; atmospheric CO_2 levels are decreasing for the first time in two hundred years; and effluent water leaving factories is cleaner than the water coming into them. Industrialized countries have reduced resource use by 80% while improving the quality of life. Among these technological changes, there are important social changes. The frayed social nets of Western countries have been repaired. With the explosion of family-wage jobs, welfare demand has fallen. The progressive and active union movement has taken the lead to work with business, environmentalists, and government to create "just transitions" for workers as society phases out coal, nuclear energy, and oil. In communities and towns, churches, corporations, and labor groups promote a new living-wage social contract as the least expensive way to ensure the growth and preservation of valuable social capital. (Hawken, A. Lovins, & L. H. Lovins, 1999, pp. 1–2)

When Deborah read this paragraph, she thought "Now that's worth working for!" And she wondered how it might be possible. In their book, *Natural Capitalism*, Hawken et al. went on to detail myriad examples of how corporations, communities, and individuals are accomplishing specific changes in this direction. They concluded that this vision of an ecologically healthy human society is not a futile utopian dream, but a do-able possibility given current trends in technology, including: hypercars that run on fuel cells; factories that restore water while making sturdy, nontoxic products; materials that are designed for durability rather than mass production; food that is grown organically; and new nontoxic materials that are stronger than steel and lighter than plastic. We propose that an important psychological ap-

Maxine

Reprinted by permission of the artist.

proach to building a sustainable society is to keep positive visions of the future in focus, and to work diligently on making them happen. A psychologically sophisticated approach to environmental problems must include ways of protecting us from overload and despair. Hope is a crucial psychological commodity for building a sustainable future, as it is for emotional intelligence in general (Goleman, 1995; Seligman, 1975; Snyder et al., 1991). The importance of providing positive images flows directly from Freudian psychology that emphasizes defenses and anxiety. With positive images of our future, we can direct more of our energy toward accomplishing our goals, and use less of it defending against negative feelings.

WORK WITH BIG IDEAS AND SMALL STEPS

Nurturing hope for a sustainable society will require diligent persever-ance. Unfortunately, when faced with huge challenges, psychologists, like most people, are liable to resort to small problems and ideas be-cause they produce less anxiety, making us feel more comfortable be-cause we are distracted from troubling realities. This book has pre-sented some big ideas for some big problems. We hope that it encourages you to keep focused on the big problems, using the big the-ories of psychology to help design a sustainable world (Winter, 2000). But we agree that it is easy to feel overwhelmed and discouraged, espe-cially because resistance from others to new ideas is often vigorous.

Instead of distracting ourselves with small *problems*, we suggest using small *steps* to work on big problems. Weick (1984) made the same suggestion decades ago, noting that people cannot solve problems if they become emotionally overwhelmed by them. He used the Yerkes–Dodson Law of arousal (Broadhurst, 1959; Yerkes & Dodson, 1908) to argue that we need optimal levels of arousal for optimal per-formance. When arousal is too high, people tend to respond with more primitive coping mechanisms, which means that more highly refined and contextually valid responses are the first to go. On the other hand, arousal that is too low also hurts problem solving. When problems seem too depersonalized or distant, people become inactive or apa-thetic. To keep arousal in the optimal moderate range, Weick sug-gested that we define problems in terms of small wins. Small wins have immediacy, tangibility, and controllability that reverse powerless-ness and apathy. For example, Alcoholics Anonymous is successful helping alcoholics because it does not insist on complete abstinence for the rest of their lives. Instead, the goal is to stay sober one day at a time. And, according to Weick, feminists have been more successful with the smaller win of promoting gender neutral language (particularly in the *APA Publication Manual*) than in the larger issue of amending the United States Constitution. Reforms in gender neutral language were adopted, he believed, because of their size, specificity, and visibility.

Specificity and visibility are the hallmarks of the behavioral approach, which breaks down large behaviors into small, measurable ones. The self-control project we outlined in the behavioral chapter is a good example of the psychology of small wins. Small wins may seem trivial at the time, but they have the advantage of facilitating success, and thus momentum and motivation for further change.

THINK CIRCLE INSTEAD OF LINE

One of the most optimistic glimpses of a positive future we have encountered lately is depicted in the video *The Next Industrial Revolution* (McDonough & Braungart, 2001). Incorporating many of the principles described by Hawken et al. (1999), McDonough and Braungart (2002) offered a similar vision of the future—"one where humanity works with nature, where technical enterprises are continually reinvented as safe and ever renewing natural processes" (from the Web site: http://www.thenextindustrialrevolution.org). Because people are generally unwilling to adopt new technologies if they mean economic decline (Hodgkinson & Innes, 2000), McDonough and Braungart worked on ways to produce environmentally friendly products and buildings without sacrificing profitability.

An important principle of the Next Industrial Revolution is that of closed systems, where nothing is added or taken away. Nature has a lot of them: The hydrological cycle, the carbon cycle, and the nitrogen cycle are a few examples. For instance, as a global system, water is never produced or depleted, but constantly transformed as rain, fog, clouds, rivers, and snow through evaporation and precipitation. Water can be polluted beyond healthy use (and far too often, it is) or cleaned by purification methods, but it operates in a closed cycle. In contrast, human-made systems usually function as linear structures, eating up inputs, and exuding wastes. Even though there is really no "away" to throw things to, we act as if there is when we fill dump sites, oceans, and water supplies with the wastes from our industrial activities.

The first industrial revolution brought unparalleled prosperity, productivity, and profits to large numbers of people, along with physical comforts, extended life spans, and increased personal mobility. But the same industrial revolution has also put billions of pounds of toxic waste into the air, water, and soil every year, some so dangerous that they will require constant vigilance by future generations; industrialization has depleted natural capital (fresh air and clean water, intact forests, healthy fish stocks and coral reefs), destroyed large amounts of habitat for many different species, and required thousands of complex regulations to keep people from poisoning each other too quickly (McDonough & Braungart, 1998).

Industrialization rests on the common sense that supports it. One belief that gave rise to the first industrial revolution is the assumption that natural resources are inexhaustible. This idea seemed accurate during the 17th through 20th centuries, when Europeans and North Americans were busy expanding their populations and colonizing other lands. But the view that natural resources are inexhaustible is clearly out of date in the 21st century. "What we thought was boundless has limits, and we are beginning to hit them" as Robert Shapiro, CEO of Monsanto put it in 1997 (quoted by McDonough & Braungart, 1998).

Instead of using the linear model, where "inexhaustible" inputs are manufactured to produce intolerable wastes, it is time to design human activities that follow natural laws of circular exchange. In this model, "wastes" must become food, just as they are in natural cycles, where organic wastes serve as fertilizers for the next generation of growth. Operating as if we belong to a closed system (which we do), we will need to change how we design and use most of our material products. In other words, we will need "cradle to cradle," rather than "cradle to grave" manufacturing designs. Does this sound unlikely? Consider a few of the many examples that Hawken et al. and McDonough and Braungart listed as "cradle to cradle" technologies already in use:

- Manufacturers rent products for service, rather than sell them for eventual disposal. When products are rented and returned to the manufacturer, incentives are enhanced for making durable and reusable parts. For example, most photocopy machines are now leased rather than sold. Designers are making floor coverings with the same goal. When you rent a carpet and pay for the service of having your floor covered, you do not have to throw it "away" when you want to replace it. Instead, you return it to the manufacturer who has produced it for its recyclability.
- Toilets in Sweden use a two-compartment bowl to separate urine from feces. Urine is sold as fertilizer, and feces as compost (Hawken et al., 1999, p. 221). Automobiles powered by fuel cells produce hot water instead of exhaust laden with dangerous heavy metals.

- Recently enacted national legislation in 29 countries requires manufacturers to take back their packaging discarded by consumers; another 9 countries have mandated the "take back" of electronic equipment; the European Union now requires that automobile manufacturers take back their used products (Gardner, 2002).
- Technologies that utilize the waste materials of other industrial or agricultural processes are beginning to spread. As of 2002, there are 25 eco-industrial parks modeled on the original one in Kalundborg, Denmark, where a fish farm, a power plant, a manufacturer of gypsum wallboard, a producer of insulin, a cement factory, local farmers, and an oil refinery, each use by-products of another's production. In this way, waste becomes food.

In each of these examples, natural resources do not end up in sewers and landfills, but are used in new production cycles, mimicking how natural systems operate. Renewable energy is another example of the circle design. Firms like British Petroleum and Shell are investing in renewable energy sources because of their greater likelihood for future markets. As Hawken et al. (1999) pointed out, "the world's fastest-growing energy technologies, outpacing even energy savings, are windpower, increasing by 26% a year, and photo-voltaics (solar cells) whose annual growth has lately ranged from 23 to 42% as manufacturers struggle to keep pace with strong demand" (p. 247).

Seeing ourselves and our activities as part of natural circular cycles is congruent with both physiological and ecological psychology. The first industrial revolution depended on the assumption that human beings are separate from nature and destined to transform it to satisfy human needs. But, as we emphasized in chapter 5, when industrial processes produce pollution and pesticides, they harm the human body and nervous system. Because we are physiological beings, wastes from agriculture and manufacturing lodge as poisons in our bodies. When we see ourselves linked at the chemical level to industrial processes, the importance of promoting benign technologies comes into view. From the vantage point of ecopsychology, this awareness means consciousness of our larger ecological identity.

LESS IS MORE

Another problem in getting people to think about our future is that many assume that sustainability will mean hardship and sacrifice. But instead of presupposing that our future, if designed for sustainability, will be Spartan and severe, consider the principle that with increased human attention, less can be more. This rule is grounded in both psychology and physics.

At the physical level, less is more means enhanced efficiency. Designers around the world are working for "Factor 10," meaning a 90% reduction in the energy and materials used to produce and run our industrial life (Schmidt-Bleek et al., 1999). If this goal sounds impossible, then consider the hideous inefficiency of the automobile as it is manufactured today. Eighty percent of the energy from the gasoline it burns is used to run and cool the engine and deal with its exhausts. Only 5% of the remaining 20% is used to move the person; the rest is used to move the car. Thus, only 1% of the total energy in gasoline goes to moving the driver—the rest is wasted. Even worse, a lot of the energy is spit out as exhaust waste, contaminating our air and contributing to global warming.

On the other hand, new hypercars designed for maximum efficiency could use only one tenth the energy it takes to manufacture and run a car. Ultra-light and durable, they are being designed to combine "Lexus comfort and refinement, Mercedes stiffness, Volvo safety, BMW acceleration, Taurus price, four-to eighteen fold improved fuel economy (that is, 80 to 200 miles per gallon), a 600 to 800 mile range between refuelings, and zero emissions ... [with] ... technologies [that] exist today" (Hawken et al., 1999, p. 25). For those readers considering career options, working on eco-efficient design and production might be a very good choice.

On the psychological end, as we discussed in chapter 3, more wealth does not bring more happiness (D. Myers, 2000). Instead, people report more fulfillment when they have close relationships, a sense of belonging to a community, and some faith in larger meanings, either of religious or spiritual dimensions. These activities do not require material wealth, and in fact, can be interrupted by harried pursuit of more money and possessions. "Affluenza," the "unhappy condition of overload, debt, anxiety, and waste resulting from the dogged pursuit of more" (Walljasper, 1997, p. 19) is hazardous to our physical and mental health. In this perspective, less (consumption) is more (pleasure and well-being).

The lifestyle of voluntary simplicity makes many of the same points (Cairns, 1998; Elgin, 1981). Voluntary simplicity (VS) is a social movement spreading through North America and Europe in which people are deliberately choosing to downscale their material possessions, in order to live "consciously, deliberately, while not being distracted by consumer culture ... taking charge of a life that is too busy, too stressed, and too fragmented, [while] consciously tasting life in its unadorned richness" (Elgin, 2000, Web posting). Using principles of Zen and other contemplative practices, VS addresses both the stressed spirit and the stressed planet through methods that increase attention to present abundance. VS teaches contemplative methods similar to those ecopsychologists use, so that people learn to appreciate and experience more from less. Resources are available on the web for supporting people interested in learning more about VS (http://www.simpleliving.net; see also the Center for a New American Dream, http://www.newdream.org). And research shows that VS is a good route to enhancing pro-environmental habits. Iwata (1999) developed a measure of VS that correlates with environmentally responsible behaviors, such as resisting impulse buying, conserving energy, and buying natural food.

Maxine

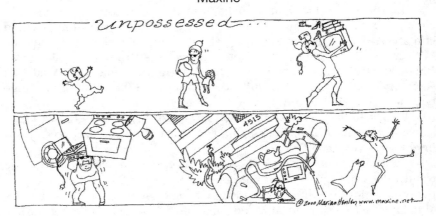

Reprinted by permission of the artist.

There's a catchy, old New England maxim that reflects some of these ideas: "Use it up, wear it out; make it do, or do without." Meadows (1991), a global systems analyst, offered another way of approaching the less is more principle, using the ideas of Gandhi:

> As a child in the middle-class Midwest [of the U.S.], I lived out of a subconscious sense of *abundance*. That sense permits security, innovation, generosity, and joy. But it can also harbor insensitivity, greed, and waste. After returning from India, I lived out of a sense of *scarcity*. That is fine when it fosters stewardship, simplicity, and frugality, but not when it leads to grimness, intolerance, and separation from one's fellows. Now I try to base my life on the idea of *sufficiency*—there is just enough of everything for everyone and not one bit more. There is enough for generosity

but not waste, enough for security but not hoarding. Or as Gandhi said, enough for everyone's need, but not for everyone's greed. (p. 17, italics hers)

Practice Conscious Consumption

Voluntary simplicity implies the obvious principle of conscious consumption, for example, not only reducing how much we buy and consume, but choosing environmentally friendly products whenever we need to make purchases. Research shows that people who hold values in line with the New Ecological Paradigm (NEP) (discussed in chap. 3) practice ecologically conscious consumer behavior (Roberts & Bacon, 1997). Specifically, those who agree that "the balance of nature is very delicate and easily upset" and "there are limits to growth beyond which our industrialized society cannot expand" are more likely to buy recycled and recyclable products, and avoid excessive packaging, polluting materials, and aerosol containers.

People make conscious consumer decisions for different reasons. Ebreo et al. (1999) analyzed conscious consumption based on two categories: concern about the conservation of natural resources (purchasing items that are reusable, refillable, biodegradable) and concern about the wider impact on natural systems (e.g., avoiding items with pesticides, or that were tested on animals). Both factors are correlated with NEP scores, and women show higher scores on both factors than men. Recycling behaviors are related to concern with conservation rather than natural systems. In general, people seem to have more unease about toxicity of products, and are least concerned about the role of animals in the development and manufacture of consumer products. Whether this is because information about animal testing and suffering is not salient enough (we think it isn't), or people do not extend their scope of justice (chap. 3) to include animals, is not yet known.

In any case, we believe that conscious consumption is one of the public's most powerful political and economic tools. Consumers have enormous economic power that can promote or delay sustainability. For example, McDonald's ceased using styrofoam containers for their hamburgers after prominent public pressure. In 1988, consumers boycotted Burger King because they imported cheap beef from tropical rainforest countries, causing major destruction of precious ecosystems. Burger Kings' sales dropped 12%. Shortly thereafter, this company canceled $35 million worth of contracts from Central American countries and announced that it would no longer continue importing rain-

forest beef (http://rainforestweb.org). Many other examples of successful boycotts exist, along with instances of successful pressure in
changing corporate practices. For example, when Deborah wrote the
first edition of this book in 1994, she called Starbucks headquarters to
inquire about their efforts to purchase fair-trade coffee (grown on
farms that pay farmers a living wage, and with shade trees so that bird
species are not annihilated). She was told that no one cares about that.
After many years of public pressure, in fall 2002, Starbucks announced
that it will buy fair trade certified coffee, will give $1 million to devas-
tated coffee farmers, and will offer fair trade certified coffee as the
"coffee of the day" on the 20th of each month (*Co-op America Quarterly*, 2002). We would prefer to see it be every day of every month, but
these changes are a big start.

Each consumer choice we make supports something—sustainable
or not. Responsible shopping is getting easier with the aid of resources
that deliver information that is not provided in the aisles of stores or
on the labels of products. For example, at the Web site, http://www.
responsibleshopper.com, you can search for keywords by brand, product, or category to find out how companies compare on pollution, recycling, animal testing, and labor practices. Co-op America's *National
Green Pages* lists goods and services that promote sustainability. The
Union of Concerned Scientists publishes the *Consumer's Guide to Effective Environmental Choices* (Brower & Leon, 1999), and several Web
sites listed in the appendix give clear, up-to-date, and immediate information on responsible consumerism. A lot of important progress is also
being made at the shareholder level with resolutions to change irresponsible company practices. For example, CVS, Longs, and Safeway
recently agreed to phase out production and distribution of mercury
thermometers because of shareholder pressure (*Co-op America Quarterly*, 2002, p. 25).

When better information leads to more responsible choices, cognitive psychology is at work. Most of us lack the essential information
we need to make responsible purchasing choices. Imagine, for example, how your choices might be affected if you knew whether a product's manufacturing process produces dangerous pollution, whether
it is horrifically inefficient, or dangerous for workers who produce it.
Because most people would avoid hurting others or the planet if they
could, responsible consumer information is crucial. Behavioral psychology is also at work with conscious consumerism because when we
choose environmentally responsible products and services, our financial reinforcers operate on providers to promote sustainable business
practices.

ACT ON PERSONAL AND POLITICAL LEVELS, ESPECIALLY COMMUNITY PARTICIPATION

Deborah didn't change Starbucks' practices, but years of political activism by many people did. Environmental devastation is driven by behaviors at both personal *and* political levels. Although psychology tends to focus on individual behavior, political work for the larger public good is equally crucial because even when we know about and would like to choose responsible behaviors, it is not always possible to do so. Consider an example.

Deborah drives a Volvo, a car that only gets 23 miles to the gallon. She knows that gasoline plays a big role in current environmental and political problems. She is outraged by the way that her country has militarized the Middle East, treating it as if it is a cheap gas station, because of our dependence on oil. A small portion of what the world pays for militarization could solve many of our environmental problems (see Fig. 8.1). Deborah is disturbed that she contributes her share to global warming and international wars by burning a fossil fuel so often. However, she drives to work every morning anyway, because her environmentally irresponsible behavior has structural dimensions beyond her immediate control: Her office is 20 miles from where she lives and there is no mass transit system. Snow and ice in the winter, and deer year round on the country road make driving a lighter weight car unsafe. Roads are built and maintained by tax dollars that she did not allocate. Yet she knows that her irresponsible behavior is contributing to environmental decline and international conflict.

For reasons like these, we believe that in order for psychology to make a viable contribution to building a sustainable world, it must also be practiced in political contexts to change the structural (economic, legal, and political) dimensions of environmental decline. That means using our citizenship to participate in public decision making. It means taking responsibility for our own behavior while working to change norms, rules, and laws that shape the behavior of many others. It means tracking and speaking out about national and international legislation. A good way to do this is to participate in political activism via Web sites such as those listed in the appendix.

But another crucial element of our problem is what is happening in our own communities. You have probably heard the dictum "Think Globally, Act Locally." We believe it's an indispensable strategy, but one that isn't enacted frequently enough. Recent research shows a disturbing gap between how people think about global versus local environmental problems. Specifically, they are more concerned about

What the World Wants

— and how to pay for it —

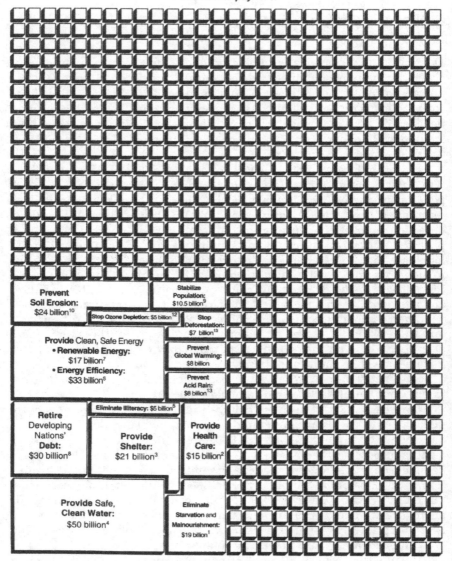

Prevent Soil Erosion: $24 billion[10]

Stop Ozone Depletion: $5 billion[12]

Stabilize Population: $10.5 billion[9]

Stop Deforestation: $7 billion[13]

Provide Clean, Safe Energy
- **Renewable Energy:** $17 billion[7]
- **Energy Efficiency:** $33 billion[5]

Prevent Global Warming: $8 billion

Prevent Acid Rain: $8 billion[13]

Eliminate Illiteracy: $5 billion[5]

Retire Developing Nations' Debt: $30 billion[8]

Provide Shelter: $21 billion[3]

Provide Health Care: $15 billion[2]

Provide Safe, Clean Water: $50 billion[4]

Eliminate Starvation and Malnourishment: $19 billion[1]

...using World Military Expenditures.

The above are annual costs of various global programs for solving the major human need and environmental problems facing humanity. Each program is the amount needed to accomplish the goal for all in need in the world. Their combined total cost is approximately 25% of the world's total annual military expenditures. Footnotes and references are [page 103]. Full explanatory text is in "Doing the Right Things," available from the World Game Institute at the address on the reverse.

Total Chart = Total Annual = World Military Expenditures: $1 trillion

= One-tenth of One Percent of Annual World Military Expenditures: $1 billion

= Amount That Was Needed to Eradicate Smallpox From the World (Accomplished 1978): $300 Million

FIG. 8.1. *(Continued)*

What the World Wants

This chart seeks to make the point that what the world needs to solve the major systemic problems confronting humanity is both available and affordable. Clearly, to portray a problem as complex and large as, for example, the global food situation, with just a small part of a single graph is incomplete, at best. The following explanations of the chart's various components are not intended as complete or detailed plans, but rather as very broad brush-strokes intended to give the overall direction, scope and strategy. The paper, "Doing the Right Things" goes into more detail and is available from the World Game Institute at the address below. (References listed at end of numbered sections contain supporting documentation, further explication, and related information.)

1. Eliminate starvation and malnourishment: $19 billion per year total; $2 billion per year for 10 years for global famine relief—spent on international grain reserve and emergency famine relief; $10 billion per year for twenty years spent on farmer education through vastly expanded in-country extension services that teach/demonstrate sustainable agriculture, use of local fertilizer sources, pest and soil management techniques, post harvest preservation, and which provide clear market incentives for increased local production; $7 billion per year for indigenous fertilizer development. Educational resources of #10 coupled with this strategy. Closely linked with #'s 2, 2A, 2B, 4, 5, 9, 10.

2. Provide health care: $15 billion per year spent on providing primary, health care through community health workers to all areas in the world that do not have access to health care. Closely linked with #'s 1, 3, 4, 5.

2A. Child health care: $2.5 billion per year spent on: a) providing Vitamin A to children who lack it in their diet, thereby preventing blindness in 250,000 children/year; b) providing oral rehydration therapy for children with severe diarrhoea; and c) immunizing 1 billion children in developing world against measles, tuberculosis, diphtheria, whooping cough, polio and tetanus, thereby preventing the death of 6–7 million children/year.

2B. Special health problems: $40 million per year for iodine addition to table salt to eliminate iodine deficiency, thereby reducing the 190 million who suffer from goiter and not adding to the 3 million who suffer from overt cretinism.

3. Eliminate inadequate housing and homelessness: $21 billion for ten years spent on making available materials, tools and techniques to people without adequate housing. Closely linked with #'s 1, 4, 5, 9.

4. Provide clean and abundant water: $50 billion per year for ten years spent on water and sanitation projects—wells, pipes, water purifying systems. Closely related to #'s 1, 2, 3, 9.

5. Eliminate illiteracy: $4.5 billion per year for ten years; $2 billion spent on a system of 10 to 12 communication satellites and their launching; $2 billion spent on ten million televisions, satellite dish receivers, and photovoltaic/battery units for power—all placed in village schools and other needed areas throughout high illiteracy areas; the rest (90% of funds), spent on culturally appropriate literacy programming and maintenance of system. Closely related to #'s 1, 2, 3, 4, 9, 10, 11.

6. Increase efficiency: $33 billion per year for ten years spent on increasing car fleet mileage to over 50 m.p.g., plus increasing

appliance, industrial processes, and household energy and materials use efficiency to state of the art. Closely linked with #'s 7, 8, 12, 13, 14.

7. Increase renewable energy: $20 billion per year for ten years spent on tax and other incentives for installation of renewable energy devices, graduated ten year phase-out of subsidies to fossil and nuclear fuels, research and development into more advanced renewable energy harnessing devices. Closely linked with #'s 6, 8, 11, 12, 13, 14.

8. Debt management: $30 billion per year for ten years spent on retiring $450 billion or more of current debt discounted to 50% face value. (Much of developing world's current debt is already discounted to 10–25% face value.) Not only helps developing countries get out of debt, but helps banks stay solvent. Closely linked with #'s 1, 6, 7, 10, 11, 14.

9. Stabilize population: $10.5 billion per year for ten years spent on making birth control universally available. Closely linked with #'s 1, 2, 3, 4, 5.

10. Reverse soil erosion: $24 billion per year for ten years spent on converting one-tenth of the world's most vulnerable cropland that is simultaneously most susceptible to erosion, the location of most severe erosion, and the land that is no longer able to sustain agriculture, to pasture or woodland; and conserving and regenerating topsoil on remaining lands through sustainable farming techniques. Both accomplished through a combination of government regulation and incentive programs that remove the most vulnerable lands from crop production; and by farmer education through vastly expanded in-country extension services that teach/demonstrate sustainable agriculture and soil management techniques. Closely linked to #1.

11. Reverse deforestation: $7 billion per year for ten years spent on reforesting 150 million hectares needed to sustain ecological, fuelwood, and wood products needs. Planted by local villagers, costs would be $400 per hectare, including seedling costs. Additional costs for legislation, financial incentives, enforcement of rainforest protection. Closely linked with #10 and 14.

12. Reverse ozone depletion: $5 billion per year for twenty years spent on phasing in substitutes for CFCs, CFC taxes, incentives for further research and development. Closely linked with #14.

13. Stop acid rain: $8 billion per year for ten years spent on combination of tax incentive, government regulation and direct assistance programs that place pollution control devices (electrostatic precipitators, etc.) on all industrial users of coal, increase efficiency of industrial processes, transportation, and appliances. Closely linked to #6, 7, 11, 14.

14. Stop global warming: $8 billion per year for thirty years spent on reducing carbon dioxide, methane and CFC release into atmosphere through combination of international accords, carbon taxes, increases in energy efficiency in industry, transportation, and household, decreases in fossil fuel use, increases in renewable energy use and reforestation. Closely linked with #'s 6, 7, 11, 12, 13.

FIG. 8.1. While the world spends approximately $1 trillion on militaries, human needs and environmental problems remain unsolved. If just 25% of the military budget were redirected to solve social and environmental problems, they could be alleviated. World Game Institute, 1994 ©, now owned by O. S. Earth. Reprinted by permission. Available online: www.worldgame.org/wwwproject/.

global issues, but feel less responsible for them (Uzzell, 2000). Unfortunately, people don't seem to notice local problems. This disconnect contributes to a widespread sense of powerlessness over increasingly worrisome global trends. Because it is difficult to effect change on a global level, local action is imperative. But people are unlikely to act locally if they do not even know about the environmental issues in their local settings.

Uzzell suggested several reasons why people fail to recognize problems on a local level. We were intrigued to see that the reasons Uzzell formulated closely follow the major chapters of this book: He suggested the following:

• From a Freudian perspective, people use denial to reduce fear and anxiety, perhaps even more so as the risks are closer. Deborah had a recent experience of this explanation when she met someone hired to incinerate nerve gas at the Umatilla Army Chemical Weapons Depot in northeastern Oregon. Despite the fact that 34 workers were sent to the hospital after suffering symptoms of nerve gas poisoning in 1999 (vomiting, chest pains, difficulty breathing) (http://www.house.gov/defazio/ 073100DERelease. shtml), the worker she met believed that incinerating the gas is very safe and did not remember anything about any hospitalized workers. Deborah, on the other hand, who lives about 60 miles from the site, is more dubious.

• From a social perspective, Uzzell urged environmental educators to teach about local problems so that students create attributions of responsibility. When environmental education focuses only on the global level, issues are too abstract, leading people to conclude that the problems are not theirs to help solve.

• From a behavioral perspective, Uzell noted that local effects of environmentally relevant behavior are not readily noticeable, so rewards and costs are not directly experienced. For example, if we recycle cans, we may never see the impact on a local level.

• Uzell also suggested that physiologically, our nervous systems are not wired to pick up small effects over a long period of time, because of sensory adaptation and limitations. We would add that the long delay between exposure and health outcomes reduces our ability to notice the physiological impacts at a local level.

• Cognitively, Uzell proposed that because dramatic, rare causes of death are overestimated (e.g., nuclear accidents), whereas more mundane, common deaths are underestimated (e.g., automobile accidents) people are less likely to pay attention to local risks that are at play everyday.

• And, we'll add, from an ecopsychology perspective, perhaps it is easier for some people to connect with an abstract notion like Gaia, than it is to hold active membership in our local communities, where disagreement with our neighbors and friends over environmental questions may be more aversive.

Fortunately, environmental psychologists have articulated principles for helping local citizens work on sustainability issues. For example, Wisenfeld and Sanchez (2002) described the importance of community participation for formulating and making decisions about local environmental resources and land uses. When local citizens are involved in community decisions, they are empowered by their responsibility, by ties among members, and by feelings of belonging to place. From interviews with participants in various local projects, such as waste incineration and organic agriculture, Wisenfeld and Sanchez showed that successful community work resulted in people examining their basic assumptions for new ways to think about and solve problems. Participation is enhanced when people feel bonded to their place, and they remain involved because they feel common risks and benefits to the community's water, air, or land use. S. Kaplan (2000) and Clinebell (1996) made similar arguments.

Strategies for engaging in community-based environmental work has been effectively developed and made widely accessible online by McKenzie-Mohr (http://www.cbsm) through his framework called "community-based social marketing" (CBSM) (McKenzie-Mohr, 2000a, 2000b). CBSM uses principles of social psychology, promoting behavior change at the community level with direct contact between people. Noting that information campaigns have limited effects, McKenzie-Mohr approached behavior change by addressing barriers and designing incentives, using such concepts as commitment, feedback, framing, modeling, norms, prompts, and social diffusion, all concepts that we have addressed in this book. CBSM has been widely used by community groups to change environmentally relevant behaviors, including composting, energy use, waste disposal, recycling, littering, reuse, resource reduction, transportation, waste reduction, and water efficiency. The Web site is a valuable resource offering research and a how-to manual online.

Another useful Web site is www.greenmap.org, which helps citizens map their local communities for green sites, such as hiking trails, wildlife reserves, cultural sites, green businesses, environmental hot spots, and public transportation options. Constructing greenmaps is a good method for citizens to work locally to provide and access better information about what is available in their communities, put pressure on local businesses to participate in environmentally responsible practices, and monitor progress toward a sustainable world.

CONCLUSIONS

Using psychology to solve environmental problems means balancing our knowledge of the complexity of our problems with a commitment to working diligently on them, especially in local contexts. It means rethinking our own consumption in light of the billions of people who now live in destitution, disentangling ourselves from the consumer culture, and promoting self-reliance and cultural integrity among all people on the planet. This goal implies a serious and difficult look at the planet's distribution of wealth, power, and environmentally damaging patterns, and a personal commitment to changing both our own behaviors as well as the larger structures that propel them.

The Cost of Inaction

One of the ways in which we contribute to environmental decline is by knowing a lot but not acting on that knowledge. Higher education is traditionally conducted along these lines. Action and activism are not typically included as key features of college classrooms, for fear they will create ideological robots out of our students. We appreciate the importance of carefully considering and debating our actions before doing them; we also believe that it is impossible to completely know the results of our behavior before undertaking it. But we also think, along with John Dewey (1929), that we do not really understand an idea until we apply it. We learn more about an idea from experiencing how it works, especially if we remain diligently open to feedback from our experience. Service learning in higher education addresses this insight about how people learn. For example, at Willamette University where Sue teaches, the importance of community involvement in college classes is acknowledged by the motto "Not unto ourselves alone are we born."

Moreover, inaction will insure that business proceeds as usual, whereas undertaking action will change us, as well as the world around us. Sometimes we will make mistakes, but we will not learn from them if we never make them.

The appendix lists some valuable sources for designing your own responses, joining others in groups or in agencies, reconsidering your consumer choices, and helping solve specific resource or pollution problems. No matter what actions you decide to take, becoming aware of your behavior, your thoughts, and your feelings, will significantly facilitate your effectiveness. But you cannot do anything for sustainability or for yourself until you begin.

As you select your actions, you will likely experience many of the defenses we discussed in this book. Keep track of them, but be careful about giving them too much power. You may feel overwhelmed. Feeling overwhelmed is a constant, recurring liability in this work because as we learn more, we learn how interconnected and colossal are the structures that are driving ecological destruction. Focusing on specific behaviors can help mitigate the experience of feeling overwhelmed, even though those feelings are likely to recur. Yet allowing ourselves to slip into despair or helplessness is the *most* destructive path—destructive because it undermines our own growth and maturity, and destructive because it insures a planetary outcome that justifies our despair. Just as we can best confront our feelings of being overwhelmed by action, so too is despair best confronted through action. In Lopez' (1990) words,

> If we become the prisoners of our own minds, if we think ourselves into despair, we can step onto wounded ground with a shovel and begin to plant trees. They will grow. They will hold the soil, provide shelter for birds, warm someone's home after we are gone. If we lose faith in ourselves, we can in those moments forget ourselves and dwell on the future of the larger community, on the blessing of neighbors. (p. 53)

And so it is essential to proceed gently, with conviction, patience, perseverance, and most of all, with trust—trust in yourself, as well as in the interconnected wholeness that embraces you. "If you take one step with all the knowledge you have, there is usually just enough light shining to show you the next step" (Williams, 1994, p. 94).

May your steps be steady, graceful, revealing, and rewarding, and may you know them as part of the greater ecological dance.

KEY CONCEPTS

Community-based social marketing
Next industrial revolution
Voluntary simplicity

6 principles:
- Visualize healthy ecosystems
- Work with small steps and big ideas
- Think circle instead of line
- Consider ways in which less is more
- Practice conscious consumption
- Act on personal and political levels

References

Abram, D. (1987). The perceptual implications of Gaia. *Revision, 9*(2), 7–15.

Abramovitz, J. N. (1998). *Taking a stand: Cultivating a new relationship with the world's forests*. Worldwatch paper no. 140. Washington, DC: Worldwatch Institute.

Agency income report (2002). Retrieved December 1, 2002, from http://www.adage.com

Alhakami, A. S., & Slovic, P. (1994). A psychological study of the inverse relationship between perceived risk and perceived benefit. *Risk Analysis, 14*(6), 1085–1096.

American Psychiatric Association. (2000). *Diagnostic and statistical manual of mental disorders* (4th ed., text revision). Washington, DC: APA.

Anderson, R. C. (1998). *Mid-course correction: Toward a sustainable enterprise: The Interface model*. Atlanta, GA: Peregrinzilla Press.

Anthony, C. (1995). Eco-psychology and the deconstruction of whiteness. In T. Roszak, M. E. Gomes, & A. D. Kanner (Eds.), *Eco-psychology: Restoring the earth, healing the mind* (pp. 263–278). San Francisco, CA: Sierra Club.

Antrobus, P. (1993). Quoted at the Global Assembly of Women for a Healthy Planet, Miami. In J. Seager (Ed.), *Earth follies: Coming to feminist terms with the global environmental crisis* (pp. 269–270). New York: Routledge.

Appleton, J. (1975). *The experience of landscape*. London: Wiley.

Arbuthnot, J., Tedeschi, R., Wayner, M., Turner, J., Kressel, S., & Rush, R. (1977). The induction of sustained recycling behavior through foot-in-the-door technique. *Journal of Environmental Systems, 6*, 353–366.

Archer, D., Aronson, E., Pettigrew, T. F., Condelli, L., Curbow, B., McLeod, B., & White, L. T. (1983). *An evaluation of the energy conservation research of California's major utility companies, 1977–1980.* Report to the California Public Utilities Commission, February 10, 1983. Energy Conservation Research Group, Stevenson College, University of California, Santa Cruz, CA.

Arnetz, B. B. (1998). Environmental illness: Multiple chemical sensitivity, sick building syndrome, electric and magnetic field disease. In A. Lundberg (Ed.), *The environment and mental health: A guide for clinicians* (pp. 115–146). Hillsdale, NJ: Lawrence Erlbaum Associates.

Arnold, R. (1993). *Ecology wars: Environmentalism as if people mattered.* Bellevue, WA: Meril Press.

Arnow, B., Kenardy, J., & Agras, W. S. (1992). Binge eating among the obese. *Journal of Behavioral Medicine, 15,* 155–170.

Aronson, E. (1994). *The social animal* (7th ed.). New York: Freeman.

Aronson, E., & O'Leary, M. (1982–1983). The relative effectiveness of models and prompts on energy conservation: A field experiment in a shower room. *Journal of Environmental Systems, 12,* 219–224.

Atkinson, R. L., Atkinson, R. C., Smith, E. E., & Bem, D. J. (1993). *Introduction to psychology* (11th ed.). Fort Worth, TX: Harcourt Brace Jovanovich.

Atyi, R. E., & Simula, M. (2002). Forest certification: Pending challenges for tropical lumber. *ITTO (International Tropical Timber Association) International Workshop on Comparability and Equivalence of Forest Certification Schemes.* Retrieved October 29, 2002 from http://www.itto.or.jp/inside/workshop/download/Overview-Paper.pdf

Bailey, R. (1993). *Eco-Scam: The false prophets of ecological apocalypse.* New York: St. Martin's Press.

Baltes, M. M., & Hayward, S. C. (1976). Application and evaluation of strategies to reduce pollution: Behavior control of littering in a football stadium. *Journal of Applied Psychology, 61,* 501–506.

Banaji, M. R., & Crowder, R. G. (1989). The bankruptcy of everyday memory. *American Psychologist, 44,* 1185–1193.

Barnes, G. E., & Prosen, H. (1985). Parental death and depression. *Journal of Abnormal Psychology, 94,* 64–69.

Baum, W. M. (1994). *Understanding behaviorism: Science, behavior, and culture.* New York: HarperCollins.

Bazerman, M. H. (1983). Negotiator judgment: A critical look at the rationality assumption. *American Behavioral Scientist, 27*(2), 211–228.

Bazerman, M. H., & Hoffman, A. J. (1999). Sources of environmentally destructive behavior: Individual, organizational, and institutional perspectives. *Research in Organizational Behavior, 2,* 39–79.

Bell, P. A., Greene, T. C., Fisher, J. D., & Baum, A. (2001). *Environmental psychology* (5th ed.). Fort Worth, TX: Harcourt College.

Bell, P. A., Petersen, T. R., & Hautaluoma, J. E. (1989). The effect of punishment probability on overconsumption and stealing in a simulated commons. *Journal of Applied Social Psychology, 19,* 1483–1495.

Bellinger, D. C., & Adams, H. F. (2001). Environmental pollutant exposures and children's cognitive abilities. In R. J. Sternberg & E. L. Grigorenko (Eds.), *Environmental effects on cognitive abilities* (pp. 157–188). Hillsdale, NJ: Lawrence Erlbaum Associates.

Bilder, R. M., & LeFever, F. F. (1998). *Neuroscience of the mind on the centennial of Freud's project for scientific psychology* (1895). Annals of NY Academy of Sciences: Vol. 843. New York: New York Academy of Sciences.

Birjulin, A. A., Smith, J. M., & Bell, P. A. (1993). Monetary reward, verbal reinforcement, and harvest strategy of others in the commons dilemma. *Journal of Social Psychology, 133*(2), 207–214.

Björkman, M. (1984). Decision making, risk taking and psychological time: Review of empirical findings and psychological theory. *Scandinavian Journal of Psychology, 25,* 31–49.

Black, J. S., Stern, P. C., & Elsworth, J. T. (1985). Personal and contextual influences on household energy adaptations. *Journal of Applied Psychology, 70,* 3–21.

Bloom, A. (1987). *The closing of the American mind: How higher education has failed democracy and impoverished the souls of today's students.* New York: Simon & Schuster.

Boaz, N. T. (2002). *Evolving health: The origins of illness and how the modern world is making us sick.* New York: Wiley.

Boring, E. G. (1957). *A history of experimental psychology* (2nd ed.). New York: Appleton-Century-Crofts.

Bostrom, A., & Fischhoff, B. (2001). Communicating health risks of global climate change. *Research in Social Problems and Public Policy, 9,* 31–56.

Bowlby, J. (1989). The role of attachment in personality development and psychopathology. In S. I. Greenspan & G. H. Pollock (Eds.), *The course of life* (Vol. 1, pp. 229–270). Madison, CT: International University Press.

Bragg, E. A. (1996). Towards ecological self: Deep ecology meets constructionist self-theory. *Journal of Environmental Psychology, 16,* 93–108.

Broadhurst, P. L. (1959). The interaction of task difficulty and motivation: The Yerkes–Dodson Law revived. *Acta Psychologica, 16,* 321–338.

Bronzaft, A. L. (2002). Noise pollution: A hazard to physical and mental well-being. In R. B. Bechtel & A. Churchman (Eds.), *Handbook of environmental psychology* (pp. 499–510). New York: Wiley.

Brower, M., & Leon, W. (1999). *The consumer's guide to effective environmental choices.* Cambridge, MA: Three Rivers Press.

Brown, L. (2001). *Eco-economy: Building an economy for the earth.* New York: Norton.

Bullard, R. D. (1983, Spring). Solid waste sites and the Black Houston community. *Sociological Inquiry, 53,* 273–288.

Bullard, R. D. (1990, Winter). Ecological inequities and the New South: Black communities under siege. *Journal of Ethnic Studies, 17,* 101–115.

Bullard, R. D. (1993). *Confronting environmental racism: Voices from the grassroots.* Boston: South End Press.

Bullard, R. D. (1994). *Dumping in Dixie: Race, class and environmental quality.* Boulder, CO: Westview Press.

Bullard, R. D. (1996). *Unequal protection: Environmental justice and communities of color.* San Francisco, CA: Sierra Club.

Bullard, R. D., & Johnson, G. S. (2000). Environmental justice: Grassroots activism and its impact on public policy decision making. *Journal of Social Issues, 56*(3), 555–578.

Burtt, E. A. (1954). *The metaphysical foundations of modern science.* Garden City, NY: Doubleday.

Bush, G. W. (2002, February 14). *President announces clear skies & global climate change initiatives.* White House press release. Retrieved August 10, 2002, from http://www.whitehouse.gov/news/releases/2002/02/20020214-5.html

Butterfield, H. (1960). *The origins of modern science, 1300–1800.* New York: Macmillan.

Cairns, J. (1998). The Zen of sustainable use of the planet: Steps on the path to enlightenment. *Population and Environment, 20*(2), 109–123.

Calahan, W. (1995). Ecological groundedness in Gestalt therapy. In T. Roszak, M. E. Gomes, & A. D. Kanner (Eds.), *Ecopsychology: Restoring the earth, healing, the mind* (pp. 216–223). San Francisco, CA: Sierra Club.

Callicott, J. B. (1994). The land aesthetic. In K. C. Chapple & M. E. Tucker (Eds.), *Ecological prospects: Scientific, religious, and aesthetic perspectives* (pp. 169–184). Albany, NY: State University of New York Press.

Cancer Research Treatment Foundation (2002). *Research.* Retrieved August 22, 2002, from http://www.ctrf.org/research.htm

Carlson, N. (1995). *Foundations of physiological psychology* (3rd ed.). Needham Heights, MA: Allyn & Bacon.

Carson, R. (1962). *Silent spring.* New York: Houghton Mifflin.

Casey, L., & Lloyd, M. (1977). Cost and effectiveness of litter removal procedures in an amusement park. *Environment and Behavior, 9,* 535–546.

Catton, W. R. (1993). Carrying capacity and the death of a culture: A tale of two autopsies. *Sociological Inquiry, 63,* 202–222.

Center for Disease Control (1999, November 19). Nonfatal and fatal firearm-related injuries—United States, 1993–1997 [Electronic version]. *Morbidity and Mortality Weekly Report, 48*(45), 1029–1034. Retrieved October 21, 2002, from http://www.cdc.gov/mmwr/preview/mmwrhtml/mm4845a1.htm

Center for Disease Control (2002, September 11). Impact of September 11 attacks on workers in the vicinity of the World Trade Center—New York City [Electronic version]. *Morbidity and Mortality Weekly Report, 51(Special Issue),* 8–10. Retrieved October, 21, 2002, from http://www.cdc.gov/mmwr/preview/mmwrhtml/mm51SPa3.htm

Chodorow, N. (1978). *The reproduction of mothering: Psychoanalysis and the sociology of gender.* Berkeley, CA: University of California Press.

Chodorow, N. (1989). *Feminism and psychoanalytic theory.* New Haven, CT: Yale University Press.

Cialdini, R. B., Kallgren, C. A., & Reno, R. R. (1991). A focus theory of normative conduct: A theoretical refinement and reevaluation of the role of norms in human behavior. *Advances in Experimental Social Psychology, 24,* 201–234.

Cialdini, R. B., Reno, R. R., & Kallgren, C. A. (1990). A focus theory of normative conduct: Recycling the concept of norms to reduce littering in public places. *Journal of Personality and Social Psychology, 58,* 1015–1026.

Clark, M. E. (1989). *Ariadne's thread: The search for new modes of thinking.* New York: St. Martin's Press.

Clayton, S. (1994). Appeals to justice in the environmental debate. *Journal of Social Issues, 50*(3), 13–27.

Clayton, S. (2000). Models of justice in the environmental debate. *Journal of Social Issues, 56*(3), 459–474.

Clinebell, H. (1996). *Ecotherapy: Healing ourselves, healing the earth.* New York: Haworth.

Cobern, M. K., Porter, B. E., Leeming, F. C., & Dwyer, W. W. (1995). The effect of commitment on adoption and diffusion of grass recycling. *Environment and Behavior, 27,* 213–232.

Cohen, M. J. (1993). Integrated ecology: The process of counseling with nature. *Humanistic Psychologist, 21*(3), 277–295.

Cohen, M. J. (1997). *Reconnecting with nature.* Corvallis, OR: Ecopress.

Collins, A. M., & Loftus, E. F. (1975). A spreading-activation theory of semantic processing. *Psychological Review, 82*(6), 407–428.

Cone, J. D., & Hayes, S. C. (1980). *Environmental problems/behavioral solutions.* Monterey, CA: Brooks/Cole.

Conn, S. (1991). The self-world connection: Implications for mental health and psychotherapy. *Woman of Power, 20*, 71–77.

Conn, S. (1995). When the earth hurts, who responds? In T. Roszak, M. E. Gomes, & A. D. Kanner (Eds.), *Eco-psychology: Restoring the earth, healing the mind* (pp. 156–171). San Francisco: Sierra Club.

Co-op America Quarterly (2002). Spring, p. 25.

Co-op America (2003). *National green pages: A directory of products and services for people and the planet.* Washington, DC: Co-op America.

Costanzo, M., Archer, D., Aronson, E., & Pettigrew, T. (1986). Energy conservation behavior: The difficult path from information to action. *American Psychologist, 41*(5), 521–528.

Covello, V. T. (1993). Public confidence in industry and government: A crisis in environmental risk communication. In G. T. Miller (Ed.), *Living in the environment: An introduction to environmental science* (7th ed., p. 572). Belmont, CA: Wadsworth.

Craig, C. S., & McCann, J. M. (1978). Assessing communication effects on energy conservation. *Journal of Consumer Research, 5*, 82–88.

Csikszentmihalyi, M. (1999). If we are so rich, why aren't we happy? *American Psychologist, 54*(10), 821–827.

Cvetkovich, G., & Earle, T. (1992). Environmental hazards and the public. *Journal of Social Issues, 48*(4), 1–20.

Damasio, A. R. (1994a). *Descartes' error: Emotion, reason, and the human brain.* New York: Grosset/Putnam.

Damasio, A. R. (1994b). Descartes' error and the future of human life. *Scientific American, 271*(4), 144.

Davidson, L. M., & Baum, A. (1996). Chronic stress and posttraumatic stress disorder. *Journal of Consulting and Clinical Psychology, 54*, 303–308.

Dawes, R. M. (1980). Social dilemmas. *Annual Review of Psychology, 31*, 169–193.

Dennis, M. L., Soderstrom, E. J., Koncinski, W. S., & Cavanaugh, B. (1990). Effective dissemination of energy-related information: Applying social psychology and evaluation research. *American Psychologist, 45*(19), 1109–1117.

Devall, B., & Sessions, G. (1985). *Deep ecology: Living as if nature mattered.* Salt Lake City, UT: Peregrine Smith.

Dewey, J. (1929). *The quest for certainty.* New York: Capricorn Books.

Diamond, I., & Orenstein, G. F. (1990). Introduction. In I. Diamond & G. F. Orenstein (Eds.), *Reweaving the world: The emergence of ecofeminism* (pp. ix–xv). San Francisco, CA: Sierra Club.

Dinan, F. J., & Bieron, J. F. (2002). *To spray or not to spray: A debate over malaria and DDT. Case teaching notes.* Retrieved August 24, 2002 from http://ublib.buffalo.edu/libraries/projects/cases/ddt/ddt_notes.html

Dominguiz, J., & Robin V. (1999). *Your money or your Life* (2nd ed.). New York: Penguin.

Dunlap, R. E., Gallup, G. H., & Gallup, A. M. (1992). *The health of the planet survey: A preliminary report on attitudes toward the environment and economic growth measured by surveys of citizens in 22 nations to date.* Princeton, NJ: The George H. Gallup International Institute.

Dunlap, R. E., & Saad, L. (2001). Only one in four Americans are anxious about the environment. *The Gallup Poll Monthly, 427*, 6–16.

Dunlap, R. E., & Van Liere, K. D. (1978). The "New Environmental Paradigm": A proposed measuring instrument and preliminary results. *Journal of Environmental Education, 9*(4), 10–19.

Dunlap, R. E., & Van Liere, K. D. (1984). Commitment to the dominant social paradigm and concern for environmental quality. *Social Science Quarterly, 65*(4), 1013–1028.

Dunlap, R. E., Van Liere, K., Mertig, A., & Jones, R. E. (2000). Measuring endorsement of the new ecological paradigm: A revised NEP scale. *Journal of Social Issues, 56*(3), 425–442.

Dunn, S., & Flavin, C. (2002). Moving the climate change agenda forward. In C. Flavin, H. French, & G. Gardner (Eds.), *State of the world 2002: A Worldwatch Institute report on progress toward a sustainable society* (pp. 24–50). New York: Norton.

Durenberger, D., Mott, L., & Sagoff, M. (1991, March/April). A dissenting voice. *EPA Journal, 17*(2), 49–52.

Durning, A. (1991). Asking how much is enough. In L. Brown (Ed.), *State of the world* (p. 169). New York: Norton.

Durning, A. T. (1992). *How much is enough? The consumer society and the future of the earth.* New York: Norton.

Durning, A. T. (1993). *Saving the forests: What will it take?* Worldwatch Paper no. 117. Washington, DC: Worldwatch Institute. Retrieved September, 22, 2002, from http://www.worldwatch.org/pubs/paper/117.html

Ebreo, A., Hershey, J., & Vining, J. (1999). Reducing solid waste: Linking recycling to environmentally responsible consumerism. *Environment and Behavior, 31*(1), 107–135.

Ehrlich, P. R., & Ehrlich, A. H. (1991). *Healing the planet: Strategies for resolving the environmental crisis* (pp. 7–10). Reading, MA: Addison-Wesley.

Ehrlich, P. A., & Holdren, J. (1971). The impact of population growth. *Science, 171*, 1212–1217.

Elgin, D. (1981). *Voluntary simplicity: Toward a way of life that is outwardly simple, inwardly rich.* New York: Morrow Quill Paperbacks.

Elgin, D. (1993). *Voluntary simplicity: Toward a way of life that is outwardly simple, inwardly rich* (rev. ed.). New York: Quill.

Elgin, D. (2000). *The garden of simplicity.* Retrieved Dec. 15, 2002, from http://www.simpleliving.net/webofsimplicity/the_garden_of_simplicity.asp

Engelman, R., Halweil, B., & Nierenberg, D. (2002). Rethinking population, improving lives. In C. Flavin, H. French, & G. Gardner (Eds.), *State of the world 2002: A Worldwatch Institute report on progress toward a sustainable society* (p. 127). New York: Norton.

Environmental Protection Agency (2002a). *Asthma and upper respiratory illnesses. Office of Children's Health Protection.* Retrieved April 30, 2002, from http://www.epa.gov/children/asthma.htm

Environmental Protection Agency (2002b). Data from the American Association of Poison Control Centers. *Office of Pesticide Programs: Pesticides and Child Safety.* Retrieved July 27, 2002, from http://www.epa.gov/pesticides/citizens/childsaf.htm

Environmental Protection Agency (2002c, July 23). *Persistant bioaccumulative and toxic chemical program.* Retrieved July 27, 2002, from http://www.epa.gov/pbt/

Environmental Protection Agency (2002d). *Technology transfer network: National air toxics assessment, estimated risk: Summary of results.* Retrieved July 27, 2002, from http://www.epa.gov/ttn/atw/nata/risksum.html

Environmental Protection Agency (2002e). *What the pesticide residue limits are on food. Office of Pesticide Programs.* Retrieved July 27, 2002, from http://www.epa.gov/pesticides/food/viewtols.htm

Environmental Working Group (2000, April). Banned pesticide, others found on Washington State apples. Retrieved July 23, 2002, from http://www.ewg.org/reports/fewbadapples/pressrelease.html

Epstein, P. R. (2000, August). Is global warming harmful to health? *Scientific American,* 50–57.

Evans, G. W., & Cohen, S. (1987). Environmental stress. In D. Stokols & I. Altman (Eds.), *Handbook of environmental psychology* (pp. 571–610). New York: Wiley.

Everett, P. B., Hayward, S. C., & Meyers, A. W. (1974). The effects of a token reinforcement procedure on bus ridership. *Journal of Applied Behavior Analysis, 7*, 1–9.

Feaster, D. J., Goodkin, K., Blaney, N. T., Baldewicz, T. T., Tuttle, R. S., Woodward, C., Szapocznik, J., Eisdorfer, C., Baum, M. K., & Fletcher, M. A. (2000). Longitudinal psychoneuroimmunologic relationships in the natural history of HIV-1 infection: The stressor-support-coping model. In K. Goodkin & A. P. Visser (Eds.), *Psychoneuroimmunology: Stress, mental disorders, and health* (pp. 153–193). Washington, DC: American Psychiatric Press.

Festinger, L., Schachter, S., & Reicken, H. (1956). *When prophecy fails*. Minneapolis, MN: University of Minnesota Press.

Finucane, M. L. (in press). The psychology of risk judgments and decisions. In S. Cameron, N. Cromar, & H. Fallowfield (Eds.), *Environmental health in Australia and New Zealand*. New York: Oxford University Press.

Finucane, M. L., Alhakami, A., Slovic, P., & Johnson, S. M. (2000). The affect heuristic in judgments of risks and benefits. *Journal of Behavioral Decision Making, 13*, 1–17.

Fischhoff, B. (1990). Psychology and public policy: Tool or toolmaker? *American Psychologist, 45*(5), 647–653.

Fisher, A. (2002). *Radical eco-psychology: Psychology in the service of life*. Albany, NY: State University of New York Press.

Flynn, L. R., & Goldsmith, E. (1994). Opinion leadership in green consumption: An exploratory study. *Journal of Social Behavior and Personality, 9*, 543–553.

Forgas, J. P. (1999). Network theories and beyond. In T. Dalgleish & M. J. Power (Eds.), *Handbook of cognition and emotion* (pp. 591–611). New York: Wiley.

Fox, J., & Guyer, M. (1978). "Public" choice and cooperation in n-person prisoner's dilemma. *Journal of Conflict Resolution, 22*, 468–481.

Fox, M. R. (1987). *Perspective in risk: Compared to what?* Paper presented to the American Society of Heating, Refrigeration, and Air Conditioning Engineers, Nashville, June 1987. Reprinted in *Vital Speeches of the Day*, September 15, pp. 730–733.

Fox, W. (1990a). *Toward a transpersonal ecology: Developing new foundations for environmentalism*. Boston: Shambala.

Fox, W. (1990b). Transpersonal ecology: "Psychologizing" ecophilosophy. *Journal of Transpersonal Psychology, 22*(1), 59–96.

Frank, L. D., & Engelke, P. O. (2001). The built environment and human activity patterns: Exploring the impact of urban form on public health. *Journal of Planning Literature, 16*(2), 202–218.

Freud, S. (1927). The future of an illusion. In P. Gray (Ed.), *The Freud reader* (p. 693). New York: Norton.

Freud, S. (1961). *Civilization and its discontents* (J. Strachey, Trans.). New York: Norton. (Original work published 1930)

Freud, S. (1949). An outline of psycho-analysis. James Strachey (Trans.). London: Hogarth.

Freud, S. (1964). Splitting of the ego in the process of defense. In J. Strachey & A. Freud (Eds.), *The standard edition of the complete psychological works of Sigmund Freud* (pp. 275–276). London: Hogarth. (Original work published 1938)

Freudenburg, W. R., & Pastor, S. K. (1992). NIMBYs and LULUs: Stalking the syndromes. *Journal of Social Issues, 48*(4), 39–61.

Frumkin, H. (2001). Beyond toxicity: Human health and the natural environment. *American Journal of Preventive Medicine, 20*(3), 234–240.

Gardner, G. (2002). The challenge for Johannesburg: Creating a more secure world. In C. Flavin, H. French, & G. Gardner (Eds.), *State of the world 2002: A Worldwatch Institute report on progress toward a sustainable society* (pp. 3–23). New York: Norton.

Gardner, G. T., & Stern, P. C. (1996). *Environmental problems and human behavior*. Boston: Allyn & Bacon.

Gardner, G. T., & Stern, P. C. (2002). *Environmental problems and human behavior* (2nd ed.). Boston: Pearson Custom Publishing.

Gaulin, S.J.C., & McBurney, D. H. (2001). *Psychology: An evolutionary approach*. Upper Saddle River, NJ: Prentice-Hall.

Gay, P. (1989). Introduction. In P. Gay (Ed.), *The Freud reader* (pp. xiii–xiv). New York: Norton.

Gazzaniga, M. S. (1998). Why can't I control my brain? Aspects of conscious experience. In M. Ito, Y. Miyashita, & E. T. Rolls (Eds.), *Cognition, computation, and consciousness* (pp. 69–80). Oxford, England: Oxford University Press.

Gazzaniga, M. S., Ivry, R. B., & Mangun, G. R. (2002). *Cognitive neuroscience: The biology of the mind*. New York: Norton.

Gelbspan, R. (1998). *The heat is on*. Cambridge, MA: Perseus Books.

Gelbspan, R. (2001 May/June). A modest proposal to stop global warming. *Sierra Magazine*, 62–67.

Geller, E. S. (1987). Applied behavior analysis and environmental psychology: From strange bedfellows to a productive marriage. In D. S. Stokols & I. Altman (Eds.), *Handbook of environmental psychology* (Vol. 1, pp. 361–387). New York: Wiley.

Geller, E. S. (1990). Behavior analysis and environmental protection: Where have all the flowers gone? *Journal of Applied Behavior Analysis, 23*, 269–273.

Geller, E. S. (1992a). It takes more than information to save energy. *American Psychologist, 47*, 814–815.

Geller, E. S. (1992b). Solving environmental problems. In S. Staub & P. Green (Eds.), *Psychology and social responsibility: Facing global challenges* (pp. 248–270). New York: New York University Press.

Geller, E. S. (1994). The human element in integrated environmental management. In J. Cairns, T. V. Crawford, & H. Salwasser (Eds.), *Implementing integrated environmental management* (pp. 5–26). Blacksburg, VA: Virginia Polytechnic Institute & State University.

Geller, E. S. (1995). Actively caring for the environment: An integration of behaviorism and humanism. *Environment and Behavior, 27*, 184–195.

Geller, E. S. (2002). The challenge of increasing proenvironmental behavior. In R. B. Bechtel & A. Churchman (Eds.), *Handbook of environmental psychology* (pp. 525–540). New York: Wiley.

Geller, E. S., Winett, R. A., & Everett, P. B. (1982). *Preserving the environment: New strategies for behavior change*. Elmsford, NY: Pergamon.

Gerber, M. S. (1992). On the home front: The Cold War legacy of the Hanford nuclear site. Lincoln, NB: University of Nebraska Press.

Gevirtz, R. (2000). The physiology of stress. In D. T. Kenny, J. G. Carlson, E. F. McGuigan, & J. L. Sheppard (Eds.), *Stress and health: Research and clinical applications* (pp. 53–72). The Netherlands: Harwood Academic Publishers.

Gigerenzer, G. (2000). *Adaptive thinking: Rationality in the real world*. New York: Oxford University Press.

Goleman, D. (1995). *Emotional intelligence: Why it can matter more than IQ*. New York: Bantam.

Goodkin, K., & Visser, A. P. (2000). *Psychoneuroimmunology: Stress, mental disorders, and health*. Washington, DC: American Psychiatric Press.

Goodman, E. (2001, October). Quoted in *Sustainable Living*, a publication of the Oregon State University Extension Service, Corvallis, OR.

Goodstein, E. (1999). *The trade-off myth: Fact and fiction about jobs and the environment*. Washington, DC: Island Press.

Gray, L. (1995). Shamanic counseling and eco-psychology. In T. Roszak, M. E. Gomes, & A. D. Kanner (Eds.), *Eco-psychology: Restoring the earth, healing the mind* (pp. 172–182). San Francisco, CA: Sierra Club Books.

Greenberg, J. R., & Mitchell, S. A. (1983). *Object relations in psychoanalytic theory*. Cambridge, MA: Harvard University Press.

Greenway, R. (1995). The wilderness effect and ecopsychology. In T. Roszak, M. E. Gomes, & A. D. Kanner (Eds.), *Eco-psychology: Restoring the earth, healing the mind* (pp. 122–135). San Francisco: Sierra Club Books.

Gregory, R. (2000). Using stakeholder values to make smarter environmental decisions. *Environment, 42*(5), 34–44.

Hacket, B. (1984). Energy billing systems and the social control of energy use in a California apartment complex. In B. M. Morrison & W. Kempton (Eds.), *Families and energy: Coping with uncertainty* (p. 298). East Lansing: Michigan State University.

Hallin, P. O. (1995). Environmental concern and environmental behavior in Foley, a small town in Minnesota. *Environment and Behavior, 27*(4), 558–578.

Halweil, B. (2002). Farming in the public interest. In C. Flavin, H. French, & G. Gardner (Eds.), *State of the world 2002: A Worldwatch Institute report on progress toward a sustainable society* (pp. 51–74). New York: Norton.

Hardell, L., Lindstrom, G. van Bavel, B., Fredrikson, M., Liljegren, G., Becher, H., & Flesch-Janys, D. (1998). Some aspects of the etiology of non-Hodgkin's lymphoma. *Environmental Health Perspectives, 106*(2), 679–681.

Hardin, G. (1968, December). The tragedy of the commons. *Science*, 1243–1248.

Hardin, G. (2002). Moral implications of cultural carrying capacity. In G. T. Miller (Ed.), *Living in the environment: Principles, connections, and solutions* (12th ed., pp. 252–253). Belmont, CA: Wadsworth.

Harper, S. (1995). The way of wilderness. In. T. Roszak, M. E. Gomes, & A. D. Kanner (Eds.), *Ecopsychology: Restoring the earth, healing the mind* (pp. 183–200). San Francisco, CA: Sierra Club Books.

Harrigan, M. (1994, January/February). Can we transform the market without transforming the customer? *Home Energy Magazine Online*. Retrieved September 4, 2002, from http://homeenergy.org/archive/hem.dis.anl.gov/eehem/94/940109.html

Hartig, T., Kaiser, F. G., & Bowler, P. A. (2001). Psychological restoration in nature as a positive motivation for ecological behavior. *Environment and Behavior, 33*(4), 590–607.

Hawken, P. (1993). A declaration of sustainability: 12 steps society can take to save the whole enchilada. *Utne Reader*, September/October, p. 56.

Hawken, P., Lovins, A., & Lovins, L. H. (1999). *Natural capitalism: Creating the next industrial revolution*. Boston: Little Brown.

Hayes, S. C., & Cone, J. D. (1981). Reduction of residential consumption of electricity through simple monthly feedback. *Journal of Applied Behavior Analysis, 14*, 81–88.

Hebb, D. O. (1949). *The organization of behavior*. New York: Wiley Interscience.

Hillman, J., & Ventura, M. (1992). *We've had a hundred years of psychotherapy and the world's getting worse*. New York: HarperCollins.

Hines, J. M., Hungerford, H. R., & Tomera, A. N. (1986–1987). Analysis and synthesis of research on responsible environmental behavior: A meta-analysis. *Journal of Environmental Education, 18*, 1–8.

Hirst, E., Berry, L., & Soderstrom, J. (1981). Review of utility home energy audit programs. *Energy, 6*, 621–630.

Hodgkinson, S. P., & Innes, M. (2000). The prediction of ecological and environmental belief systems: The differential contributions of social conservatism and beliefs about money. *Journal of Environmental Psychology, 20*, 285–294.

Hogan, D. (2001, November 23). Greenbacks Take Stand for Powerful Portland, Oregon, Timber Industry. *The Oregonian*. Retrieved March 27, 2003 from http://search.epnet. com/direct.asp?an=2W61883602899&db=nfh.

Hollender, J. (1990). *How to make the world a better place: A guide to doing good*. New York: William Morrow.

Home Energy Magazine (2001). *Web audit tool providers*. Retrieved September 6, 2002, from http://www.homeenergy.org/webaudit.otheraudits.html

Hornik, J., Cherian, J., Madansky, M., & Narayana, C. (1995). Determinants of recycling behavior: A synthesis of research results. *Journal of Socio-Economics, 24*, 105–127.

Howard, G. S. (2000). Adapting human lifestyles for the 21st Century. *American Psychologist, 55*(5), 509–515.

Howard, G. S. (2002). *How should I live my life: Psychology, environmental science, and moral traditions*. New York: Rowman & Littlefield.

Hunt, M. (1993). *The story of psychology* (p. 154). New York: Anchor Books.

Hutton, R. R. (1982). Advertising and the Department of Energy campaign for energy conservation. *Journal of Advertising, 11*(2), 27–39.

Hwang, A. (2002, January/February). Exportable righteousness, expendable women. *Worldwatch* (pp. 24–31). Washington, DC: Worldwatch Institute.

Intergovernmental Panel on Climate Change (2001). *IPCC third assessment report—climate change 2001*. Retrieved November 8, 2002, from http://www.ipcc.ch/

Irvine, K. N., & Warber, S. (2002). Green healthcare: Practicing as if the natural environment really mattered. *Alternative Therapies, 8*, 76–83.

Iwata, O. (1999). Perceptual and behavioral correlates of voluntary simplicity lifestyles. *Social Behavior and Personality, 27*(4), 379–386.

Jacobson, J. L. (1992). *Gender bias: Roadblock to sustainable development*. Worldwatch paper no. 110. Washington, DC: Worldwatch Institute.

Jacobson, J. L., & Jacobson, S. W. (1996). Intellectual impairment in children exposed to polychlorinated biphenyls in utero. *New England Journal of Medicine, 335*, 783–789.

James, W. (1929). *The varieties of religious experience*. New York: Modern Library.

Jerdee, T. H., & Rosen, B. (1974). Effects of opportunity to communicate and visibility of individual decisions on behavior in the common interest. *Journal of Applied Psychology, 59*, 712–16.

Kabeer, N. (2001). *Reversed realities: Gender hierarchies in development thought*. New York: Verso.

Kahn, P. H. (1999). *The human relationship with nature: Development and culture*. Cambridge, MA: MIT Press.

Kaiser, F. G., Ranney, M., Hartig, T., & Bowler, P. (1999). Ecological behavior, environmental attitude, and feelings of responsibility for the environment. *European Psychologist, 4*(2), 59–74.

Kals, E., & Maes, J. (2002). Sustainable development and emotions. In P. Schmuck & W. P. Schultz (Eds.), *Psychology of sustainable development* (pp. 97–122). Boston: Kluwer.

Kals, E., Schumacher, D., & Montada, L. (1999). Emotional affinity toward nature as a motivational basis to protect nature. *Environment and Behavior, 31*(2), 178–202.

Kanner, A. D., & Gomes, M. E. (1995). The all-consuming self. In T. Roszak, M. E. Gomes, & A. D. Kanner (Eds.), *Eco-psychology: Restoring the earth, healing the mind* (pp. 77–91). San Francisco, CA: Sierra Club.

Kaplan, R. (2001). The nature of the view from home: Psychological benefits. *Environment and Behavior, 33*(4), 507–542.

Kaplan, R., & Kaplan, S. (1989). *The experience of nature*. Cambridge, England: Cambridge University Press.

Kaplan, S. (1992). Environmental preference in a knowledge-seeking, knowledge-using organism. In J. H. Barkow, L. Cosmides & J. Tooby (Eds.), *The adapted mind: Evolutionary psychology and the generation of culture* (pp. 581–598). New York: Oxford University Press.

Kaplan, S. (1995). The restorative benefits of nature: Toward an integrative framework. *Journal of Environmental Psychology, 15*, 169–182.

Kaplan, S. (2000). Human nature and environmentally responsible behavior. *Journal of Social Issues, 56*(3), 491–508.

Kaplan, S., & Kaplan, R. (1982). *Cognition and environment: Functioning in an uncertain world*. Westport, CT: Greenwood Publishing Group.

Kaplan, S., & Talbot, J. F. (1983). Psychological benefits of a wilderness experience. In I. Altman & J. F. Wohlwill (Eds.), *Behavior and the natural environment* (pp. 163–203). New York: Plenum.

Kasser, T., & Kanner, A. (2004). *Psychology and consumer culture: The struggle for a good life in a materialist world*. Washington, DC: American Psychological Association.

Kates, R. W. (1994). Sustaining life on the earth. *Scientific American, 174*(4), 114–122.

Katzev, R., & Johnson, T. (1984). A social-psychological analysis of residential electricity consumption: The impact of minimal justification techniques. *Journal of Economic Psychology, 3*, 267–284.

Keepin, W. (1992). Toward an ecological psychology. *ReVision, 14*, 90–99.

Keller, S. E., Schleifer, S. J., Bartlett, J. A., Shiflett, S. C., & Rameshwar, P. (2000). Stress, depression, immunity and health. In K. Goodkin & A. P. Visser (Eds.), *Psychoneuroimmunology: Stress, mental disorders, and health* (pp. 1–26). Washington, DC: American Psychiatric Press.

Kellert, S. T., & Wilson, E. O. (Eds.). (1993). *The biophilia hypothesis*. Washington, DC: Island Press.

Kennedy, R. F. (2001, November 24). Better gas mileage, greater security. *The New York Times*, editorials.

Kerr, N. L. (1989). Norms in social dilemmas. In D. Shroeder (Ed.), *Social dilemmas: Psychological perspectives* (pp. 287–313). New York: Praeger.

Kitzhaber, J. (2002, September 25). *Keynote address at the Forest Futures Conference*. Willamette University, Salem OR.

Knott, A. (2000). Legislators with timber ties happy to help the industry. *The Center for Public Integrity*. Retrieved October 4, 2002, from http://www.public-i.org/50states_01_082900.htm

Kohler, W. (1947/1975). *Gestalt psychology: An introduction to new concepts in modern psychology*. New York: New American Library.

Koyre, A. (1968). *From the closed world to the open universe*. Baltimore, MD: Johns Hopkins.

Kuo, F. E., & Sullivan, W. C. (2001). Aggression and violence in the inner city: Effects of environment via mental fatigue. *Environment and Behavior, 33*(4), 543–571.

Laituri, M., & Kirby, A. (1994). Finding fairness in America's cities? The search for environmental equity in everyday life. *Journal of Social Issues, 50*, 121–140.

Langer, E. (1983). *The psychology of control*. Beverley Hills, CA: Sage.

Lawrence, R. J. (2002). Healthy residential environments. In R. B. Bechtel & A. Churchman (Eds.), *Handbook of environmental psychology* (pp. 394–412). New York: Wiley.

Lazarus, R. S. (1966). *Psychological stress and the coping process*. New York: McGraw-Hill.

Lazarus, R. S., & Folkman, S. (1984). *Stress, appraisal and coping*. New York: Springer.

LeCouteur, D. G., McLean, A. J., Taylor, M. C., Woodham, B. L., & Board, P. G. (1999). Pesticides and Parkinson's disease. *Biomedicine and Pharmacotherapy, 53*, 122–30.

Lee, K. N. (1993). *Compass and gyroscope: Integrating science and politics for the environment*. Washington, DC: Island Press.

Leonard-Barton, D. (1981). The diffusion of active-residential solar energy equipment in California. In A. Shama (Ed.), *Marketing solar energy innovations* (pp. 243–257). New York: Praeger.

Leopold, A. (1949). *A sand county almanac: And sketches here and there*. New York: Oxford University Press.

Leopold, A. (1993). *Round river: From the journals of Aldo Leopold*. New York: Oxford University Press.

Lewin, K. (1959). *Field theory in social science* (p. 228). New York: Harper & Bros.

Lifton, R. J. (1993). From a genocidal mentality to a species mentality. In S. Staub & P. Green (Eds.), *Psychology and social responsibility: Facing global challenges* (pp. 17–29). New York: New York University Press.

Lomborg, B. (2001). *The skeptical environmentalist: Measuring the real state of the world*. Cambridge, England: Cambridge University Press.

Lopez, B. (1990). *The rediscovery of North America*. New York: Vintage.

Lord, C. G., Lepper, M. R., & Preston, E. (1984). Considering the opposite: A corrective strategy for social judgment. *Journal of Personality and Social Psychology, 47*, 1231–1243.

Lord, K. R. (1994). Motivating recycling behavior: A Quasi-experimental investigation of message and source strategies. *Psychology and Marketing, 11*, 341–358.

Lovins, A. B. (2002). Technology is the answer (but what was the question?) In G. T. Miller (Ed.), *Living in the environment: Principles, connections, and solutions* (12th ed., pp. 361–362). Belmont, CA: Wadsworth/Thomson Learning.

Lovins, A. B., & Lovins, L. H. (2001, July/August). Fool's gold in Alaska [Electronic version]. *Foreign Affairs*. Retrieved August 10, 2002, from http://www.rmi.org/images/other/E-FAFoolsGold.pdf

Lovelock, J. (1979). *Gaia: A new look at life on earth*. New York: Oxford University Press.

Lovelock, J. (1990). *The ages of Gaia: A biography of our living earth*. New York: Bantam.

Lundberg, A. (1998). Environmental change and human health. In A. Lundberg (Ed.), *The environment and mental health: A guide for clinicians* (pp. 5–23). Hillsdale, NJ: Lawrence Erlbaum Associates.

Lundberg, A., & Santiago-Rivera, A. L. (1998). Psychiatric aspects of technological disasters. In A. Lundberg (Ed.), *The environment and mental health: A guide for clinicians* (pp. 57–66). Hillsdale, NJ: Lawrence Erlbaum Associates.

Lynn, M. (1992). Scarcity's enhancement of desirability: The role of naive economic theories. *Basic and Applied Social Psychology, 13*(1), 67–78.

Mack, J. (1992). Inventing a psychology of our relationship to the Earth. In S. Staub & P. Green (Eds.), *Psychology and social responsibility: Facing global challenges* (pp. 237–247). New York: New York University Press.

MacKenzie, J. J. (2000). *Oil as a finite resource: When is global production likely to peak?* Retrieved September 25, 2002, from http://www.wri.org/wri/climate/jm_oil_001.html

Macy, J. R. (1983). *Despair and personal power in the nuclear age*. Philadelphia: New Society Publishers.

Maddock, C., & Pariante, C. M. (2001). How does stress affect you? An overview of stress, immunity, depression and disease. *Epidemiologia e Psichiatria Sociale, 10*(3), 153–162.

Mahler, M. S. (1972). On the first three subphases of the separation-individual process. *International Journal of Psycho-Analysis, 53*, 333–338.

Mainieri, T., Barnett, E. G., Valdero, T. R., Unipan, J. B., & Oskamp, S. (1997). Green buying: The influence of environmental concern on consumer behavior. *Journal of Social psychology, 137*, 189–204.

Martin, G., & Pear, J. (2002). *Behavior modification: What it is and how to do it* (7th ed.). Englewood Cliffs, NJ: Prentice-Hall.

Maser, C. (1988). *The redesigned forest*. San Pedro, CA: R.E. Miles.

Masterson, K. (2002, March 14). Fuel efficiency rules cut out of energy bill: Lawmakers yield to auto industry. *Houston Chronicle*, p. 1.

Matlin, M. W. (2002). *Cognition*. New York: Wadsworth Thompson Learning.

Mayer, B. (2000). *The dynamics of conflict resolution*. San Francisco, CA: Jossey-Bass.

Mazumdar, S., & Mazumdar, S. (1993). Sacred space and place attachment. *Journal of Environmental Psychology, 13*, 231–242.

McDonough, W., & Braungart, M. (1998). The NEXT industrial revolution. *Atlantic Monthy* [Digital edition]. Retrieved January 11, 2003 from http://www.theatlantic.com/issues/98oct/ industry.htm

McDonough, W., & Braungart, M. (2001). Invitation to a revolution: The next industrial revolution. Retrieved January 11, 2003, from http://www.thenextindustrialrevolution.org/context.html

McDonough, W., & Braungart, M. (2002). *Cradle to cradle*. New York: North Point Press.

McGinn, A. P. (2002). Reducing our toxic burden. In C. Flavin, H. French, & G. Gardner (Eds.), *State of the World, 2002: A Worldwatch Institute report on progress toward a sustainable society* (pp. 75–100). New York: Norton.

McKenzie-Mohr, D. (2000a). Fostering sustainable behavior through community-based social marketing. *American Psychologist, 55*(5), 531–537.

McKenzie-Mohr, D. (2000b). Promoting sustainable behavior: An introduction to community-based social marketing. *Journal of Social Issues, 56*(3), 543–555.

McNeil, B. J., Pauker, S. G., Sox, H. C., & Tversky, A. (1982). On the elicitation of preferences for alternative therapies. *New England Journal of Medicine, 306*(21), 1259–1262.

Meadows, D. H. (1991). *The global citizen*. Washington DC: Island Press.

Medin, D. L., Ross, B. H., & Markman, A. B. (2001). *Cognitive psychology* (3rd ed., pp. 540). Fort Worth, TX: Harcourt College.

Merchant, C. (1983). *The death of nature: Women, ecology and the scientific revolution*. San Francisco: Harper, San Francisco.

Milgram, S. (1974). *Obedience to authority*. New York: Harper.

Miller, G. T. (1993). *Living in the environment: An introduction to environmental science* (7th ed.). Belmont, CA.: Wadsworth.

Miller, G. T. (2002). *Living in the environment: Principles, connections and solutions* (12th ed.). Belmont, CA: Wadsworth/Thompson Learning.

Miller, G. T. (2003). *Environmental science* (9th ed.). Pacific Grove, CA: Brooks/Cole.

Miller, T. A., & Keller, E. B. (1991). What the public thinks. *EPA Journal, 17*(2), 40–43.

Mohai, P. (1992). Men, women, and the environment: An examination of the gender gap in environmental concern and activism. *Society and Natural Resources, 5*, 1–19.

Moore, C. (1996). *The mediation process: Practical strategies for resolving conflict*. San Francisco, CA: Jossey-Bass.

Moore, D. W. (2001). Energy crisis: Americans lean toward conservation over production. *The Gallup Poll Monthly, 428*, 14–15.

Morgan, M. G. (1993, July). Risk analysis and management. *Scientific American*, 32–41.

Motavalli, J. (2002a). The case against meat. *The Environmental Magazine, 8*(1), 26–32.

Motavalli, J. (2002b). The fight against highly toxic mercury in the environment has just begun. *The Environmental Magazine, 8*(3), 26–33.

Myers, D. (1992). *The pursuit of happiness: Who is happy and why*. New York: William Morrow.

Myers, D. (1993). *Social psychology* (4th ed.). New York: McGraw-Hill.

Myers, D. (2000). The funds, friends, and faith of happy people. *American Psychologist, 55*(1), 56–67.

Myers, D. G. (2002). *Social psychology* (7th ed.). New York: McGraw-Hill.

Myers, G. J., & Davidson, P. W. (2000). Does methylmercury have a role in causing developmental disabilities in children? *Environmental Health Perspectives, 108*(3), 413–420.

Myers, N. (1984). *The primary source: Tropical forests and our future.* New York: Norton.

Nadakavukaren, A. (2000). *Our global environment: A health perspective* (5th ed.). Prospect Heights, IL: Waveland Press.

Naess, A. (1985). Identification as a source of deep ecological attitudes. In M. Tobais (Ed.), *Deep ecology* (pp. 256–270). San Diego: Avant Books.

Naess, A. (1988). *Self realization: An ecological approach to being in the world.* Quoted in B. Devall. *Simple in means, rich in ends: Practicing deep ecology* (p. 43). Salt Lake City: Peregrine Smith.

National Institute of Mental Health (2002). *Depression.* Retrieved October 4, 2002, from http://www.nimh.nih.gov/publicat/depression.cfm

National Research Council (2001, June 6). *Leading climate scientists advise White House on global warming.* National Academy of Sciences, Washington, DC. Retrieved November 8, 2002, from http://www4.nationalacademies.org/news.nsf/(ByDocID)/854F0F191BB3912385256A6300697720?OpenDocument

Nevin, J. A. (1985). Behavior analysis, the nuclear arms race, and the peace movement. In S. Oskamp (Ed.), *International conflict and national public policy issues. Applied Social Psychology Annual, 6.* Beverly Hills, CA: Sage.

Nevin, J. A. (1991). Behavior analysis and global survival. In W. Ishaq (Ed.), *Human behavior in today's world* (pp. 39–49). New York: Praeger.

Newton, D. E. (1996). *Environmental justice.* Santa Barbara, CA: ABC-CLIO.

Nicholsen, S. W. (2002). *The love of nature and the end of the world: The unspoken dimensions of environmental concern.* Cambridge, MA: MIT Press.

Opotow, S. (1990). Moral exclusion and injustice: An introduction. *Journal of Social Issues, 46*(1), 1–20.

Opotow, S. (1994). Predicting protection: Scope of justice and the natural world. *Journal of Social Issues, 50*(3), 49–63.

Opotow, S. (2001). Social injustice. In D. Christie, R. Wagner, & D. Winter (Eds,). *Peace, conflict and violence: Peace psychology for the 21st century* (pp. 102–109). Upper Saddle River, NJ: Prentice-Hall.

Opotow, S., & Clayton, S. (1994). Green justice: Conceptions of fairness and the natural world. *Journal of Social Issues, 50*, 1–12.

Opotow, S., & Weiss, L. (2000). Denial and moral exclusion. *Journal of Social Issues, 56*(3), 475–490.

Orbell, J. M., van de Kraght, A. J., & Dawes, R. M. (1988). Explaining discussion-induced cooperation. *Journal of Personality and Social Psychology, 54*, 811–819.

Oregon Department of Forestry (2000, September). *Northwest Oregon state forests management plan: Legal and policy mandates.* Retrieved August 20, 2002, from http://www.odf.state.or.us/StateForests/nwfinal/21-D-Mandates.prn.pdf

Ornstein, R., & Ehrlich, P. (2000). *New world, new mind: Moving toward conscious evolution.* Cambridge, MA: Malor Books, ISHK.

Oskamp, S. (2000). A sustainable future for humanity? How can psychology help? *American Psychologist, 55*(5), 496–508.

Oskamp, S., Harrington, M. J., Edwards, T. C., Sherwood, D. L., Okuda, S. M., & Swason, D. C. (1991). Factors influencing household recycling behavior. *Environment and Behavior, 23*, 494–519.

Pallak, M. S., Cook, D. A., & Sullivan, J. J. (1980). Commitment and energy conservation. In L. Bickman (Ed.), *Applied social psychology annual* (Vol. 1, pp. 235–254). Beverly Hills, CA: Sage.

Pardini, A. U., & Katzev, R. D. (1983–84). The effects of strength of commitment on newspaper recycling. *Journal of Environmental Systems, 13*, 245–254.

Parkinson's Action Network (2002). *The cost of Parkinson's disease.* Retrieved July 29, 2002, from http://www.parkinsonsaction.org/oldsite/cost.html

Parsons, R., & Hartig, T. (2000). Environmental psychophysiology. In J. T. Cacioppo, L. G. Tassinary, & G. G. Berntson (Eds.), *Handbook of psychophysiology* (2nd ed., pp. 815–848). Cambridge, England: Cambridge University Press.

Perkins, H. W. (1991). Religious commitment, Yuppies values, and well-being in postcollegiate life. *Review of Religious Research, 32*, 244–251.

Perls, F. (1969). *Ego, hunger, and aggression: The beginning of gestalt therapy.* New York: Random House.

Perls, F. (1971). *Gestalt therapy verbatim.* New York: Bantam.

Perls, F. (1978). *The gestalt approach: An eyewitness to therapy.* New York: Bantam.

Peurifoy, R. Z. (1995). *Anxiety, phobias and panic: A step-by-step program for regaining control of your life.* New York: Warner Books.

Piel, G. (1994, March 21). Defusing the "Population Bomb." *The Nation, 258*(11), 376–380.

Pierce, J. C., Dalton, R. J., & Zaitsev, A. (1999). Public perceptions of environmental conditions. In R. J. Dalton, P. Garb, N. P. Lovrich, J. C. Pierece, & J. M. Whitely (Eds.), *Critical masses: Citizens, nuclear weapons production, and environmental destruction in the United States and Russia* (pp. 97–129). Cambridge, MA: MIT Press.

Pirages, D. C., & Ehrlich, P. R. (1974). *Ark II: Social response to environmental imperatives.* San Francisco, CA: Freeman.

Platt, J. R. (1973). Social traps. *American Psychologist, 28*, 641–651.

Ponting, C. (1991). *A green history of the world: The environment and collapse of great civilizations.* New York: St. Martin's Press.

Porterfield, S. (2000). Thyroidal dysfunction and environmental chemicals—Potential impact on brain development. *Environmental Health Perspectives, 108*(3), 433–438.

Powers, R. B., Osborne, J. G., & Anderson, E. G. (1973). Positive reinforcement of litter removal in the natural environment. *Journal of Applied Behavior Analysis, 6*, 579–586.

Prezant, D. J., Weiden, M., Banauch, G. I., McGuinness, G., Rom, W. N., Aldrich, T. K., & Kelly, K. J. (2002). Cough and bronchial responsiveness in firefighters at the World Trade Center site. *New England Journal of Medicine, 347*(11), 806–815.

Renner, M. (2001, September/October). The killing of US alternative energy R&D. *World Watch* (p. 11). Washington, DC: Worldwide Institute.

Researchers implant spinach gene into pig (2002, January 24). Kyodo News Service, Japan Economic Newswire, International News.

Reser, J. P. (1995). Whither environmental psychology? The transpersonal ecopsychology crossroads. *Journal of Environmental Psychology, 15*, 235–257.

Revkin, A. C. (2003, January 8). Environment and science: Danes rebuke a "skeptic." *The New York Times*, p. A7.

Riebel, L. (2001). Consuming the earth: Eating disorders and ecopsychology, *Journal of Humanistic Psychology, 41*(2), 38–58.

Ritter, M. (2002, January 13). Response to terror: Ground-zero workers air concerns over health impact. *Los Angeles Times*, p. A5.

Roberts, J. A., & Bacon, D. R. (1997). Exploring the subtle relationships between environmental concern and ecologically conscious consumer behavior. *Journal of Business Research, 40*, 79–89.

Robertson, I. (1987). *Sociology*. New York: Worth Publishers.

Robertson, J.A.L. (2000). *Decide the nuclear issues for yourself: Nuclear need not be unclear*. Retrieved October 12, 2002, from http://www.magma.ca/~jalrober/Decide.htm

Rodgers, W. H. (1994). *Environmental law* (2nd ed.). St. Paul, MN: West Publishing.

Roszak, T. (1992). *The voice of the earth: An exploration of eco-psychology*. New York: Simon & Schuster.

Roszak, T. (1994). Green guilt and ecological overload. In M. Walker (Ed.), *Reading the environment* (pp. 534–538). New York: Norton.

Ryan, J. D. (1992). *Life support: conserving biological diversity*. Worldwatch paper no. 108. Washington, DC: Worldwatch Institute.

Saad, L. (2001). Americans mostly "green" in the energy vs. environment debate. *The Gallup Poll Monthly, 426*, 33–37.

Sarafino, E. P. (1998). *Health psychology: Biopsychosocial interactions*. New York: Wiley.

Sattler, B. (2002). Environmental health in the health care setting. *American Nurse, 34(2)*, 25–38.

Schlosser, E. (2001). *Fast food nation: The dark side of the all-American meal*. Boston: Houghton Mifflin.

Schumaker, J. F. (2001). Dead zone. *New Internationalist, 336*, 34.

Schmidt-Bleek, F. et al. (1999). Statement to government and business leaders, Wuppertal Institute, Wuppertal, Germany. In P. Hawken, A. Lovins, & L. H. Lovins (Eds.), *Natural capitalism*. Boston: Little, Brown. www.faktor10.at/Englisch/index_en.html

Schnelle, J. G., Gendrich, J. G., Beagle, G. P., Thomas, M. M., & McNees, M. P. (1980). Mass media techniques for prompting behavior change in the community. *Environment and Behavior, 12*, 157–820.

Schultz, P. W. (1998). Changing behavior with normative feedback interventions: A field experiment on curbside recycling. *Basic and Applied Social Psychology, 2*(1), 25–36.

Schultz, P. W. (2000). Empathizing with nature: The effects of perspective taking on concern for environmental issues. *Journal of Social Issues, 56*(3), 391–406.

Schultz, P. W. (2001). The structure of environmental concern: Concern for self, other people, and the biosphere. *Journal of Environmental Psychology, 21*, 327–339.

Schultz, P. W., Shriver, C., Tabanico, J., & Khazian, A. (in press). Implicit connections with nature. *Journal of Environmental Psychology*.

Schwartz, S. H. (1977). Normative influences on altruism. In L. Berkowitz (Ed.), *Advances in experimental social psychology* (Vol. 19, pp. 221–279). New York: Academic Press.

Scull, J. (n.d.). *Eco-psychology: Where does it fit in psychology?* Retrieved January 6, 2003, from http://www.island.net/~jscull/ecopsych.htm

Seager, J. (1993). *Earth follies: Coming to feminist terms with the global environmental crisis*. New York: Routledge.

Seed, J., Macy, J., Fleming, P., & Naess, A. (1988). *Thinking like a mountain: Towards a council of all beings*. Philadelphia: New Society Publishers.

Seligman, M.E.P. (1975). *Helplessness: On depression, development and death*. San Francisco, CA: Freeman.

Sewell, L. (1995). The skill of ecological perception. In T. Roszak, M. E. Gomes, & A. D. Kanner (Eds.), *Eco-psychology: Restoring the earth, healing the mind* (pp. 201–215). San Francisco, CA: Sierra Club.

Sewell, L. (1999). *Sight and sensibility: The eco-psychology of perception*. New York: Tarcher/Putnam.

Shapiro, E. (1995). Restoring habitats, communities and souls. In T. Roszak, M. E. Gomes, & A. D. Kanner (Eds.), *Eco-psychology: Restoring the earth, healing the mind* (pp. 224–239). San Francisco, CA: Sierra Club.

Shepard, P. (1982). *Nature and madness*. San Francisco: Sierra Club.

Sherman, J. (2000). *Life's delicate balance: A guide to causes and prevention of breast cancer.* New York: Taylor & Francis.

Simon, J. L. (1981). *The ultimate resource.* Princeton, NJ: Princeton University Press.

Simon, J. L., & Kahn, H. (1984). *The resourceful earth: A response to global 2000.* New York: Basil Blackwell.

Sitter, S. (1993). Interview on National Public Radio "All Things Considered," May 19, 1989. Quoted in J. Seager. *Earth follies: Coming to feminist terms with the global environmental crisis* (p. 221). New York: Routledge.

Skinner, B. F. (1948). *Walden two.* New York: Macmillan.

Skinner, B. F. (1953). *Science and human behavior.* New York: The Free Press.

Skinner, B. F. (1971). *Beyond freedom and dignity.* New York: Knopf.

Skinner, B. F. (1985). Toward the cause of peace: What can psychology contribute? In S. Oskamp (Ed.), International conflict and national public policy issues. *Applied Social Psychology Annual, 6.* Beverly Hills, CA: Sage.

Skinner, B. F. (1990). To know the future. *The Behavior Analyst, 13,* 103–106.

Skinner, B. F. (1991). Why we are not acting to save the world. In W. Ishaq (Ed.), *Human behavior in today's world* (pp. 19–29). New York: Praeger.

Slovic, P. (2000). *The perception of risk.* London: Earthscan Publications.

Slovic, P., Finucane, M., Peters, E., & MacGregor, D. G. (2002). The affect heuristic. In T. Gilovich, D. Griffin, & D. Kahneman (Eds.), *Heuristics and biases: The psychology of intuitive judgment* (pp. 397–420). New York: Cambridge University Press.

Slovic, P., Fischhoff, B., & Lichtenstein, S. (1979). Rating the risks. *Environment, 21,* 14–20, 36–39.

Slovic, P., Fischhoff, B., & Lichtenstein, S. (1985). Characterizing perceived risk. In R. W. Kates, C. Hohenemser, & J. X. Kasperson (Eds.), *Perilous progress: Technology as hazard* (pp. 91–123). Boulder, CO: Westview Press.

Slovic, P., Flynn, J., Mertz, C. K., Poumadere, M., & Mays, C. (2000). Nuclear power and the public: A comparative study of risk perception in France and the United States. In O. Renn & B. Rohrmann (Eds.), *Cross-cultural risk perception: A survey of empirical studies* (pp. 55–102). Dordrecht, The Netherlands: Kluwer Academic.

Snyder, C. R., Harris, C., Anderson, J. R., Holleran, S. A., Irving, L. M., Sigmon, S. T., Yoshinobu, L., Gibb, J., Langelle, C., & Harney, P. (1991). The will and the ways: Development and validation of an individual-differences measure of hope. *Journal of Personality and Social Psychology, 60,* 570–585.

Spedden, S. E. (1998). Risk perception and coping. In A. Lundberg (Ed.), *The environment and mental health: A guide for clinicians* (pp. 103–114). Hillsdale, NJ: Lawrence Erlbaum Associates.

Speth, G. (1993). The global environmental challenge. In G. T. Miller (Ed.), *Living in the environment: An introduction to environmental science* (7th ed., p. 21). Belmont, CA: Wadsworth.

Spretnak, C. (1990). Ecofeminism: Our roots and flowering. In I. Diamond & G. F. Orenstein (Eds.), *Reweaving the world: The emergence of ecofeminism* (pp. 3–14). San Francisco, CA: Sierra Club.

Stein, S., & Spiegel, D. (2000). Psychoneuroimmune and endocrine effects on cancer progression. In K. Goodkin & A. P. Visser (Eds.), *Psychoneuroimmunology: Stress, mental disorders, and health* (pp. 105–151). Washington, DC: American Psychiatric Press.

Stern, P. C. (1992). What psychology knows about energy conservation. *American Psychologist, 47*(10), 1224–1232.

Stern, P. C. (2000). Psychology and the science of human-environment interactions. *American Psychologist, 55,* 523–530.

Stern, P. C., & Dietz, T. (1994). The value basis of environmental concern. *Journal of Social Issues, 50,* 65–84.

Stern, P. C., Dietz, T., & Kalof, L. (1993). Value orientations, gender, and environmental concern. *Environment and behavior, 25*(3), 322–348.

Stiffler, L. (2002, April 18). Hanford's unfinished business after countless delays and billions of dollars, the tide may be turning in cleanup of huge nuclear waste site. *Seattle Post-Intelligencer*, p. A1.

Strachey, J., & Freud, A. (Eds.). (1964). *The standard edition of the complete psychological works of Sigmund Freud.* London: Hogarth.

Strange, P. G. (1992). *Brain biochemistry and brain disorders.* New York: Oxford University Press.

Swanson, J. L. (1995). The call for Gestalt's contribution to ecopsychology: Figuring in the environmental field. *Gestalt Journal, 18*(1), 47–85.

Swanson, J. L. (2001). *Communing with nature.* Corvallis, OR: Illahee Press.

Thogersen, J. (1996). Recycling and morality: A critical review of the literature. *Environment and Behavior, 28*, 536–558.

Thomashow, M. (1995). *Ecological identity: Becoming a reflective environmentalist.* Cambridge, MA: MIT Press.

Tickner, J. (1997, May). Pesticide impacts on human health: Precautionary principle [Electronic version]. *The Newsletter of the Science and Environmental Health Net, 2*(4). Retrieved July 24, 2002, from http://www.pmac.net/precaut.htm

Trenberth, K. E. (2001). Stronger evidence of human influences on climate: The 2001 IPCC assessment. *Environment, 43*(4), 8–19.

Tversky, A., & Kahneman, D. (1983). Extensional versus intuitive reasoning: The conjunction fallacy in probability judgment. *Psychological Review, 90*, 293–315.

Ulrich, R. S. (1981). Natural versus urban scenes: Some psychophysiological effects. *Environment and Behavior, 13*(5), 523–556.

Ulrich, R. S. (1983). Aesthetic and affective response to natural environment. *Human Behavior & Environment: Advances in Theory & Research, 6*, 85–125.

Ulrich, R. S. (1984). View through a window may influence recovery from surgery. *Science, 224*(4647), 420–421.

Ulrich, R. S., Simons, R. F., Losito, B. D., Fiorito, E., Miles, M. A., & Zelson, M. (1991). Stress recovery during exposure to natural and urban environments. *Journal of Environmental Psychology, 11*, 201–230.

Union of Concerned Scientists (1992). World scientists' warning to humanity. Statement available from the *Union of Concerned Scientists*, 26 Church St., Cambridge, MA 02238.

Union of Concerned Scientists (2002, October 22). *UCS examines the Skeptical Environmentalist by Bjørn Lomborg.* Retrieved November 15, 2002, from http://www.ucsusa. org/global_environment/global_warming/page.cfm?pageID=533

United Nations Secretariat (1999). *Population Newsletter.* Retrieved November 14, 2001, from http://www.un.org/popin/news68.pdf

U.S. Census (2000). Poverty among individuals according to the official poverty measure. *Poverty in the United States.* Series P60-214, Table A. Retrieved November 9, 2002, from http://www.ssc.wisc.edu/irp/faqs/faq3dir/povtab00-one.htm

U.S. Department of Agriculture Forest Service (1990). *Summary: Final environmental impact statement, Umatilla National Forest,* p. S-29.

U.S. Department of Health and Human Services (2001, December 13). *Overweight and obesity threaten U.S. health gains. Communities can help address the problem, Surgeon General says.* Retrieved July 24, 2002, from http://www.hhs.gov/news/press/2001pres/ 20011213.html

U.S. Department of Health and Human Services (2002, July 17). *HHS launches new campaign to encourage physical activity and healthy behaviors for kids.* Retrieved July 24, 2002, from http://www.hhs.gov/news/press/2002pres/20020717b.html

Uzzell, D. L. (2000). The psycho-spatial dimensions of global environmental problems. *Journal of Environmental Psychology, 20*, 307–318.

Van Houten, R., Nau, P., & Marini, Z. (1980). An analysis of public posting in reducing speeding behavior on an urban highway. *Journal of Applied Behavior Analysis, 13*, 383–395.

Van Liere, K. D., & Dunlap, R. (1978). Moral norms and environmental behavior: An application of Schwartz's norm-activation model to yard burning. *Journal of Applied Social Psychology, 8*, 174–188.

Van Liere, K. D., & Dunlap, R. E. (1980). The social bases of environmental concern: A review of the hypotheses, explanations, and empirical evidence. *Public Opinion Quarterly, 44*, 181–197.

Van Vugt, M. (2002). Central, individual, or collective control? Social dilemma strategies for natural resource management. *American Behavioral Scientist, 45*(5), 783–800.

Vining, J., & Ebreo, A. (1992). Predicting recycling behavior from global and specific environmental attitudes and changes in recycling opportunities. *Journal of Applied Social Psychology, 22*, 1580–1607.

Vining, J., & Ebreo, A. (2002). Emerging theoretical and methodological perspectives on conservation behavior. In B. Bechtel & A. Churchman (Eds.), *Handbook of environmental psychology* (pp. 541–558). New York: Wiley.

Vlek, C. (2000). Essential psychology for environmental policy making. *International Journal of Psychology, 35*(2), 153–167.

Vonnegut, K. (1990). Notes from my bed of gloom: Or, why the joking had to stop. *New York Times Book Review*, April 11, p. 14.

Walljasper, J. (1997). Affluenza—warning: Materialism may be hazardous to your health. *Utne Reader*, September/October.

Wang, T. H., & Katzev, R. D. (1990). Group commitment and resource conservation: Two field experiments on promoting recycling. *Journal of Applied Social Psychology, 20*, 265–275.

Wason, P. C. (1960). On the failure to eliminate hypotheses in a conceptual task. *Quarterly Journal of Experimental Psychology, 12*, 129–140.

Watson, D., & Tharp, R. (2002). *Self directed behavior: Self modification for personal adjustment*. Pacific Grove, CA: Brooks/Cole.

Weenig, M.W.H. (1993). The strength of weak and strong communication ties in a community information program. *Journal of Applied Social Psychology, 23*, 1712–1731.

WEFA, Inc. (1998). *Global warming: The high cost of the Kyoto protocol*. Retrieved August 20, 2002, from http://www.api.org/globalclimate/wefa/ntl98.pdf

Weick, K. E. (1984). Small wins: Redefining the scale of social problems. *American Psychologist, 39*(1), 40–49.

Weiss, B. (1997). Pesticides as a source of developmental disabilities. *Mental Retardation and Developmental Disabilities Research Reviews, 3*, 246–256.

Weiss, B. (1998). Behavioral neurotoxicity. In A. Lundberg (Ed.), *The environment and mental health: A guide for clinicians* (pp. 25–41). Hillsdale, NJ: Lawrence Erlbaum Associates.

Weiss, B. (2000). Vulnerability of children and the developing brain to neurotoxic hazards. *Environmental Health Perspectives, 108*(3), 375–381.

Weiss, B., & Landrigan, P. J. (2000). The developing brain and the environment: An introduction. *Environmental Health Perspectives, 108*(3), 373–374.

Werner, C. M., Turner, J., Shipman, K., Twitchell, F., Dickson, B., Bruschke, G., & vonBismarck, W. (1995). Commitment, behavior, and attitude change: An analysis of voluntary recycling. *Journal of Environmental Psychology, 15*, 197–208.

Wessely, S. (2002). Protean nature of mass sociogenic illness: From possessed nuns to chemical and biological terrorism fears. *British Journal of Psychiatry, 180*(4), 300–306.

White, R. (1991). *"It's your misfortune and none of my own": A history of the American West*. Norman, OK: University of Oklahoma Press.

White, R. (1998). Psychiatry and eco-psychology. In A. Lundberg (Ed.), *The environment and mental health: A guide for clinicians* (pp. 205–212). Hillsdale, NJ: Lawrence Erlbaum Associates.

White, R., & Heerwagen, J. (1998). Nature and mental health: Biophilia and biophobia. In A. Lundberg (Ed.), *The environment and mental health: A guide for clinicians* (pp. 175–192). Hillsdale, NJ: Lawrence Erlbaum Associates.

Who gave, who got. (2001). *The Mother Jones 400*. Retrieved August 23, 2002, from http://www.motherjones.com/web_exclusives/special_reports/mojo_400/chart.html

Whole Terrain (2001/2002). In *Utne Reader*, January–February 2003, p. 20.

Wicker, A. (1969). Attitudes versus actions: The relationship of verbal and overt behavioral responses to attitude objects. *Journal of Social Issues, 25*, 41–78.

Widegren, O. (1998). The new environmental paradigm and personal norms. *Environment and Behavior, 30*, 75–100.

Wiesenfeld, E., & Sanchez, E. (2002). Sustained participation: A community based approach to addressing environmental problems. In B. Bechtel (Ed.), *Handbook of environmental psychology* (pp. 629–643). New York: Wiley.

Williams, K., & Harvey, D. (2001). Transcendent experience in forest environments. *Journal of Environmental Psychology, 21*, 249–260.

Williams, T. T. (1994). *An unspoken hunger: Stories from the field*. New York: Pantheon.

Wilson, E. O. (1984). *Biophilia: The human bond with other species*. Cambridge, MA: Harvard University Press.

Wilson, E. O. (2002). *The future of life*. New York: Knopf.

Wilson, T. D. (2002). *Strangers to ourselves: Discovering the adaptive unconscious*. Cambridge, MA: Belknap Press.

Winett, R. A., Hatcher, J. W., Fort, T. R., Leckliter, I. N., Love, S. Q., Riley, A. W., & Fishback, J. F. (1982). The effects of videotape modeling and daily feedback on residential electricity conservation, home temperature and humidity, perceived comfort, and clothing worn: Winter and summer. *Journal of Applied Behavior Analysis, 15*, 381–402.

Winter, D. D. (1996). *Ecological psychology: Healing the split between planet and self*. New York: HarperCollins Text.

Winter, D. D. (2000). Some big ideas for some big problems. *American Psychologist, 55*(5), 516–522.

Winter, D. D. (2002). (En)Gendering sustainable development. In P. Schmuck & W. P. Schultz (Eds.), *Psychology of sustainable development* (pp. 79–95). Dordrecht, The Netherlands: Kluwer.

Winter, D. D., & Cava, M. M. (in press). The psycho-ecology of war. *Journal of Social Issues*.

Wishful thinking: Wise use cowboys try to rewrite the constitution. (1994, January/February). *Sierra*, p. 40.

World Health Organization (2000, September). *Air pollution* (Fact Sheet No. 187). Retrieved September 15, 2002, from http://www.who.int/inf-fs/en/fact187.html

World Resources Institute (1998–1999). Global trends, population and human well being: Population growth—stabilization. *World Resource Institute*, Washington, DC. Retrieved November 9, 2002, from http://www.wri.org/wr-98-99/popgrow.htm

World Resources Institute (2000–2001). *Global topics: Forest ecosystems*. Retrieved from http://www.wri.org/wr2000/forests.html

World Resources Institute (2001). *Facts and figures: Environmental data tables, energy and resource use*. Table ERC.5: Resource consumption [Data file]. Available from World Resources Institute Web site, http://www.wri.org/trends/index.html

Worldwatch Institute (2002a). *Low-access forests and their level of protection in North America*. Retrieved March 27, 2003, from http://www.wri.igc.org/wri/gfw/gfw_namerica.html

Worldwatch Institute (2002b). *Report calls for rapid scaling up of efforts to preserve health of forests and provide economic benefits*. Retrieved October 4, 2002, from http://www.worldwatch.org/alerts/pr980402.html

Wright, R. (1995, August 28). The evolution of despair. *Time, 146*(9), 50.

Yates, S. (1982). *Using prospect theory to create persuasive communications about solar water heaters and insulation*. Unpublished doctoral dissertation, University of California, Santa Cruz.

Yates, S., & Aronson, E. (1983). A social psychological perspective on energy conservation in residential buildings. *American Psychologist, 38*, 435–444.

Yerkes, R. M., & Dodson, J. D. (1908). The relation of strength of stimulus to rapidity of habit-formation. *Journal of Comparative Neurology and Psychology, 18*, 459–482.

Zelezny, L. D., Chua, P. P., & Aldrich, C. (2000). Elaborating on gender differences in environmentalism. *Journal of Social Issues, 56*, 443–458.

Zoumbaris, S. J., & O'Brien, T. P. (1993). Consumption behaviors hinge on financial self-interest. *American Psychologist, 48*, 1091–1092.

Zukier, H. (1982). The dilution effect: The role of the correlation and the dispersion of predictor variables in the use of nondiagnostic information. *Journal of Personality and Social Psychology, 43*, 1163–1174.

Appendix:
How To Do It

T here are excellent guides available for how to enhance your environmentally responsible behavior. The quickest and easiest is the following list, "101 Ways to Heal the Earth" (Context Institute, 1989, www.context. org). In addition, the Web sites and books provide more detailed help for improving individual behavior, local communities, and environmental policy.

101 Ways to Heal the Earth
© In Context Institute. Reprinted with permission.

1. Insulate your home.
2. Buy energy-efficient appliances.
3. Caulk and weatherstrip doors and windows.
4. Install storm windows.
5. Close off unused areas in your home from heat and air conditioning.

6. Wear warm clothing and turn down winter heat.

7. Switch to low wattage or fluorescent light bulbs.

8. Turn off all lights that don't need to be on.

9. Use cold water instead of hot whenever possible.

10. Opt for small-oven or stove-top cooking when preparing small meals.

11. Run dishwashers only when full.

12. Set refrigerators to 38°F, freezers to 5°F, no colder.

13. Run clothes washers full, but don't overload them.

14. Use moderate amounts of biodegradable detergent.

15. Air-dry your laundry when possible.

16. Clean the lint screen in clothes dryers.

17. Instead of ironing, hang clothes in the bathroom while showering.

18. Take quick showers instead of baths.

19. Install water-efficient showerheads and sink-faucet aerators.

20. Install an air-assisted or composting toilet.

21. Collect rainwater and graywater for gardening use.

22. Insulate your water heater. Turn it down to 121°F.

23. Plant deciduous shade trees that protect windows from summer sun but allow it in during the winter.

24. Explore getting a solar water heater for your home.

25. Learn how to recycle all your household goods, from clothing to motor oil to appliances.

26. Start separating out your newspaper, other paper, glass, aluminum, and food wastes.

27. Encourage your local recycling center or program to start accepting plastic.

28. Urge local officials to begin roadside pickup of recyclables and hazardous wastes.

29. Encourage friends, neighbors, businesses/local organizations to recycle and sponsor recycling efforts.

30. Use recycled products, especially paper.

31. Reuse envelopes, jars, paper bags, scrap paper, etc.

32. Bring your own canvas bags to the grocery store.

33. Encourage local governments to buy recycled paper.

34. Start a recycling program where you work.

35. Limit or eliminate your use of "disposable" items.

36. Urge fast food chains to use recyclable packaging.
37. Avoid using anything made of plastic foam. It is often made from CFCs, and it never biodegrades.
38. If your car gets less than 35 mpg, sell it, buy a small fuel-efficient model, and spend whatever money you save on home energy efficiency.
39. Maintain and tune up your vehicle regularly, and keep tires properly inflated for maximum gas mileage.
40. Join a car pool or use public transportation to commute.
41. Write to automobile manufacturers to let them know that you intend to buy the most fuel efficient car on the road.
42. Reduce your use of air conditioning.
43. Encourage auto centers to install CFC recycling equipment for auto air conditioners. Freon is released during servicing to become both a greenhouse gas and an ozone layer destroyer.
44. Remove unnecessary articles from your car. Each 100 lbs. of weight decreases fuel efficiency by 1%.
45. Don't speed; accelerate and slow down gradually.
46. Walk or use a bicycle whenever possible.
47. Urge local governments to enact restrictions on automobile use in congested areas downtown.
48. Enjoy sports and recreational activities that use your muscles rather than gasoline and electricity.
49. Buy products that last, and buy used items whenever possible.
50. Rent or borrow items that you don't use often.
51. Maintain and repair the items you own.
52. Use colored fabrics to avoid the need for bleach.
53. Use natural fiber clothing, bedding, and towels.
54. Don't buy aerosols, halon fire extinguishers, or other products containing CFCs.
55. Write to computer chip manufacturers and urge them to stop using CFC-113 as a solvent.
56. Invest your money in environmentally and socially conscious businesses.
57. Avoid rainforest products, and inform the supplier or manufacturer of your concerns.
58. Use postcards instead of letters for short messages.
59. Eat vegetarian foods as much as possible. Meat makes less efficient use of land, soil, water, and energy, and cows emit 300 liters of methane per day.

60. Buy locally produced foods; avoid buying foods and other products that must be trucked in from great distances.
61. Read labels. Eat organic and less processed foods.
62. Start a garden; plant a garden instead of a lawn.
63. Water the garden with an underground drip system.
64. Support organic farming and gardening methods; shun chemical fertilizers, herbicides, and pesticides.
65. Compost kitchen and garden waste, or give it to a friend who can.
66. Inform schools, hospitals, airlines, restaurants, and the media of your food concerns.
67. Stay informed about the state of the Earth.
68. Talk to friends, relatives, and coworkers about reversing global climate change.
69. Read and support publications that educate about long-term sustainability (like this one).
70. Start a global climate change study group.
71. Educate children about sustainable living practices.
72. Xerox this list and send it to 10 friends.
73. Go on a citizen diplomacy trip and talk with those you meet about averting global climate change.
74. Get involved in local tree planting programs.
75. Join an environmental organization. If they're not involved with climate change, then get them involved.
76. Support zero population growth.
77. Support work to alleviate poverty. Poverty causes deforestation and other environmental problems.
78. Donate money to environmental organizations.
79. Support programs that aim to save rainforest areas.
80. Support solar and renewable energy development.
81. Work to protect local watershed areas.
82. Pave as little as possible. Rip up excessive concrete.
83. Encourage sewage plants to compost their sludge.
84. Write your senator now in support of environmental protections, such as improving fuel efficiency.
85. Write your congressperson now in support of protecting pristine areas, such as the Arctic National Wildlife Refuge.
86. Support disarmament and the redirection of military funds to environmental restoration.

87. Write letters to the editor expressing your concern about climate change and environmental issues.

88. Support electoral candidates who run on environmental platforms.

89. Run for local office on an environmental platform.

90. Attend city council meetings and speak out for action on climate change issues.

91. Organize a citizens' initiative to put a local "climate protection program" into place.

92. Learn how to lobby. Lobby your local, state, and national elected officials for action on climate change and environmental issues.

93. Organize a demonstration at a plant that uses toxic chemicals.

94. In place of TV and the stereo, spend time reading, writing, drawing, telling stories, making music.

95. Live within the local climate as much as possible, rather than trying to isolate yourself from it.

96. Strive to establish good communications with friends, neighbors, and family, including learning conflict resolution skills.

97. Spend time seeing, hearing, and rejoicing in the beauty of the Earth. Feel your love for the Earth. Make serving the Earth your first priority.

98. Learn about the simpler, less resource-intensive lifestyles of aboriginal peoples.

99. Think often about the kind of Earth you would like to see for your grandchildren's grandchildren.

100. While doing small things, think big. Think about redesigning cities, restructuring the economy, reconceiving humanity's role on the Earth.

101. Pray, visualize, hope, meditate, dream.

WEB RESOURCES

In the last few years, the World Wide Web has become the premier resource for up-to-date information about environmental problems. Particularly useful are the many sites that include "Take Action," routes for you to express your concern to lawmakers and public officials, organize citizens in your community, and implement other forms of activism. The following are some of our favorites:

Action Network
http://actionnetwork.org/

Gives information on a variety of problems and provides e-mail alerts and free faxes to legislators.

Basel Action Network
http://www.ban.org/

Seeks environmental justice by working to prevent toxic trade (toxic waste, toxic products, and toxic technology).

Center for Environmental Citizenship
http://www.envirocitizen.org/index.asp

Dedicated to educating, training, and organizing a diverse, national network of young leaders (especially college students) to protect the environment.

Center for Science in the Public Interest
http://www.cspinet.org/

Promotes safety and food quality.

Conservation Economy
http://www.conservationeconomy.net

Outlines what a sustainable society looks like with information about 57 dimensions for a conservation economy (including renewable energy, community planning, sustainable agriculture, etc.); comprehensively integrates social, natural, and economic capital to demonstrate that a sustainable society is both desirable and achievable.

Community-Based Social Marketing
http://www.cbsm.com

A valuable resource for people designing psychology-based strategies for community interventions regarding composting, energy efficiency, recycling, reuse, transportation, waste reduction, and water efficiency.

Common Dreams News Center
http://www.commondreams.org/

Assembles a large collection of news articles and opinions on environmental and peace issues.

Co-op America
http://www.coopamerica.org

Gives practical steps for using consumer and investor power to promote environmental responsibility and social justice; includes Green Pages, information about shareholder actions, boycotts, investments, sweatshops, and sustainable wood products.

Essential Information
http://www.essential.org/

Founded in 1982 by Ralph Nader, this site provides provocative information on important topics usually neglected by the mass media and policymakers.

Defenders of Wildlife
http://www.defenders.org/

Works to protect native wild animals and plants in their natural communities through new approaches to habitat conservation and leadership on endangered species issues.

Earth Island Institute
http://www.earthisland.org/home_body.cfm

Posts selected articles from its widely used *Earth Island Journal*, and provides action opportunities on a wide range of environmental problems.

Ecological Footprint Quiz
http://www.MyFootprint.org

How many acres does it take to support your lifestyle? How does your footprint compare with that of most North Americans? Take the quiz online and find out.

Enviro-Link
http://www.envirolink.org

Provides access to thousands of online environmental resources.

Environmental Defense
http://www.environmentaldefense.org/home.cfm

A leading national organization that links science, economics, and law to create solutions to environmental problems.

Environmental Research Foundation
http://www.rachel.org/home_eng.htm

Provides understandable scientific information about human health and environmental justice.

The Environment Site
http://www.environmentsite.org/

Visitors to the site make a free donation (funds come from sponsors) that goes toward reducing CO_2 emissions. No personal information is required for a visitor to make the donation. Sponsors send payments to fund donations that go directly to the Alliance to Save Energy. These donations support energy efficiency projects that reduce or avoid greenhouse gas emissions.

Friends of the Earth
http://www.foe.org/

International organization with local chapters working on high profile (often litigation) efforts to create a more healthy, just world.

Greenhouse Network
http://www.greenhousenet.org/

Works to educate and unite business, government, students, civic organizations, community leaders, and citizens in the effort to stabilize the climate.

Greenpeace USA, Inc.
http://www.greenpeaceusa.org/

Uses nonviolent direct action to expose global environmental problems and promote solutions.

Grist Magazine
http://www.gristmagazine.com

"Gloom and doom with a sense of humor!" Online environmental magazine that doesn't pull punches or accept advertising.

League of Conservation Voters
http://www.lcv.org/

Devoted full-time to shaping a pro-environment Congress. Through their *National Environmental Scorecard*, LCV holds Congress accountable for environmental decisions. They also run regional offices to build coalitions, promote grassroots power, and train the next generation of environmental leaders.

National Audubon Society
http://www.audubon.org/

A national network of community-based chapters dedicated to protecting birds and other wildlife and their habitat. Promotes environmental education programs and advocacy.

National Wildlife Federation
http://www.nwf.org/

> Educates and assists individuals and organizations of diverse cultures to conserve wildlife and other natural resources.

The Nature Conservancy
http://nature.org/

> Works to preserve plants, animals, and natural communities, promoting biodiversity and protection of habitat.

Natural Resources Defense Council
http://www.nrdc.org/

> NRDC advocates environmentally responsible policies, using law and lobbying to promote wildlife and wild places.

Northwest Coalition for Alternatives to Pesticides
http://www.pesticide.org/

> Works to protect people and the environment by advancing healthy solutions to pest problems.

Population Connection
http://www.populationconnection.org/

> Formerly known as Zero Population Growth (ZPG), Population Connection works to slow population growth and achieve a sustainable balance between the Earth's people and its resources.

Population Reference Bureau, Inc.
http://www.prb.org/

> Provides timely and objective information on U.S. and international population trends and their implications for policymakers, educators, the media, and concerned citizens.

Psychologists for Social Responsibility
http://www.psysr.org

> Uses psychological knowledge and skills to promote peace and social justice; the Environmental Protection and Justice Action Committee works on sustainability issues and their intersection with peace.

Responsible Shopper
http://www.responsibleshopper.org

> Organized by Co-Op America (see earlier), Responsible Shopper gives information about environmental and social responsibility records for thousands of products, companies, and name brands.

Save Our Environment Action Center
http://www.saveourenvironment.org/

A collaborative Web site of the nation's most influential environmental advocacy organizations, organized to increase public awareness and activism.

Second Nature: Education for Sustainability
http://www.secondnature.org/

Dedicated to transforming higher education by assisting colleges and universities integrate sustainability as a core component of education.

Sierra Club
http://www.sierraclub.org

Organizes a wide range of environmental action issues to promote responsible use of natural resources. Keeps a useful updated log of legislative actions and ways to express your opinions about them.

Transfair USA
www.transfairusa.org

Maintains an up-to-date list on merchants who sell fair trade coffee (coffee grown sustainably and sold at a fair price).

Vegsource
http://www.vegsource.com/veg faq/environment.htm

Provides discussion boards and useful information on vegetarian lifestyles, recipes, food risks, and diet-related diseases.

Working for Change
http://www.workingforchange.com

A comprehensive Web site of resources for promoting social and environmental justice; includes ActForChange.com, a site especially designed for taking action, as well as ShopForChange.com, a site where merchants donate 5% to progressive causes.

Worldwatch Institute
http://www.worldwatch.org/

Offers interdisciplinary research with a global focus and accessible writing about building a sustainable world.

World Wildlife Fund
http://www.worldwildlife.org/

The largest privately supported international conservation organization in the world, WWF is dedicated to protecting the world's wildlife and wild lands.

Union of Concerned Scientists
http://www.ucsusa.org/index.html

Provides a scientifically trained voice on policies regarding automobiles, food, environment, energy, and security; writes readable public policy statements that are widely circulated and highly regarded.

20/20 Vision
http://www.2020vision.org/

Promotes environmental restoration and elimination of weapons of mass destruction; each month focuses on a different issue and organizes mechanisms for opinions to be transmitted to political leaders.

BOOKS

Here are a few books we recommend for increasing environmentally helpful behaviors.

Christensen, K. (1990). *Home ecology*. Golden, CO: Fulcrum.

A humorous and useful guide for personal changes you can make in your home or residence.

Dominguez, J. R. (1999). *Your money or your life: Transforming your relationship with money and achieving financial independence.* New York: Penguin Putnam.

This book (as well as an audio tape set and workbook available from Sounds True) teaches people how to get off the production/consumption treadmill by examining personal financial attitudes, practices, and identities; a powerful tool for achieving financial independence and lower consumption habits.

Hayes, D. (2000). *The official earth day guide to planet repair*. Washington, DC: Island Press.

Take an Eco-IQ quiz, and then read this guide to "everything you need to know about global warming so you can help repair the planet." Accessible, but thorough, information on energy, transportation, and household contributors to global warming, and painless ways to reduce your impact.

Martin, G., & Pear, J. (2002). *Behavior modification: What it is and how to do it.* Englewood Cliffs, NJ: Prentice-Hall.

A clear guide to using behavioral principles to change your own behaviors, as well as others'.

Watson, D., & Tharp, R. (2002). *Self directed behavior: Self-modification for personal adjustment* (8th ed.). Belmont, CA: Wadsworth.

This is a detailed text and discussion of how to arrange self-control projects. Although the authors do not deal with environmental behaviors in particular, their approach is easily applied. It is particularly useful for attempts to change the most habitual behaviors.

Author Index

Subject Index

DATE DUE

FEB 26 2011			

Demco, Inc. 38-293